From the Eye of the Hurricane

Alex Higgins

From the Eye of the Hurricane

•

My Story

<u>headline</u>

First published in 2007 by
HEADLINE PUBLISHING GROUP

1

Cataloguing in Publication Data is available from the British Library

Hardback ISBN 978 0 7553 1659 5
Trade paperback ISBN 978 0 7553 1660 1

Typeset in Sabon by Avon DataSet Ltd, Bidford on Avon, Warwickshire

Printed and bound in Great Britain by
Mackays of Chatham plc, Chatham, Kent

Headline's policy is to use papers that are natural, renewable and
recyclable products and made from wood grown in sustainable forests.
The logging and manufacturing processes are expected to conform
to the environmental regulations of the country of origin.

HEADLINE PUBLISHING GROUP
A division of Hachette Livre UK Ltd
338 Euston Road
London NW1 3BH

www.headline.co.uk
www.hodderheadline.com

Endpaper photographs:
(Front) Alex Higgins lines up a shot during the 1982 World Championship
final © Action Images/Sporting Pictures
(Back) Alex Higgins is helped by paramedics after being stabbed
in 1997 © MEN Syndication

To my family – Elizabeth, Alexander, Isobel, Anne, Jean, Lauren and Jordan.

Contents

●

Acknowledgements

●

First, and most importantly, I'd like to thank my mother and father, Elizabeth Stockman Higgins and Alexander Higgins. The journey might have been hard, bringing up my three sisters and I, but the way was sublime. I would never have made my mark on the world without their support and guidance. Rest in peace Mum and Dad. From Sandy, your son.

To my three sisters, Isobel, Anne and Jean. Thank you all. We have always been in touch through thick and thin. Rare girls, all with different talents of your own and all good mothers. I will always love the three of you. From your brother Sandy.

To Lauren and Jordan. I am so proud of the people you have become. You are the shining lights that keep me going. Thank you both, for everything. All my love. Your dad.

To Siobhan. I have always loved you and still do. It's a pity I didn't meet you at the beginning of my career. I hope you are well. Good luck Shiv. Your Wiry Man. PS My regards to your lovely mother.

To the snooker clubs that have played a part in my life: The Jampot, Donegall Rd, The Crown, Shankhill Rd, The Oxford, Royal Avenue, The Shaftesbury, Shaftesbury Square, The Bakers Club, North Street, The Buffs Club, centre of Belfast, the Sports Club, High Street, the YMCA, Bradbury Place, St Pats, Queen Street. All these places played their own part in me learning my job. I learned to be shrewd on a snooker table by watching individual players in each of these clubs. In particular, I want to mention Billy Bennett and Sammy Bailey. Watching them play billiards was a joy. Two gentlemen, and a great influence when I was a member of the YMCA. God bless them and all the Belfast players who helped me on my way. And thanks also to the Masters Club, Stockport, where I practised ten hours a day, watched over by Big Brian my referee. Cheers to all of you. Alex.

To Cooper and Ronnie and all the lads in the Royal Bar, Sandy Row. I know you think I'm a nuisance but I also know you all care about me nevertheless. That football on a Saturday should be banned – it interrupts my racing. All the bext, Alex.

To Peter Wake and associates – the Legal Eagles in Aussie. Some of the best times of my life. G'day mates. Alex.

To black and white television, which instilled in me my dream of becoming a player like Joe Davis, John Pulman, Fred Davis and Ray Reardon. Watching them drove me to practise, practise, practise. I might have cocked up plenty of times but with the right amount of practice I knew I could beat anyone, both past and present.

To my great friend Doug Perry. He managed me the way anyone should be managed. He was honest and upstanding and did the best he could have done without the financial resources or clout of others. I loved Doug Perry like a brother. Rest in peace Doug. Alex.

To Jimmy White. A good friend. I sometimes think the worst thing that happened to you was meeting me. You started to play like me when you could have been developing your own style. But you still did brilliantly. Thank you for all your support. God bless you. Alex.

To Louis Copeland, master tailor, a chip off the old block just like his late father, a quiet little man with an astute mind. Thank

Acknowledgements

you Louis and also your wonderful staff, you have been great to me over the years. I'm sure you would have given me a job in your men's fashion emporium because of our mutual love of textiles, materials etc. You made me look good, and with your garments on my back I felt good. Love, Alex.

To my dear friend Rafe, the proud landlord of the Gunmakers Arms who over the years has stood by me through thick and thin. My best wishes for your future. Rock on Rafe. Alex.

To Sheila and Tony O'Beirne who encouraged me and helped me on my way on the ladder of becoming a good snooker player. I have never forgotten our nights in Windmill Street with all the various characters in Herbert Holt's snooker club. All my love, for your kindness, Sandy.

To Michael Dillon, the proprietor of Gerry's Bar, Dean Street, Soho. What a sweetie you are. I love meeting all the wonderful people from the showbiz and theatrical world. As long as I draw breath I will always call in to meet your wonderful mixture of clientele. Thank you, Michael. Yours, Alex.

To everyone at Headline Publishing and in particular to Mr David Wilson and the delightful Rhea Halford, who encouraged me to open up and be frank in regards to the content of my book. My appreciation to these two people, plus my publicist Helena Towers, for all the work with the impetuous genius with a snooker cue. All your patience is surely a virtue. And to Jane Butcher and Marion Paull for your work on the text. Thank you all. Hurricane.

To David Hendon, who I have never met, but who has been so instrumental in making sure that I got all my snooker facts correct in the writing of this book. Thank you David. For all your help. Alex.

And finally, to the Higgins fans over and around the world. I applaud you. You turned up when I needed you. You were disappointed numerous times. But we did have our glorious days together and that won't be forgotten. Thank you, the Hurricane Higgins brigade, from the bottom of my soul. Our motto: We defy. The Hurricane.

1

From humble beginnings

•

The winter wind had been blowing most of the night and it had kept my mum awake. Mum was always tired in those days, looking after the family – Dad, Isobel and Anne – in a tiny council house in Abingdon Street, Sandy Row, Belfast. The girls were no sooner fed and dressed when it all started. My mum, Elizabeth, was taken to the hospital by a neighbour, and hours later, just after dark, while the cold wind still blew outside, a little hurricane arrived in the maternity ward. I was screaming at the top of my voice, which was the start of something that would get me into trouble time and time again during my turbulent life. My dad, Alex, was delighted to have a son at last, whom he could take to football matches, and later that evening he was in the pub with a cigar in one hand and a pint of Guinness in the other to wet the baby's head. The newspaper in his pocket was folded at the racing pages and the date on the top read Friday, 18 March 1949.

I weighed in at just over 4lb, a minute kid, but strong just the same. Isobel and Anne were just as pleased to have a brother as Mum and Dad were to have a son. Isobel was so fascinated by my size that she used to put me in a shoebox and push me around the floor like it was a pram. 'Come on baby Sandy, we'll go for a walk and don't you be bold now for Isobel,' she'd say. The family used to roar with laughter when she did it. Years later, when Monty

Python did the famous four Yorkshiremen sketch, I found it so funny when one of them said, 'We were so poor, we lived in t'shoebox in t'middle o'road' because it was so close to home. Growing up with Isobel, Anne and, later on, Jean was great. We were a close bunch and still are.

Happy memories I certainly have of my childhood, but life wasn't easy in the immediate years after the war. Europe had been torn apart, millions were displaced and England and Northern Ireland were still on wartime rations. Food was basic, but then so was almost everything else in Belfast. There was some work to be had, but wages were very low and that didn't leave much for luxuries, if you could get them anyway. My dad was a labourer who worked on building sites and sometimes on the tracks on the railways. He was a hard worker, very strong and lean, but he wasn't a big man. A lot like me, I guess. My mum worked so hard to give us all a little extra. Not only did she keep the house immaculate, and all of us as well, but she had a job as a cleaner and also used to go potato picking.

I can still see Mum now, heading out of the home before we'd left for school, hurrying to catch a lorry waiting at the end of the street, which would take her and some of the other local women, and a few men, to the outskirts of Belfast. On arrival at the fields what they had to look forward to was a day spent literally bent over double, picking potatoes for a pittance. At night Mum would come home tired, sore and cold, covered in mud with her meagre wage and a few potatoes for the pot. She would then get the dinner started and eat with us after getting washed. Isobel, Anne and Jean would help with the cooking and the housework. By the time I was older, I was usually out at a local snooker hall, the Jampot, or somewhere else, earning a few bob. I grew up in a very happy family environment on that council estate, where kids got by on their wits. Everyone was into some scam or other.

We didn't have supermarkets back then, but the local shops were fairly well stocked – mainly with black-market goods. I was always a skinny kid. Whether that was because of the basic foods we had to eat or because I was just born that way, I never fathomed, but as I made my way to put on my dad's bets, the fellas on the street corners were always telling me that I would make a great jockey. They would gather in groups to make their wagers with the illegal bookie's runners – there was no betting allowed off the course in those days. Horses played a big part in my life as I grew up, not least because of the rag-and-bone men, who would come round the streets. We kids would get old jam-jars and worn-out clothes to sell to them. I used to love the horses and as I fed them apples I would dream of being a jockey when I grew up. My dad used to laugh at my wild dreams of becoming a professional sportsman. He would often tease me in his broad Ulster accent, 'Go away wit yourself young Sandy.' He always called me Sandy, as did everyone else in the family.

I liked school well enough, but I wasn't very academic, although I did realise the importance of a good education and, contrary to common belief, I went to classes most of the time. I attended two very good schools in Belfast, which sadly aren't there any more. As a junior I went to Mabel Street primary and then on to Kelvin secondary school. There were some tough lads in my classes, but I tended to stay out of trouble, by staying out of their way. I got on well with most of the teachers. I wasn't an unruly kid. In fact, I was quite a good student, who liked to learn. We had an art master, Mr Clarke, who was hilarious, a real eccentric. He was six foot something and drove a bubble car. It was such a laugh to see him squeeze into it. Mr Walsh was the PE master and he used to put us through the hoops all right. Maybe that's another reason why I was so slim. All in all, most of the teachers and kids were a good lot, although a few teachers could be cruel and sadistic. It was a different era and the standards of acceptable behaviour weren't the same as they are now.

My first real exposure to snooker must have been when I was about eleven years old. I was determined to find a way to get some money so that my eldest sister could go out dancing on a Saturday night. In those postwar years, a lot of people couldn't read or write or do basic maths, so to earn a few pennies kids would go to the snooker halls and keep score for the players. The nearest one to us was the Jampot club just off the Donegall Road, where I still live. The club, which the schoolmasters used to call the Gluepot club because their pupils were never out of it, was the epitome of every snooker hall you have ever imagined in the forties and fifties. We have all seen them in the old black-and-white films, dark and dingy with clouds of cigarette smoke hanging over the tables. Well, the Jampot was just like that. It was run by a lovely man, Harry McMillan, and he would let us in, although he knew that we shouldn't be there until we were at least fifteen. But we were poor kids with nowhere to go, so rather than throw us out, he turned a blind eye. He once said that he did it to stop us getting into bad ways. At least in the club we didn't vandalise anything or learn how to rob.

I actually started to play about one month after joining Kelvin, so I was dead chuffed when I discovered that the teachers had a snooker table in the common room. I often asked if I could practise on it at playtime, but they never let me. Honest, I'd have been happy to stay at school — but I had to play. It was in my blood. So I used to pop round to the Jampot at lunchtime. A nice man named Trevor used to let us in and tell us to go up to the back of the hall where we could play in the dark for free. Trevor was a six foot four or five chain-smoker. What I remember most about him is his black Brylcreemed hair with a parting up the middle, just like Betty Boop's. I think Trevor helped me learn to play snooker because I was well-mannered and very keen and would do odd-jobs around the hall. Mostly I was self-taught, though. I watched and learned.

In the club the men would play a game called life pool in which they all had three lives. They would each put, say, 2/6d (12p) in the pool and then play the game till all were eliminated. The last man in was the winner and took the pot. When I was keeping score for the players I had to concentrate on what was happening on the table all the time, and it was this intense watching of the game that got me fascinated by snooker. I can still remember now that I used to think to myself that certain players shouldn't take certain shots, and that they would have been better off going for another ball. I used to get sixpence (2½p) per game to keep score. This was supposed to be paid by the winner of the pot, but sometimes they would only give you a penny, and so I would have to mark more games to get my stake. That's what I was really after – to get into the main life-pool game. When I had built up the required 2/6d, I used to take to the table. I preferred to play the men rather than other boys because the challenge was better, and it made me play a harder game.

These men didn't give you any quarter for being a kid. They would play me like I was a grown-up and, needless to say, I lost my stake more often than I won the pot when I first started playing. There were some infamous hard men around and when the skinny kid won the pot they would often try to club me with their cues. Mum always gave me sixpence for my lunch and more often than not it would become my starting point to raising the money to play at the Jampot, probably another reason why I remained so skinny.

Other ways I'd get the money to play came from visiting uncles and aunties in the Shankill, who'd give me a little something for being 'such a sweet young lad'. Hard to believe now, I know, but back then I knew which side my bread was buttered, so it was all sweetness and light with me. Getting hold of that stake money was all important. We referred to one of Mum's cousins as auntie, and she would often visit us and give 2/6d to Isobel, Anne and Jean. More often than not, I was out on these occasions, but if I came home to be told that she had called in, I'd be off like a shot, racing after her, telling her I was Sandy Higgins, just to get the 2/6d to play another game. I'm sure she never really knew if I was related to her or not because she very rarely met me in the house. Dad used to give me 2/6d pocket money each week and that always went on a game. I'd also get some of my mates to give me their pocket money and we would split the winnings if I won. Watching the men play was my way of learning the game. I always had a quick brain and still do today. My memory is my best asset and is the secret of my success as a world-class snooker player.

Even though in those early days I spent a lot of my time in the Jampot, playing the men and hustling for Isobel's dance-club money, I never dreamed of being a professional player. In the fifties, snooker wasn't really recognised as a proper sport by the powers that be. Don't get me wrong here, there were professional players who made a good living from playing the game, but the entertainment value just wasn't there.

It wasn't really until the 1970s, when television producers started to notice the entertainment value of the players, that the game really came into its own. I have to say, though, that since I left the circuit the game has never been the same. I know that sounds a bit arrogant – perhaps it is – but in my view snooker has reverted back to the dark days of serious and boring players. Today, there isn't any entertainment value – snooker is played by people who are good at it, purely for the money. I never played for the money or the records. I played, and still play today, simply because I love the game. I still do some exhibitions and I always have a laugh with the crowds.

Ken Doherty is a great friend of mine and I enjoy playing him, even though he beats me a lot. I love Ken because of his wicked sense of humour. He can give me back as much as I give him in a game and he is very quick-witted. Ken Doherty and a few players like him are the lifeblood of snooker in the twenty-first century. He isn't just a great player, but also a great entertainer, with both his wit and the way he plays his game. It is a joy to watch Ken playing. The crowds love him and he is a well-deserving champion who is a great ambassador not only for the game of snooker, but for his country as well.

After I grew a bit and could fully reach the table, I graduated to playing better snooker players, and for this I had to move to the Shaftesbury snooker club in the square of the same name. The Jampot was a bit of a rough-and-ready club, but the Shaftesbury had some class. It was there I first met Maurice Gill, who was the Irish amateur champion. I was still making my stake money by marking cards, even at the Shaftesbury, but I was so excited about the prospect of playing real snooker men. I got noticed by a lot of players and my play improved so much that I very often had to handicap myself in order to get a game. Maurice was one of my main targets, not to play, but to watch. I also used to love watching Willie Maxwell, Alan Sproule and Georgie McLachey, who was affectionately known as 'The Bug'. These guys would play a game called sticks. An odd number of players, sometimes as many as seven, each took turns in potting balls. The winner was the one who had the highest number of points at the end of play. It was by watching these guys while I marked points for them that I actually learnt to pot balls. The time I spent at the Shaftesbury really turned me into a serious player because I learnt not only to play well, but to analyse myself and my play. I was very critical of myself and often spoke out loud my thoughts about my playing ability during matches. I used to do this at tournaments later on, to the joy of the crowds.

I might not have been considering the possibility of playing snooker as a full-time profession, but somewhere in my heart I think I always knew I was going to 'make it', doing something even if it wasn't snooker. That belief stemmed partly from an odd moment that happened years before I'd even seen a snooker table. I must have been about seven years old when a gypsy woman knocked on our door and my mum, being the kind soul she was, invited her in for a cup of tea. I was watching, wide-eyed, when the gypsy returned the favour by reading Mum's tea-leaves and she told her that there was a budding star in the family. I think Mum thought that person would be Anne, who was, and still is, a talented person. But the prophecy struck a chord with me and I never forgot that day.

My dad couldn't read or write, not because he was uneducated, but due to an accident he had as a kid when he was run over by a lorry and suffered a serious head trauma. The injury left his brain unable to comprehend or recognise the written word, a bit like dyslexia. So from an early age I used to read the paper to him, pick out the horses and write out his bets. That's how I got interested in betting on the dogs and horses. From what the gypsy said, I thought I would make my fortune by becoming a famous jockey. The snooker was just a means to an end, a way to earn a few quid for those luxuries kids like: sweets and pop.

Hustling and keeping score wasn't my only source of income – as young Sandy Higgins I was known in the family as the money machine. I was up to all sorts of schemes. I never stole anything in my life, apart from a few sweets from the shop, and I always earned my money in an honest and hard-working way.

8

Isobel, Anne and Jean would help me in my endeavours and we would sort of share the profits. I say 'sort of' because Isobel usually took the lion's share.

We had a firewood round in the week where we would, or rather I would, collect fruit crates and other kinds of wooden boxes, chop them up with a hatchet, reducing them to small sticks, and then sell them to neighbours to start their coal fires. If it wasn't firewood it would be something else. By myself or with a mate, I would sometimes go around collecting scrap metal – steel, iron, brass, copper – and sell it on in order to pay for the cinema and other teenage pursuits. Another great idea I had was to run regular weekly raffles in the six weeks leading up to Christmas. All the locals knew me and that I was honest with my raffles. I would sell the tickets all week and divide the money fifty-fifty. I would use 50 per cent to buy the raffle prizes, and I always made sure that the raffle was drawn in someone else's house, and that the winners got their prizes. My reputation for being honest was my greatest asset and I used to make a small fortune to buy presents for the family. As I've said, my three sisters, Mum, Dad and I had a lot of happy times in my childhood and we were a very close-knit family. I miss Mum and Dad so much these days. Mum died in 1993 and Dad in 2003. Dad was so proud of me when I started playing professionally and the girls used to come with me on the road when I was in competition and doing exhibitions.

One time, after I'd become professional, I was playing in a local club and Anne decided she was going to bring me my lunch each day. Anne knew that if she didn't bring me something I wouldn't eat all day. On this particular occasion it was steak and onion sandwiches, but when she got to the club she saw I was very busy playing, so she just left this brown-paper-wrapped sandwich on the counter and told the man behind what it was.

He was too busy watching me and didn't hear what she said. A few minutes later he noticed the parcel sitting on the counter. Well, your man panicked and started shouting that there was a bomb on the counter and we should all get out while he called the bomb squad. So we all walked over to take a look at this supposed deadly device and I just picked it up and started to unwrap it as they all put their heads in their hands waiting for the bomb to go off. 'It's only my sandwich, you idiots,' I said, and went back to the table to finish the game, cool as you like. Well, I would recognise my own lunch, wouldn't I?

When I told Anne about it later she said it would have been funny to see the papers the next day with the headlines 'Army bomb squad blows up the Hurricane's lunch'. We still laugh about it today. There are so many great stories to tell about my sisters and me and I love them so much. Jean and Anne still live in Belfast and still look after their Sandy. Thank God.

Isobel went to Australia about thirty years ago with her husband and since then they have made a good living with their own glazing business, specialising in coloured glass. Isobel's daughter, Julie, is now married to Francesco Quinn, the son of Hollywood film legend Anthony Quinn, and lives in Los Angeles. Anne still sings when she isn't running her hairdressing business, where Jean also works. Hairdressing has been a big part of our family. Before she moved away, Isobel also owned a salon. Perhaps that's part of the reason I've always cared about how I look. The girls would never hear of me going out not looking my best.

Anne, Jean and I often meet up for a drink and a chat about the old days. One story I want to tell you is about the time I was playing across the border in Ireland. It's a bit unsavoury, I admit, but it makes me laugh. Unlike a lot of the other snooker players, I used to stay behind and have a drink to socialise with the people who had come to see us play, instead of just picking up my appearance money and going home. That's what the majority used to do, but I don't think that's on. Never have. Anyway, I was talking to a group of people and one fella asked me to give him a lift home as he wanted me to meet his wife.

Now this chap was a greyhound breeder and after a few more drinks I parted with £200 for what was described to me as the new 'Mick the Miller', a famous greyhound who won the Derby twice. I took the hound outside and as I opened the door of my Mini Cooper it jumped into the back and laid down, so I thought it was a great dog. You see, although I owned a car, I couldn't drive. Still don't. So I always had someone to drive me to the matches but, as you can imagine, there isn't a whole lot of room in such a small car for two adults, plus my cue. So a dog that immediately, and quietly, settled in the back was ideal. I thought I was on to a winner – no hassle and with electric speed – so I'd been told. Now I couldn't look after this thing, so I took it round to Anne's house and told her I had a big bunny rabbit for her to keep for me, and then in comes the dog. Well, it took one look at Anne, growled at her and then jumped on the settee and claimed it for himself.

Whenever Anne went near him, he'd growl and she would back off. Now Anne is telling me to get this animal out of the house, so I give her a few hundred quid and leg it out the front door before she knows what's happening. Anne knows about as much as I do when it comes to looking after greyhounds, so she thinks the dog must be hungry and that's why it's growling. In her wisdom she decides that the dog would like to have a bowl of beef broth, which she'd made that very evening. Not surprisingly, she didn't have any dog food in the house. So she gives the dog a big bowl of the soup and goes to bed. The next day she wakes up and comes downstairs to find that the dog has shit everywhere. None too pleased, she gets her next-door neighbour to help her put the lead on the dog, which is still growling, and drag it out of the house. Little did she know that the soup had given the animal diarrhoea.

So they take this growling, shitting greyhound on a walk, and as they pass through the churchyard they notice a wedding is taking place. They peek a look into the church from the main entrance, with the dog lagging behind them. Well, at this point the dog decides to unload himself of the rest of the contents of his bowels, right in the entrance of the church. It wasn't exactly the place, or the time, for such behaviour and so Anne and the neighbour try to drag the dog away, but it is too late. They look at each other in horror as they see the bride coming up the aisle and out of the church . . . straight into the mess. Well as much as it was disgusting, they both fell about laughing and dragged the dog along as it continued to leave a trail along the path.

When she got home Anne decided to take the dog to the vet. She drags the poor animal along the road to the surgery and it's still growling at her. The vet examines the dog and tells Anne that it wouldn't win any raffles if it bought every ticket, never mind a race. I had been sold a pig in a poke and it cost me another £25 to have the poor animal put to sleep. Apparently, the dog was in great pain with its back legs and it was better to have it put down rather than let it suffer. That was in the early 1980s and Anne has only recently forgiven me for it. She spent the money I had given her on a new settee, a new carpet and gallons of air freshener and disinfectant.

In the late fifties and early sixties things in general became a little better, but the area where I grew up wasn't a priority for the council, and so my life just became more humdrum with future prospects looking increasingly dismal. In 1964 I left school, without any certificates worth their salt, but I did get some good reports. I applied for and got a job at the Irish Linen Company in Belfast. This huge factory was owned and run by Sir Graham Lorimer, a well-known industrialist. My wages were £2 11s (£2.60p) a week and I considered myself lucky to get that job and work for such a good company. I gave Mum £2 a week for my keep and kept the eleven shillings for myself.

My main job was to take Sir Graham's messages around the factory and around town. A 'runner' I guess you'd call it and I was very proud to have the job. I was given money from petty cash to get the bus and sometimes, if the message was really urgent, a taxi. Now, Sir Graham was a wise old man, a bit like Midas in the respect that everything he touched turned to gold. Some of that gift must have rubbed off on me. All day long I would think about nothing except playing snooker, and when I finished work I would go straight to the Jampot and play till they closed. During the day I would pocket the expenses money and run from one address to another. I was a fit lad and I'd get the job done all right. I was never reprimanded at work for being late or not pulling my weight, but by going about it that way – using my wits – by the time I was done for the day I'd have enough money to start playing a frame as soon as I arrived at the club.

I have to tell you that by this time in my life I was like any other teenager, fed up with authority and of being poor without any real prospects. My relationship with my mum and dad wasn't too good either. I was under a lot of pressure to join my dad labouring, but I didn't fancy that. I wanted to better myself and Mum and Dad were always going on at me to stop gambling in the snooker halls. 'That is no way to make a living,' was their common refrain. To be honest, I never fancied working for a living. I preferred to stay out most of the day and all of the night. I would often come home with the milk as the house was rising, and I'd quietly slip into my pit like a vampire for a few hours' kip.

My mum used to try all sorts of tricks to get me out of bed. Her favourite was to pretend that the house was on fire, but one day that little trick backfired on both of us, if you'll excuse the pun. Mum had been out to the shops and on her return she was met by a pall of smoke coming from the front room. She rushed outside and called on the neighbours to help, which they did by forming a line and filling up buckets to pour on the flames while waiting for the fire brigade. Someone asked her if I was up yet and she suddenly realised that I was probably still in bed. Well, she rushed inside and up the stairs into my room. Sure enough, there I was happily asleep in the land of Nod.

'Quick, Sandy, will you get out, the place is on fire!' she shouted as she shook me.

I looked around to see if there was any smoke, but the fire was being contained by the buckets of water and the smoke hadn't quite reached my room.

'Oh Mum,' I said, 'will yer ever leave me alone with your tricks. I'm not getting up.'

'Oh please, Sandy, please will you ever get up, the house really is on fire this time.'

I must have sensed the panic in her voice and it was that that woke me up. I thought I would check it out and as I got to the top of the stairs I could see the smoke and people rushing around with buckets. Mum grabbed my arm to take me down with her, but I broke free and went back for my suit – I wasn't going to let a good piece of tailoring go to ruin. I've always liked to look sharp.

I loved my parents, but I was fed up with being told what to do and, like so many other teenagers, I rebelled. This just led to more arguments and so I decided to leave home and seek my fortune on the mainland. I got talking to some mates one day and one mentioned an advert in the paper for stableboys at a training yard in England. I wrote a letter to Eddie Reavey at the stables in East Hendred, Wantage, Oxfordshire. Now Eddie was an Ulsterman himself and liked to give the Belfast boys a chance, so he invited me over for a month. I wanted to become a champion jockey but I had no illusions about it. I saw being a stablelad as a means to an end. My mum and dad didn't really want me to leave Belfast – for all we were arguing a fair bit, we hated being apart at any time.

I was about fifteen and a half years old when I got the boat from Belfast to Liverpool. The whole family came to see me off. Mum and Dad were very upset that I was leaving. Dad kept saying his only son was going away and he would miss me so much. Mum was in bits. As for me, I was so thrilled to be going away to England and seeking my fortune that I didn't really see my parents' tears and the pain that they were feeling. I had a plan, and I was single-minded about achieving it. I don't see that as being selfish – something I've been accused of often, I'm sure. I see it as taking an opportunity to make your own things happen in life. That's what I was trying to do. That's what I've always tried to do.

That ferry journey marked my leaving childhood in more ways than one. Accompanying me on the boat, the *Ulster Queen*, were Dermot Wisdon and Davy Copeland, both already recruited by Reavey and, at twenty, both a lot older than me. They had spotted a pretty girl of about eighteen boarding the ferry and had their eyes on her. But they settled into a few drinks in the bar first, and as I was too young to drink, I slipped out and stole the girl from under their noses. She and I hid in a lifeboat, where I had my first taste of sex on the high seas. Dermot and Davy went bananas when they realised we'd disappeared but I made sure I didn't surface until just before we docked in Liverpool. To this day they don't know exactly what happened with the girl. I just told them I had fallen asleep. My big adventure had begun in the best possible way.

2

A racing certainty

•

It is probably fair to say that racing is the great sporting love of my life, even more than snooker and that's saying something. Racing has always been deep down in my heart. I've never fallen out of love with racing, unlike snooker. That's the story that is going to unfold over the course of this book.

As a kid I had big hopes of being a jockey in England and started at the Reavey stables with that in mind. I had ridden a bit in Belfast on wild unbridled ponies at a place called Barnett Park, about four miles from the city centre. These animals had no head collar, no reins, no bridle. If you could get close enough, you would grab a pony's mane and jump on as they took off under you. When things got hairy you would just throw yourself off, rolling when you hit terra firma. So I had a little bit of experience with horses. Well, you have to start somewhere.

Davy Copeland, who'd been on the boat over with me, after he'd been visiting friends and family back home, was one of the top stablelads. He mostly stayed in the yard and was in charge of a group of us. Basically, Davy got to do most of the best jobs, while the mere minions, including me, did all the mucking out and menial jobs. Like me, he had been recruited through an Eddie Reavey advert, five years earlier, and was a very amiable man and a very good jockey.

Most of the lads stuck together within their own groups, that is to say we looked after certain horses together, so it made sense to socialise within that group. I used to take off most nights to the youth club in the village to dance. We also used to play a fair bit of darts – so much so that Davy and I, along with some of the other lads, joined the local Rose and Crown pub team. At the oche, Davy was the main man, and whenever we played he used to wipe the floor with me. He was, and still is, a very good dart player.

That said, I wasn't half bad myself, and I saved our team many a defeat by coming good at the last minute, which is a typical Higgins trait. We used to take our girlfriends along with us when we played away. I didn't have a lot to do with girls then, but I did like to try my luck when I saw a filly I fancied, as my experience on the boat proved. Davy had a regular girlfriend, Wendy, and she often introduced me to other girls, mostly because Davy and I would usually go into the village together, so it was either me playing gooseberry or Wendy fixing me up. You see, there was a very strong camaraderie among the lads, not so much because we were mostly Irish and from the same background, but more that we were all away from our families. We missed the warmth and safety that a family atmosphere gives you and so we became our own little family away from home and looked out for each other.

Wendy fixed me up with one of the village girls one night. Her name was Susan and I really fancied myself with her. We went off to the Rose and Crown and at closing time we walked back to the stables. I was sure my luck was in and so we all went to our 'house', by which I mean our little lovenest that we'd built in the back of one of the barns, hidden behind a wall of straw bales. It was like a front parlour. It had a settee and a couple of old moth-eaten armchairs, a coffee table with some candles on it and a rug that had seen better days. It wasn't much, but I felt sure it was bound to wow the lovely Susan straight into my arms.

Needless to say, I tried it on after we got comfy but Susan wasn't having any of it. The old Higgins charm wasn't working that night, or most other nights, to be honest, as far as women were concerned in those days. Hard to believe, I know. Well, I ended up getting the hump and giving Susan a mouthful of my thoughts on how I expected the evening to go. This lovely, feisty girl stared straight at me, folded her arms and, with a look that only a woman can give, laid into me with her own verbal outburst. Well, I could see that I wasn't going to win the match this time, so I turned on my heels and, giving out to her again, marched off to my bed. As I walked away all I could hear was Davy and Wendy laughing like a pair of those fairground clowns. Davy Copeland never lets me forget about that night.

We would finance our nights out with some very ingenious ideas. Although I didn't play a great deal of snooker during that time at the stables, sometimes we would go down to the youth club, where I would win us our beer money for the night by playing the local lads at snooker. I would usually try to win games in record time to get to the pub and the girls quickly. Other times we would simply use our devious minds to come up with quick and clever ideas to get the money. One little stunt we used to pull was to climb over the fence of the Plough pub, fill a few carrier bags with empty beer bottles and a few soda siphons, then pass them over to one of the other lads. As everything was reused and to make sure you brought them back, beer bottles, pop bottles and soda siphons had a deposit on them. So we used to nick the bottles from the back of the pub and then take them inside to redeem the deposits. The Plough was well known for its card school in the room out the back, and we would often get our stake money this way for the poker games. In all the months we did that, not once did anyone catch us out.

As head lad, Davy had the privilege, along with some of the other experienced lads, of riding the horses out to exercise each day and the lesser lads used to envy them that, especially as those of us left behind had to clean out the muck and put fresh straw in the stables. After this we would wash down and sweep the yard ready for the horses to come back. Now most of us got on very well, but there was a bit of conflict from time to time and I wasn't immune to that, surprise, surprise.

There was a lad from the Republic of Ireland who fancied himself a bit. He was what was known as a travelling head lad. He would accompany the horses when they went to race meetings and was in charge of the lads while they were at the courses. His name was Michael and he didn't like me. He lived in his own caravan with his wife at the stables and one day he just pissed me off big time. I can't remember what started it off, but you can be sure it was something quite trivial. Anyway, he took a swing at me first and as it landed I swung out and caught him on the side of his face.

I recovered quicker and laid into him, as he did into me. So there we stood in the middle of the yard, punching the crap out of each other with the other lads cheering us both on. After a couple of minutes Davy came on the scene and pulled us apart. He gave us both a dressing down and made us shake hands. I didn't want to, but in the end Michael kept pushing his hand forward and eventually I took it. Michael left the yard a few weeks later and moved on to somewhere else, but it wasn't over the fight. He was just a travelling type of man. I heard that he died of a heart attack at the age of fifty.

After doing our chores in the morning, a few of the lads would head down to the village of East Hendred where we'd meet the other lads coming back with the horses after their morning run. We'd take the horses and walk them through the village, or sometimes we would ride them back to the stables after giving them a bit of a rest. My first-ever ride on a racehorse was on a 15-hands-high filly named Bonnies Trust. I loved this horse and she seemed to like me as well, but that wasn't true for all the horses in the yard. One in particular absolutely hated me.

Hunters Gold was a fast, strong and often moody horse. You see, horses know if you are frightened of them. If they sense this or any kind of caution, you are in trouble, because a strong horse will take full advantage of it to have a go at you. Hunters Gold must have smelt the wariness on me, for from the very moment we met he hated me. If I was walking another horse in front of him, he would deliberately move up and bite me. Mum sent me a jumper for Christmas and that bloody horse bit the shoulder out of it in sheer spite. The other lads thought it was hilarious and Davy offered to get Wendy to darn it for me, but Hunter had ripped the whole shoulder off – there was nothing to darn.

One morning I was walking down to the village as usual and Davy met me with Hunters Gold. Now I don't know if he thought of it as a joke or not, but he gave me the rein to that bloody horse. I took no chances. Being all too aware of the damage his teeth could inflict, I stood as far away as I could without letting go. I also tried to avoid any direct eye contact with him as I felt that was maybe setting him off. But all my precautions counted for nothing. Being a cold morning I had on my duffle coat and as I started to walk him, suddenly the local milk lorry came roaring past revving its engine. Hunter spooked. He reared up and stretched the rein, trying to break free. I was pulled off my feet and spun round, my left arm coming out of the coat. As I fell on the ground, reins still in hand, Hunter started trampling on the coat arm and got caught up in it. His leg went inside the arm and he tried to run off, dragging me for a few yards before stopping. Davy caught up with us and calmed him down, thank God, before any more damage was done. I had a lucky escape that day, I know it. I often wonder what might have happened to me – whether I'd ever have had a snooker career if my arm had still been in that coat sleeve as those flashing hoofs came clattering down on it. My bones would have been smashed to pieces, I'm certain, and my cuing action would have been totally different. Who knows what that might have meant.

Despite the best endeavours of Hunter and a few other inmates of the stables, I loved those horses. There is nothing on this earth like feeling the power and strength of a racehorse beneath me. I have met many racing-car drivers and motorbike riders in my time, and they too talk of the exhilaration of being in control of a powerful machine at speeds that defy the imagination. I admire them so much, but they have no idea of the feeling of having a powerful animal in your control. A speeding car or bike can be stopped fairly quickly, but a racehorse is something extra to contend with. These beautiful, graceful creatures have a natural instinct for speed and, mixed with their love of the open air and freedom, they are a force to be handled with great skill. Their brains are quick and their legs quicker still, and there is no greater experience than to be onboard one of these creatures when they are let go to reach their cruising speed. I miss that excitement and the adrenalin rush very much.

With the horses back in their stables, there wasn't that much to do after lunch. We could ride some of the horses if we liked, or be assigned some more menial jobs. Me, I used to skive off to do my betting. The wages for stablelads are lousy. We got just 35s (£1.75p) a week all found, but the food was good. In fact, it was too good and there was always plenty of it. I was always hungry and eating meals cooked by the lovely ladies from the village was a sure-fired way of putting on the pounds, something a wannabe jockey doesn't need. I certainly never had the will power of Davy Copeland to eat just enough to keep the body fuelled.

Margaret Pill, Mrs Liddle and dear Mrs Hillier were partly responsible for Sandy Higgins putting on too much weight ever to be seriously considered a jockey – well, I had to blame someone for putting on two stone in just under two years. I am also by nature a fairly lazy person – now there's something a lot of people don't like to admit. So, in the afternoon, after a heavy lunch, I used to sneak off to the bookies near the stables in a vain attempt to subsidise my meagre wages. The Tin Hut, as it was known, was the not-so-salubrious establishment of a character named Ted Chesney and it was here that I could be found most afternoons. Eddie and his wife Jocelyn often caught me in there with other lads and subsequently sacked us all – till teatime that is when Jocelyn would come along and tell us that she had persuaded Eddie to give us another chance. Sometimes it was Eddie telling us that he had persuaded Jocelyn to give in. I was sacked and taken on more times than I can remember.

I had a great relationship with both Eddie and Jocelyn in the near-enough two years I spent at the stables. I admired and loved them both. They had a genuine affection for all the lads and girls who worked at the stables, and made us feel like we were part of a huge family. There was one particular incident that I can pinpoint as being the moment that brought me even closer to them and their family. I was riding around the yard one day when I found a purse. It had a few quid and a piece of jewellery in it and anyone finding it might have been tempted just to pocket it. I didn't. I had seen the purse before and knew it belonged to their daughter Ann.

Ann often rode her pony Dizzy around the yard and so I guessed that she had dropped it. I took the purse into the house and handed it over to Jocelyn. She took my hand and called out to Ann. As Ann entered the room Jocelyn told her that I had found her purse, and the kid was over the moon. There turned out to be over £5 in there. I was given a reward and a huge thank-you, and from that moment on the family treated me a bit better than most of the other lads. They appreciated my honesty. The Reavey kids got on well with all the lads and we never felt that they were pulling rank on us. They did their fair share of the chores as well.

I left after about twenty-two months when Eddie, finally at the end of his tether, called me into the house and told me that it would be better if I went back home. This time he meant it and I knew he meant it. I had had enough by then anyway. I just wasn't enjoying it any more. I said a sad goodbye to all the lads and I knew I would miss it once I was actually back home. As for Davy Copeland, well he went on to better things. He married Wendy and they settled in the village and had three children, two boys and a girl. Davy and Wendy eventually divorced and Wendy and the kids still live in and around the village. Davy has had an illustrious career in the racehorse business. He rode a big winner – Commander in Chief – in the Cambridgeshire, and went to Germany where he became respected as 'The Horseman', a nickname he earned after helping to train Tempera, which Frankie Dettori rode to victory in the German Derby. After that he went to America where he spent eleven years working with some of the top trainers and horses, a few of whom won the Kentucky Derby. I am very honoured to be able to say that Davy Copeland is my friend. We can often be seen in a few pubs around Belfast these days, reminiscing about the old times. Davy came back to his roots some years ago, when he retired from the racing business, and is now head of housekeeping at the Europa Hotel in the city centre.

I never forgot my time at the Reavey stables and I can honestly say, with my hand on my heart, that the days I spent there were the happiest of my life. I really mean that. I have had some great times in my life and been treated very well, but those few brief months I will always remember. I stayed in touch with the Reaveys and often called in if I wasn't too far from there when I was on tour. After Eddie died, I used to phone more often and talk to Jocelyn about Eddie and the stables. They both formed an important part of how I developed as a young man and for that I will always be deeply grateful.

3

London belongs to me

•

It must have been around August 1966 when I arrived back home.
I got a job working at another stables outside Belfast, but that
lasted a few weeks only, and I went back to the family home. It
was the end of the summer and Dad had organised a ten-day
family holiday with his sister and her husband, so we all got the
boat over to England and the train to the Isle of Dogs. We had no
sooner got there and unpacked when Mum started to complain
to Dad that she wasn't happy with the place (or her in-laws), and
after a few days they all packed their bags and departed for
home. Not me, of course. I was quite happy to stay. We'd paid for
the full ten days and I'd already got to know a number of the
blokes who hung around the local snooker hall in Poplar. In fact,
one of them – a certain Ronnie Bender – helped me sort out digs
once I had to move. I was very happy to find a job and had no
intentions of going back to Belfast. There was nothing there for
me except more of the same. I liked my independence and wasn't
looking forward to being at home again at my age.

I got a job on the night shift at a paper mill in the East End
– Limehouse, to be precise – and started to pay my way. The
work was hard but I enjoyed it. My job was basically unloading
the paper as it flew – literally – off the presses. I also had to keep
the machines running. As paper and cardboard went through the
process, it dried out and often clogged up the rollers, so the

whole thing would grind to a halt. I'd have to climb underneath the press to work the paper free and release the jam. The mill produced paper and cardboard from old paper products – newspapers, magazines, books, boxes and paperbacks. You name it, the mill made paper from it. The books were stored in a series of huge warehouses and rooms; the newspapers and magazines were stored separately. I used to work mainly in the old-books warehouse and I started to notice that we got a lot of erotic paperbacks. Today, the material in these books wouldn't even make you blink, but in the 1960s it was very raunchy stuff.

There was an opportunity to be had here and no mistake, and I wasn't about to let it slip. A bit of my own recycling would do nicely, so I thought. I would fill my sack each morning before leaving the mill after my shift, and head down to a little bookshop two miles away. I got sixpence (2½p) for each one – not a fortune, but if you multiply that by twenty books or so, it was enough in the mid sixties to buy five pints of beer, although drinking in smoky pubs was not really my scene then. I much preferred to go up to the West End and play snooker for money in the better snooker halls. I met some very colourful characters in those halls. I was making a nice little living out of playing my favourite sport for money during the day and working at the mill throughout the night (plus my lucrative little sideline in bookselling, of course). Before long I was playing a regular crowd of serious players for decent money. I didn't always win the frames, but I won enough to make myself a reputation for being a fair, clean and skilled player. Even at this point, though, with money coming in and a reasonably structured set of games on a fairly consistent basis, I still never once imagined that I could turn professional and make a fantastic living from the sport. The possibility never entered my head, to be honest.

London was changing as a capital city and there were lots of opportunities for anyone who wanted to better themselves, and by that I mean the previously kept-down working class. I was very naïve at that time. By now it was 1967 and The Beatles were wooing the Americans, the Stones were wooing everyone else and I was wooing no one, but that wasn't worrying me. At that stage in my life I wasn't really interested in anything except snooker and gambling, which for me went hand in hand. When I wasn't up in the West End, I'd spend my time in the hall in Poplar. Ronnie Bender and I had hit it off almost immediately. That's why he was so helpful in finding me digs after I'd been kipping on a mate's sofa for a few days. Ronnie was a great lover of snooker and encouraged me hugely to keep playing and practising. We became friends and one evening he invited me to join him at Walthamstow dog track. I hadn't been to the dogs since I'd arrived, so I was delighted to take up his offer.

I didn't have a huge amount of cash to bet with, but Ronnie did – at the beginning of the evening anyway. He was having a bad run and I knew exactly how much he was losing because I was the one putting his bets on. He said to me just as we arrived, 'Can you put a series of bets on for me, son? The bookies round here think I'm just too damn lucky. So if I go to put me money on, the odds disappear.' I was happy to oblige. It must have been about halfway through the meeting when Ronnie decided to up the ante. He handed over a bundle of cash and whispered the trap numbers and combinations he wanted me to bet on. We were standing in a very noisy area of the track and what with that, and the fact that I sometimes struggled to pick up everything he was saying because of his broad London accent, I misunderstood what he said and put the bet on incorrectly.

When he looked at the slips I handed over to him he started to have a right go at me. At first I didn't know why he was pissed off, I just knew from his tone that he was. Big time. Well, the

Higgins luck was in that night and to both our surprises, and my good fortune, the dogs I put down won most of the races. Ronnie said something about the luck of the Irish and sent me off to collect the winnings, which came to a hefty sum. My pockets were bulging with all the cash, and I got a bit scared that I might be robbed. I needn't have worried. I didn't know it at the time but the fact that I'd been seen with Ronnie was enough to protect me one hundred per cent. My fortuitous error seemed to mark a turn in Ronnie's fortunes and he went on to back the next four winners. By the end of the night he'd done very nicely indeed, thank-you very much and, as a thanks to me, he slipped me a £100 bonus. I'd honestly never had so much cash in one go. I felt like a king that night.

Our friendship grew from there but it was a long time until I realised just who this man was, one of London's most notorious gangsters. Remember, I was young and impressionable and Ronnie's swagger and know-how around town impressed me – for a time anyway. Ronnie, some of his mates (most of whom I hardly knew or didn't want to know, to be honest) and I would go out occasionally, when I could afford it, and we had some great times. It all came to an end when one of the most infamous incidents in London's crime history occurred, and Ronnie was there.

The date was 28 October 1967. The place, 'Blond Carol' Skinner's flat. The event, Reggie Kray killing Jack 'The Hat' McVitie. According to the transcripts of the trial, a couple of years later, Ronnie was standing near Reggie when the gun Reggie intended using to shoot McVitie jammed. Reggie apparently turned to Ronnie, took a knife from him and finished the job. After that evening, everything seemed to change and Ronnie and I drifted apart – not that I knew what had happened. I might have socialised a bit with that crowd, but I was nowhere near 'in', thank God. It was another two years before the world, including me, knew about the McVitie murder and Ronnie's involvement in it. I never saw Ronnie commit a violent act. He didn't need to because he had an air of menace about him. I do, however, remember a fight breaking out one night in the snooker hall in Poplar. This big bloke hit another guy who went down like he'd been shot. The big bloke grabbed a snooker triangle, put it over the fella's head as he lay on the ground and dragged him around the table with it. He then hooked the triangle over the place where the spider was kept and proceeded to give the helpless bugger the kicking of his life. I had no idea what the fight was about but I was just glad it wasn't me and, like everyone else, I looked the other way.

I soon got into a daily routine of stopping off at the book-shop at about 8 a.m. after my shift, and going back to the flat to sleep until 1 or 2 p.m. Then, with my cue under my arm, I would take the N98 bus up west and walk around the various snooker halls till I saw a familiar face. I was just working, eating and playing snooker, and still had little time or inclination for girls or drinking. In those lonely times in that big city it was difficult to get to know girls anyway, so I just didn't bother.

One of my favourite places to go was Herbert Holt's place in Windmill Street, just off Shaftesbury Avenue. I met some great players there, and they were a totally different crowd from the East End mob. One of the chaps, Derek Cox, was a lovely guy, a pianist with the London Philharmonic, and we used to play some very serious snooker, for money. He was a better, or should I say more consistent, player than I was, and I learned a lot from him about playing a slower game, because even then I would charge round the table potting balls. That probably came from the early days at the Jampot, where we would try to finish the frame as quickly as possible, grab our winnings and get on to the next table to start all over again. Being fleet of foot also helped to avoid a box round the head from the bad losers.

Derek used to beat me at the start, but as I practised more and more, I started to get the better of him. Then one night, out of the blue, he put his cue away in its case and handed it to me. 'Alex,' he said, 'I'm fed up playing now and you are such a good player these days, take my cue and use it well. I won't need it any more.' With that he shook my hand, turned away and walked out the door. I never saw him again.

For me, the club was a home from home. If you've ever lived in a big city on your own, you will know what I mean. In Poplar I knew no one, except the snooker-hall blokes. I would sit on the N98 bus going up to town and the only person I spoke to was the conductor. I met a smashing couple in the club one night, Tony and Sheila O'Beirne, who lived in Guildford in Surrey, and they sort of adopted me. They were like a second mother and father to me. Tony loved snooker and, although he wasn't a great player, he loved to watch and play the game. Many a time Tony and I would find ourselves still in Holt's club at 2 a.m. and Tony would drive me home in his little Alpha Romeo sports car.

I often used to look out for the O'Beirnes later on, when I made it big, but I never met them again. Sheila was always looking out for me and would invite me over to join them whenever they were out socialising. They even invited me down to stay with them in Guildford on a number of occasions. That was quite an experience. If Sheila was driving, it was white knuckles all the way. She drove that Alpha like she was Stirling Moss – great fun. They helped me out many times when I was having a bad night and lost all my money. Sheila would often slip me a pound for my fare home and breakfast. 'Get a fry-up in the morning, Alex. You look like you need a good meal,' she'd say. One time they came up to town to see me and gave me £50 so I could get a ticket to go home and visit my family for a few weeks. These days people might read something sinister into such generosity, but back then and with these genuine people, it was just an act of kindness. They were wonderful people and will forever be deep in my heart. God bless you both, and thank-you for all you did for me.

I was getting restless again. The flat was beginning to look like a war zone and I was beginning to feel very lonely. I needed to have that family warmth again. I missed my mum, who was so loving and caring. I even missed the nagging about getting a job from Dad, and my sisters telling me to pull myself together. They always wanted the best for me. So it was a fairly easy decision to make really, and the moment I arrived back in Belfast, which must have been in the autumn of 1967, I had a strong feeling that things were about to get better.

4

Back home again

•

Mum and Dad were just as happy to have me home as I was to be back in Belfast, but I have never been someone who doesn't pay their way. My parents taught us all the value of honesty and standing your round, so I had to find a way of contributing to the housekeeping as well as being able to go out. At first, I couldn't find a job with a decent wage, so I ended up signing on and going back to the snooker halls to play for money. At least it was an honest, if not honourable, way of making a living. I had been improving my game while hustling the snooker halls of London, so I was much better at it this time round.

As time went by, I did find work and I had all sorts of jobs, including a few with textile companies. One I really liked was as a cutter with a company called Magee's, which made clothes from Harris Tweed. I continued to subsidise my wages, though, making a few quid each week by playing money games in the snooker halls. After all, I was good enough.

By now the Troubles had divided the people of Northern Ireland completely, but I decided I didn't want anything to do with sectarianism. I had returned to a land where there were places you only went to if you were either Catholic or Protestant. I was born a Protestant and refused to be drawn into this madness. So I would frequent all the main clubs in Belfast, some Catholic and some Protestant. To be honest, I can't remember which was which. I never really cared because I just wanted to play snooker for love and money, not politics. I was always a loner and was never approached to join any gangs. In fact, the only thing I was ever asked to join was the Boys Brigade, which I was in for just a few weeks.

My old haunt, the Jampot, was now owned and operated by Cecil Mason, who I knew from playing snooker with over the years. The club was now, sadly, coming to an end and was mostly used as a bingo hall, so I started to play at the Shaftesbury club. We used to play all sorts of different games, for money of course, including life pool, which I first came across at the Jampot some years earlier. In this version, each player was allocated a colour and if your coloured ball was potted, you lost one of your three lives. Last player standing won the pot. We used to say 'Fares please' when we went to collect our winnings off the other players. Starting off my day with about 12/6d (62p), I would have enough for five games at 2/6d per game, which meant I had to win at least one game in five to stay even, and at those odds I usually came off the better each day. Whether I was working or on the dole, I used to give Mum keep money, and the rest of my cash I would use to get in on the games. I still didn't drink much. In fact, I didn't start drinking seriously until I was about nineteen or twenty. It was just snooker that got my adrenalin going.

Most weeks I would be up, but occasionally I would lose all my money and be skint by Monday. Then I'd have to wait until Thursday to get my next lot of dole money or my wages. Sometimes, if I was broke, I would go over to the Belfast City YMCA snooker centre and earn some money marking for the league players. This helped me improve my game as I was marking for good amateur players, such as Tommy McBride, Campbell Martin and Billy Caughey, who had class and were dedicated. I also really enjoyed watching two classy billiards players, Sammy Bailey and Billy Bennett. They were in their sixties but they still regularly knocked 400+ breaks.

After about three months or so of hanging around the YMCA I got my chance. One of their team members failed to turn up and I offered to step in and take his place. I won my frames that night. I was so proud of myself. There I was, still a little wet behind the ears, and playing in a real team. It felt good to belong to such an auspicious group of people. I used to go to the club almost every day to play and practise, although gambling was frowned upon. Well, after all, they were a Christian organisation. So playing for money within the league structure was a no-no, but it didn't stop us gambling among ourselves when we weren't playing actual matches. The edge of having money on the table made the games more competitive and therefore made us better players, and of course winning gave us cash in our pockets to have a few jars – which in those days meant three halves of Guinness for me.

I continued to go to the other halls to play for money, but being in the YMCA team started to give me some dignity about myself. Mum and Dad didn't really have much to say on the subject. They didn't encourage me or discourage me in any way. I suppose they didn't really know what I was up to most of the time but at least they did know I wasn't up to anything bad. I used to love bringing home a fish supper for Mum and Dad if I'd had a good night playing. As I said earlier, I wasn't a big drinker then and so when the halls closed I would usually go straight home, via the chip shop.

While all this was going on, I got it into my head to enter the 1968 Northern Ireland amateur championship. I felt my play was improving enough – and I was smarter as well with my waistcoat and tie (we didn't wear bow-ties). Just before my first match in the competition, Alfie Sanderson, chairman of the Mountpottinger club, where the competition was being held, took me aside and told me that I had the ability to win it. I don't mind telling you, despite the fact I was pretty cocky, even back then, that little chat with Alfie lifted me off my feet. I felt so proud that he had so much confidence in me that I almost cried with pride. He shook my hand, put his other hand on my shoulder and said, 'Alex, you have the ability and the skill. Go get that cup.' I looked at him and couldn't reply. I just nodded confirmation, turned and walked to the table.

The place was packed to the rafters and the line of 'spectators' extended down the stairs. Those at the top relayed the commentary to those below. I had been out till about 4 a.m. that morning, playing an exhibition match in Londonderry, but I had managed to get some sleep and what I lacked in energy was made up by the atmosphere and my team-mates' confidence in me.

I wasn't playing just for myself, but for them as well. I beat Maurice Gill, a great player and a real gentleman, 4–1 in the final and the hall exploded with cheers like I had never heard before. I almost looked around to see who had walked in the room when I suddenly realised it was me, young Alex Higgins, the skinny kid from Abingdon Street, Sandy Row, who all the clapping was for. I can still see myself at that table taking that winning shot. As I turned to the crowd to show them the trophy, I saw Alfie standing to one side. He gave me a thumbs-up and I read his lips – 'Well done, kiddo. I knew you could do it.'

I think my over-riding sensation that night was one of relief. I was elated, of course, but I'm not really one to show my emotions publicly. It doesn't happen often. I knew I had the ability and I was pleased that I hadn't let anyone down, most of all Mum and Dad. After the presentation of the trophy, and the

£8 worth of gift vouchers for the local shops, I went out for a beer with a mate, then straight home, with my fish and chips.

Mum and Dad had decided they didn't want to come to see me play because they couldn't stand the thought of me losing and them being there to see the look of disappointment on my face. This is the love they had for me and I fully understood that. So that night, before I had set off, they both hugged and kissed me. 'Good luck, son,' Dad had said proudly. I could feel the tears welling up in us all and turned away for a moment. As I turned back, I could see that their eyes were wet too. Dad hugged me again and whispered, 'I'm so proud of you, son. Just do your best and you will win this.' Then he patted my shoulder and they went off to play bingo. Later that night the bingo caller made an announcement that a local lad named Alexander Higgins had won the final and Mum told me the hall erupted in applause. Everyone was proud that a kid from their community was doing well.

Winning that championship introduced me to a new world and I was determined to make the best of it. Offers of exhibitions came flooding in and, although there wasn't any great money to be had, at least I was making a living from the game. I certainly wasn't what anyone could term a professional at that stage, but I knew I could have a shot at it, and that I'd earned the right to have that chance. Muhammad Ali has always been my sporting hero, and round about then I'd read something about the fact that Ali used to wear extra heavy boots when training. It's a bit like wearing a hat all day, and then when you take it off, your head still feels the weight and thinks you're still wearing it. Well, that's what Ali did. He fooled his legs into thinking they still carried that heavy weight, and then, just before he left the dressing room, he would change into his lightweight boots, and that made it easier for him to keep on the move and avoid those heavy punches. I did the same, just used a different method. When I first started playing in the league I was determined to push myself, to make things harder so I would be forced to improve. Instead of wearing heavy boots, I'd often give my opponents an 80–100 advantage. I'd still beat them, most of the time. It worked, and winning the Northern Ireland amateur championship was the proof.

Beating Maurice Gill so easily gave me real confidence for entering the All-Ireland amateur championship a short time later. I started the tournament with some pretty good snooker, even if I say so myself. As the players got knocked out one by one, my belief in myself increased and that had a positive effect on my game. I was consistently making breaks of 60–90 and I reached the final, where I was to meet a top-class player by the name of Gerry Hanway. I won, but not easily. Twelve months later it was a different story. Was I over-confident by then? Perhaps, for when the Northern Ireland amateur came round again, I was beaten by Dessie Anderson, who snatched the title just as I had done the previous year. Oh well, easy come, easy go.

In 1970, the YMCA team, captained by me, played in the final of the John Player UK team championship. The tournament was open to teams from across the United Kingdom. You played a series of rounds within your own region – Northern Ireland, England, Scotland and Wales – and the winners from each of the regional tournaments went into the hat for the semi-finals. We were drawn at home and won our way through to the final against the Welsh. All told, we'd played about fifteen matches to get there.

The three players in our team – Billy Caughey, Jacky Shannon and me – knew we'd have to buckle down and work hard if we were to pull it off. We had been in Bolton, Lancashire, where the final was to be played, for a few days before the matches started, mainly practising, but also out on the lash as well. We'd even presented a local beauty queen with a shillelagh one night. All that had to stop. This was serious now. We wanted to win.

The final consisted of three rounds, with each player playing two frames, and the scores were cumulative. I decided to put Billy in first because I thought he'd be able to hold his own against Welsh champion Terry Parsons. I was wrong. Billy was slaughtered over the two frames and we were something like 100 points behind as I stepped up to take my turn in the second round against John Shepherd. When I stepped away again after the two frames, we were 90 points in the lead. I'd played beautiful, fast snooker and had blown John away.

So it was down to Jacky to steer us home to victory, and he did, but only just. Incredibly, given that it was a cumulative score from three players on each team, the championship went down to a black-ball finish. The Welsh lad, Mel Jones, had a shot for glory into the side pocket – and missed with the finest of cuts into the middle pocket. Jacky didn't give him a second chance and we were champions, with £300 in our pockets. We almost didn't get that. The YMCA wanted to take the prize money for their funds but we refused. We'd been playing all over the country to get to the final, footing all our own expenses, and we weren't about to be out of pocket for being victorious.

A six-frame final isn't exactly going to keep the fans happy for a whole evening, so the organisers had enlisted the help of former world champion, John Pulman, to entertain the crowds with some trick shots after the match was over. John had been sitting watching the action on the table and was impressed enough by what he saw in me to suggest that, instead of the fancy tricks, he and I should play a match. Playing the great John Pulman in front of a big crowd – I wasn't about to turn that down. He was my absolute idol when I was a kid. He played some fantastic snooker that night, with regular 50+ breaks, and won most of the frames, but I managed to sneak a couple off him and was pleased with how I'd played. As we shook hands at the end he said to me, 'I'll have to watch you in the future, son.' I remember thinking, 'And I like the stylish way you dress and the way you carry yourself. That's a look I'd like for me.' The seed for another aspect of the Higgins image was planted that night.

Winning that trophy was not only a highlight of the year, but a turning point in my career. Mum and Dad and the girls were so proud of me and they all came to meet us at the station when we arrived home.

Belfast has always been proud of its sporting sons and daughters, who represent the city as a community, and we are all equally as proud of each other. The *Belfast Telegraph* did a huge piece on us and for some reason they used the picture of me getting presented with the trophy. Billy insisted that it was me who had won it, so I should go and get it, but I considered that I did it as part of a team and not as an individual. I knew that sometimes I played badly in the team, and it just so happened that it was Billy's turn to be shite during that tournament. That's all fine, but it was still a team victory in my view.

Anyway, the picture drew a lot of attention and some months later I was approached by Bolton snooker player Jimmy Wolsey to play some exhibition matches against John Spencer at the same venue as the John Player tournament, the Bolton Institute of Technology. This was a first of its kind – an amateur playing the world champion – and it drew good crowds. I was paid £30 for the week and this was, I suppose, really my first professional booking. Being an amateur, I was given a 14 point lead in each frame, but I didn't need it. I'd have beaten Spencer even without the handicap, and as I thought about that on my way back to the hotel after the final night's play, I began to seriously consider snooker as a possible full-time way of life. I often wonder what might have happened to me if Mel Jones hadn't over-cut that black ball and the picture hadn't been printed in the paper. But he did, and it was, and I was on the road to becoming a professional player.

I liked Lancashire and so I decided to stay a while. I needed my independence again after being back at home for so long, especially as I couldn't really take girls back with me. Mum would always look for faults in them and it became a bit off-putting. Don't get me wrong. I loved Mum, but I was a normal, hot-blooded male and I needed my space. During my stay in England at that time I lived all over the north – Accrington, Blackburn and a nice little town with a typically northern name, Oswaldtwistle. I used to go to all the best working-men's clubs and two in particular, the Post Office club in Blackburn and the Elite in Accrington, where I sometimes played Dennis Taylor and Jimmy Meadowcroft for 2/6d a game. Usually I'd come out on top by simply playing them off against each other. I had an advantage over them that they could never fathom and that was my excellent memory, which I used to outwit my fellow players.

I knew Dennis always played a safe game and that Jimmy would always go for long shots, so I tried to set up play accordingly. I'd engineer a long shot for Jimmy, knowing he would miss the shot more times than he would make it. The ball would then go down table for Dennis's shot. He would never, or rarely, take a chance, so he would safety play the ball and that way his score was usually low. Playing to opponents' weaknesses is a critical strategy in any sport and snooker is no exception. It is not merely a case of playing your own game and hoping the person you are up against cocks up. You have to structure the table so you are in charge but to do that you've got to be able to remember how the other player thinks and plays. My memory never let me down. I made a living doing this for months and my game improved immensely.

My next break came when I met some very influential and rich local men at the Post Office club. I was practising there for eight hours at a time, and then I would go home to have something to eat and head back to the tables. I still had a social life, don't worry, and would often go to the pub or a disco, but to be honest my mind wasn't on wine, women or song at that point. All I wanted to do was get good enough to be able to turn pro. My break came in the guise of John McLaughlin and his business partner Jack Leeming. They had made their fortune out of bingo halls and were bored, so they decided to start managing snooker players. I was taken on by them and they put me up in a nice flat, bought me some respectable clothes and gave me a regular wage of £35 a week, which was really good money back then.

John, Jack and another friend of theirs, Dennis Broderick, used to play at lunchtimes and I'd join in from time to time. We became great friends. To this day I regard the three of them, and their wives, as being among the most loyal and dear friends I have ever had. They were my first managers and they got me regular exhibition games at £25 a time.

I remember that time vividly. Isobel, my eldest sister, was following my progress and could see that I was developing into something a bit special. Now, Isobel has a fast brain on her, and she told me I should enter a challenge match at the Ambulance Drill Hall in Accrington against Spencer. The prize money was good and Isobel was so sure about her brother's ability that she was willing to put her money where her mouth was. She offered to put up the £100 entry fee for a share of the spoils. I thought about it and decided that it would be unfair of me to expect Isobel to take the risk. I was willing to give it a go, though, and found myself 4–1 down, but I fought back to clinch a 5–4 victory.

Back home again

There had been no handicap this time. I'd won fair and square. If I'd been contemplating turning professional before then, that victory crystallised my decision. I was too late to enter the 1971 World Championship – the governing body insisted you had a three-month probationary period before you were fully professional (not that I ever heard of anyone else having to go through that) – but my sights were firmly set on 1972.

5

People's champion

•

Whenever winter starts to creep up on us, weather forecasters start to predict storms and hurricanes. Most people refer to the year of the big hurricane as being 1987, and then someone else will say, 'No, the biggest one was in 1994.' Well, for snooker fans, it was 1972. That was the year that the mother of all Hurricanes blew through their lives. John McLaughlin and Jack Leeming named me 'The Hurricane' when they managed me. John said it was because of the way I played my shots. Jack says it was because it went so well with Higgins. I wanted to be called 'Alexander the Great'. He was a figure in history I admired. I wanted to make history and become the greatest snooker player ever, so I thought the name would be appropriate. However, Muhammad Ali was already called 'the greatest' and it may have looked as though I was cashing in on that title. It would have been disrespectful and, let's face it, conceited. Whatever the reason, the name stuck, and in 1972 every snooker fan in the world would stand up and applaud my winning the World Championship as Alex 'Hurricane' Higgins.

I played my last exhibition match of 1971 on 23 December in Accrington and after the match Jack handed me some presents – an airline ticket to Belfast and two weeks' wages. I was well set for a much-needed break, or so you'd think, but a few hours later, at 3 a.m. on Christmas Eve morning, I was on the phone to Jack, asking him to come and pick me up at the Ace of Spades casino just down the road from him. I had lost all my wages on the tables. Jack didn't say anything. He loved playing roulette so he had some empathy with me. He just picked me up and drove me to his house, where he cooked me breakfast and we chatted for ages. He arranged another flight for me, and I arrived home later that day, skint, cold, pissed off with myself and tired, but I knew that I would have a great family Christmas and I looked forward to the new year when I would get a crack at being the world champion.

January arrived with a huge hangover. I spent the first day of 1972 resting as I had to play in the Irish Professional the next day, against Jack Rea, the man who had held the title for almost twenty years.

The competition started on 2 January and was played at a different venue every night to make it accessible to as many people as possible over the course of the week. On the first night, I beat Jack 5–4 and, as the score suggests, it wasn't an easy match by any standards. I played an attacking strategy and my tactics paid off, but only just. Jack was a great player and a great entertainer and it was a close-run thing right up to the last ball dropping into the pocket.

On 7 January, at Graignamanagh in Co. Kilkenny, the final match of the tournament was played, although that was not supposed to happen until the next day at the Gresham Hotel in Dublin. My score of 28–12 made it impossible for Jack to win and I was crowned champion.

As my profile and reputation began to grow, John and Jack realised I needed more support. Jack even bought me a suit. They appointed our friend Dennis Broderick to travel with me, keep me company and help me out with arrangements. I used to travel the country with Dennis, who at that time was a rep for a firm of

Lancashire bar fitters. You could say we sort of dovetailed. Dennis was very good to me and I used to love travelling round the country with him as he did his job. 'Mr Motorway' I called him. I used to play snooker whenever I could at the clubs where he was negotiating his deals. Sometimes my playing got noticed and I'd be asked to put on an exhibition. Who knows, I may even have impressed an owner or two and got Dennis the contract. I'd like to think so.

After winning the Irish Professional title, I went back home to prepare for the big one, the competition that would make or maybe break me. Back then, the World Championship was a long drawn-out affair spanning a number of months. I'd actually beaten Jack Rea, 19–11, a few weeks prior to the Irish Professional and now I was drawn in the quarter finals against John Pulman. I had met him a few times, and played a friendly with him after the John Player UK team championship in 1970, but I was always in awe of him. I used to call him Mr Pulman out of utter respect. Now here I was, a 'wet behind the ears' professional player, playing my idol.

John was a tactician and didn't approve of my wild style of play. He tried to take the pace off the game by taking his shots very calmly and slowly, a tactic designed to unease the young upstart, but it didn't work. Whenever I came on to the table I would do my Hurricane act, eye up the ball, chalk the cue and straight down into the shot. 'Bang', I'd whack the balls and they would roar up the table, hit the cushions and crash into the pockets while I was lining up the next shot. I could see John out of the corner of my eye, and he just kept shaking his head in disbelief.

My adrenalin levels were bursting and, the more I put down, the better I felt. I just kept up the onslaught and it worked. I won 31–23 and was elated at the fact I had beaten a man who had won the championship eight times. John later complimented me on my game, and I partied for two nights on adrenalin reserves. I think John always had a great affection for me, he was always very gracious. I loved John Pulman and wanted to emulate him. Throughout my career he played a major role in how I played and looked.

Next came the semi-finals – eventually. My opponent, Rex Williams, changed the date four or five times. Not only was this inconvenient, but it cost me money. I actually missed some exhibitions due to those shenanigans.

Williams could run, but he couldn't hide, and eventually we met. So here I was in the semi-finals of the big one and cocky as hell, which was almost my downfall. I found myself on the brink of defeat and realised, to my credit I suppose, that if I didn't rethink my game plan sharpish, Rex would destroy me.

At one point he was slaughtering me with one win after another, and I ended up nine down. I changed my game, slowing down the pace and planning every shot, and I could see that Rex was now getting overly confident. Slowly I managed to pull back the score until, at the end of the following three days, I was up for once. I was bloodied, sore of ego, but recovering and getting stronger with each pot. The score stood at 30–28 to me, but Rex wasn't going quietly and he drew level.

We had one more game to play and I was playing for all my life was worth. Rex broke and took a 20 lead, and then he made a fatal mistake by missing the blue. The Hurricane was straight in. I took four reds and four colours but then I was stumped. I took a step back and looked at the state of play. I'm a naturally attacking player, but I also realise that defence is sometimes the best form of attack, and this was one such moment. I played a safety shot and tucked the cue ball behind one of the colours on the bottom cushion. Rex was stuffed and I cleaned up, winning my way to the final. Now all I had to do was beat John Spencer, which wasn't going to be easy. Fortunately, I thought, I had a rehearsal to go to a few days prior to the final, with John Spencer himself. If I could beat him then, surely I would have the psychological advantage and glory would be mine.

Our rendezvous was a money match at Radcliffe Civil Hall. At the time, I was living in Blackburn and so I travelled to and from Radcliffe each day for the match. On the third and final day I had a meeting with Ted Lowe in the Piccadilly Hotel in Manchester –before play began. I can't remember now what the meeting was about, but if Ted was involved, it had to be important. I arrived in plenty of time for my 10.30 sit down with Ted, only to realise I'd been a very silly boy and left my suitcase, with my change of clothes for the match, back in Blackburn. It meant I had to rush back home, pick up my gear and then head straight to Radcliffe. I arrived late, tired and hassled, and suddenly a six-frame lead was turned around by Spencer to be a six-frame deficit for the Hurricane. My dress rehearsal for world glory was not going well.

I re-grouped, though, for the final session and pulled it back to all square with a frame to go. Spencer was visibly shaken by my rampant comeback and suggested we play best of three to decide the winner. 'No way,' I thought. 'I'm on a roll.' So I said that we only needed to play one frame to decide – perhaps not my best decision as Spencer fluked a red and went on to win with a 70 break. I didn't really care. I'd seen fear in his eyes when he bottled it and asked for the best of three decider. The World Championship was just three days away and I knew then that I would win. Goodnight Spencer, goodbye everyone else. The Hurricane had well and truly arrived.

The venue was a typical British Legion club in Selly Oak, Birmingham, and they had put on the World Championship because no one else wanted to do it. Gathered in that huge hall were about 350 to 400 people of all ages who loved snooker and wanted to see the Hurricane win. The place was buzzing and so was I, throughout the whole match. I was learning by the second, adjusting, improvising. There was no quietness anywhere. These fans were dragging chairs, dropping glasses and even walking past us on the other side of the table to go to the toilets. This was not traditional snooker etiquette at all and I loved it. The venue and the snooker-mad crowd were more than good enough for me. Looking back, this was the moment when everything began to change, not that we realised it at the time. No one could possibly have known that this match wasn't only going to save me, it was going to bring about the rejuvenation of snooker.

The match started off fairly OK, by which I mean that both John and I were playing well. I ended the day just up. The next day we were both off our game a bit —one of us would play well for one frame, and then for the next the same player would be a disaster. It goes like that sometimes. John eventually found the edge and ended the day up at 13–11. I was staying just eight minutes' walk away from the venue and after breakfast I would walk up to the hall and practise for about two hours. This just smoothed out my nerves and I was fully relaxed by the time the match started. On the third day – a day that has subsequently gone down in the annals of snooker history – I started off very poorly and that form stayed with me into the afternoon session. John had started well and before long he was three frames in front. I just couldn't seem to catch up to level pegging, until the last frame and that is when fate stepped in. John was one frame up and I was on the last red.

I was on the last red but didn't have a shot, so I decided to play safe and left the cue ball snookered next to the pink. John played a hard shot and the referee called a foul, saying John had hit the pink first. I didn't call the referee's attention to the shot. It was his decision. Well, talk about a snooker player 'scorned'. John hit the roof and I was awarded a free shot (quite rightly, he'd fouled) and won the game to leave the score 18–18. John was livid and for an hour afterwards he called that ref all the names under the sun. Talk about a bad loser!

John insisted that from that point onwards officials be present to adjudicate any further decisions by the ref, which is something I have never seen since. I was astounded but kept my mouth shut. I decided to let my cue do the talking for once. Pity I didn't do that more often in life. Anyway, I made my way back to the hotel, happy with how the day had ended, given my erratic form. I say 'hotel' but actually it was a B & B called The Pebbles. Whenever I mentioned it to anyone, I called it The Peebles so no one could recognise where I was staying.

I must admit I had a few laughs at The Pebbles with a 20-stone giant called Bernard, who had been sent to look after me by Dennis and Jack. Bernard's main job was to make sure I was out of bed, dressed, watered and fed before he kicked me out the front door to walk to the venue. He would then go back to the breakfast room and devour anything that was left in there. After that, he would make sure my clothes were ready for the evening session and go back to bed. Jack gave him special permission to give me a big slap every morning to wake me up and it worked. Bernard is the only man who ever gave the Hurricane a slap and lived to tell the tale.

The Thursday started well for me. I took the first frame and led 19–18, but John wasn't going away without a fight and came back in the next frame. He then objected to a shot I took and said it was a deliberate miss, insisting that the referee, his auntie, uncle and anyone else who would listen, rule on it in his favour.

He didn't get the vote and we carried on. The afternoon session went one way then the other and we ended up 21–21. The evening session was a blinding one for me. I took six frames one after the other, and we ended the night with the score at 27–21. I went back to the digs walking on air. The next day was pretty shitty for us both as there was a power cut. We'd had many of those over the week, but this one was the worst, not so much for me, but for John and his wife. They left their hotel room to go to the hall and got stuck in the lift for about half an hour while I walked there and practised until he turned up. Needless to say, he was more than a bit put out and, perhaps not surprisingly, I took the opening frame to go seven up. John came back at me with all pistons firing and narrowed my lead to just four frames. If you put someone such as John Spencer under pressure, he will pull all his experience and skill together to come right back at you. That was a valuable lesson to learn. The evening session was no different and we went one way then the other to finish with me still four frames to the good at 32–28. The following day was to be the final one of the year-long tournament and would determine whether I was to become the newest and youngest world snooker champion.

As usual Bernard roused me with a big slap and I woke with a jolt and nearly smacked him one back, but was glad I didn't because I suspect my hand would have come off a lot worse than his chin. Big lad, that Bernard. I went down to breakfast and started to eat my fry-up. Midway through I leaned back for a minute to contemplate the immense day ahead and Bernard snatched my plate away and started to eat it himself, in between telling me to get my arse in gear and down to the hall. I was running late if I wanted to get a few frames of practice in before the match started. I walked down and played two very good frames out of the five I had time for, scoring 100 breaks in each.

The session started well with John missing a long yellow, allowing me to make a 40 break and win the frame.

I wasn't really feeling too well on that final day because the constant pressure of the press was beginning to wear me down. I wasn't used to it at that time. Added to that, John Spencer was in no frame of mind to be taking prisoners, and his reply to me taking the first frame was to hit me with an extended period of what I can only describe as great snooker. He took the next three frames, leaving me just two frames ahead. The Hurricane had to live up to his persona, so I pulled myself together, took a deep breath and deliberately sauntered over to the table, looking as though nothing in the world was bothering me. I was trying to do that walk John Wayne used to do, but it didn't quite come off. I knew it, so I stood at the table, chalking my cue, and saying to myself, 'Kiddo, this is your day, go and get it.'

I won the next two frames 96–16 and 88–14. I was now a comfortable four in front and there weren't many frames to play. Finally, the evening session came, the final countdown and the final chance for me to be world champion of 1972. John was leading 38–28 in the first frame when he missed a red that he should have potted easily. That gave me the courage to go for it and I won the frame 62–38. All I now needed was to take the next frame and Alexander Gordon Higgins, a.k.a. the Hurricane, would become the youngest ever world snooker champion. I walked to the table thinking what would Ali do if he was up on points but needed to reassert his position as world heavyweight champion? Answer: go for a knock-out, so I followed suit. I made a break of 94, John didn't pot his ball and I took the frame, the title, the trophy and the glory by making 46 to beat him 140–0.

To say I was elated would be an understatement. Spencer had

played at his best. He'd been determined to win – and Alex Higgins had beaten him fair and square. I had said all along that I would throw my arms up in the air and shout, 'I am the greatest,' but to be honest with you, I bottled out. In later times I would have done it, but I wasn't quite there yet with the celebrity status thing, so I thought it better to be calm, cool and collected – which I pulled off with aplomb, I might add. The first prize of £480 wasn't going to buy much of a champagne lifestyle, but the good news for me was that forces were already at work planning to bring the game, and the Hurricane, into every home in the land and many more abroad.

In March 1972 I was approached by Thames Television to take part in a documentary about the changing face of sport. It turned into a documentary about the Hurricane and how I was altering the image of snooker. What I hadn't realised was that in winning the title at the age of twenty-two, I had unwittingly made young people sit up and question the image of snooker as an old man's game. Suddenly, here I was, a mere youngster myself, becoming a mentor to other young people. I didn't set out to change snooker. I just wanted to play. And win. And make some money. What happened next was out of my hands. I didn't deliberately start the ball rolling – it just happened.

It is all to do with timing, I guess. As always. For almost three decades society had been rebuilding itself. It had been torn apart by a world war within living memory and by the mid 1960s society had started to change its perceptions. We had the first signs of revolution with the age of the hippies, the transcendental meditation experience, free love, sex, drugs and rock and roll. As we entered the seventies, the young people of the next generation were looking for their own identity and they chose sport. We lived in the age of the sporting hero as well as the music idol. Georgie Best had arrived, and now Hurricane Higgins. Fans were looking for guidance from people like us. We were the ones they were seeking to emulate. After all, we were of their generation and, as John Lennon put it, we were all working-class heroes, the people's champions.

6

Women in my life

•

I was playing an exhibition match in Portsmouth on St Patrick's
Day 1974 and, after the match, I decided on a night out to
celebrate the most important day in an Irishman's calendar, with
the intention of letting the fun run all night and on into my
birthday the following day. So, there I was, a little after
11 o'clock, drinking champagne in the Playboy club. Now, if
you've ever been to one these places, you will know that they have
the most gorgeous girls working for them, and this club was no
different.

When the second bottle arrived it was attached to a tall, leggy
blonde with the loveliest of smiles. Yes, Higgie fell in love. I asked
her to bring over another bottle right away and while she was
doing that I wrote a note with my room number on it. When she
came back I asked her what her name was. 'Kim,' she replied. I
pretended I didn't hear her and beckoned her closer. As she
leaned towards me I slipped the note into her bra, whispering,
'Come and see me later, there's my hotel and room number.' She
just smiled, winked and said, 'Maybe.' Then she turned away and
did the sexiest walk I have ever seen. Even catwalk models don't
walk like Kim. I got back to the hotel, much the worse for the
champagne, and had no sooner started to undress when I heard
a knock on the door. I opened it, half expecting to see one of the
hotel staff, and was more than pleasantly surprised to see Kim

standing there with another bottle of champagne. 'I thought you might need some room service, sir,' she said with a wink and a smile. The magic was still there, clearly.

We had the most fabulous night and got little sleep. The next day was my twenty-fifth birthday. I had to be in Exeter for an exhibition match and I asked Kim if she would like to come with me. I was quite struck with her, for obvious reasons. We got a car to take us to the exhibition hall and when we arrived the organisers surprised me with a huge cake in the shape of, and decorated like, a snooker table with twenty-five candles. I was so happy that day. I played the matches and did my usual socialising with the fans who had come to see the Hurricane play.

My mind, however, wasn't on the fans or the cake. My thoughts, and my eyes, were firmly focused on Kim, and she appeared to be in much the same situation. Every time I looked up at her she just smiled, winked and mouthed to me that she wanted me. We eventually got back to the hotel, with the cake in tow. The cake went on top of the wardrobe and we went on top of the bed. Another great night of sex was had by all and in the early hours I eventually fell asleep, with another day and another match ahead of me. Only problem was this one was miles away and in my excitement I had forgotten to book an early morning call. I suddenly woke up with just twenty minutes to get ready and get to the station to catch my train. I jumped out of bed, throwing everything into my case as I dressed. Kim was fast asleep as I ran out the door.

Fortunately, the station was just across the road and I made the direct train to Manchester with a few minutes to spare. That gave me time to write a quick note to Kim. I'd been in such a rush I hadn't had time to say goodbye. A porter kindly agreed to deliver it to the room. My note read: 'Thanks for a lovely time, Kim and I hope you enjoy the cake. Love, Alex.' I never heard from her again, but I am sure Kim has told that story herself over the years. For all those who have never believed her, here is the proof.

When I went to Australia for the first time, I stayed a couple of months. It wasn't all snooker, although the Aussies loved the game as much as we did in the UK, mostly because they could gamble on it. They like to bet on anything over there and are probably second to the Chinese in their love of wagering. It was early 1973 when I met Cara, a lovely, and wild, Aussie woman. Cara Hasler was a blind date fixed up by an old mate, the journalist Phil Wilson, and what a date that turned out to be. A date with destiny wouldn't be overstating it.

Cara was four years older than I was, and a lot wiser. She had a German father and an Irish mother and we both had a love of the race-track and gambling – not necessarily a good combination to keep me on the straight and narrow, but it worked for us, most of the time. Many a great day was had at the track. We were a fun couple, cut from the same piece of cloth, but the logistics of our relationship were strange to say the least. I would spend as much time as I could with Cara in Australia when I was there, and she also came with me to England, but she had a high-class beauty salon in Australia and it was difficult for her to come back with me all the time.

When we were in England we lived in a flat in Manchester that was sub-let by Alex Stepney, the Manchester United goalkeeper. I knew Alex fairly well, and used to go to see United play from time to time. We'd occasionally go out for a drink together. Willie Morgan used to come as well sometimes. When Alex decided to rent the place out I said to him that I would take it. In 1974 I went back to Australia to do some more exhibitions and tournaments and, as usual, hooked up with Cara. We were living together again and spending a lot of time with each other.

I loved being with her. She was fun and when she talked about getting married, I didn't flinch. Spending time with Cara only strengthened my feelings for her and I went into the marriage with a lot of love in my heart. Our relationship was a good one. I even had a nickname for her. Cara Beverley Hasler was her full name and so her initials were CBH. I used to call her Crievous Bodily Harm for fun. So, on 11 April 1975, in a lovely picturesque church in Sydney – St Edmonds chapel at Darling Point – we said 'I do' and Cara became Mrs Alexander Gordon Higgins. It was a great day and I still smile when I think about it. Cara's family pulled a lot of favours and as we emerged from the church we had to go through an arch made by Australia's top jockeys. Her father had arranged it. He is a well-respected racehorse trainer and breeder.

It had to be one of the most written-about weddings in the world that year. Even Ray Reardon, another yearly visitor to the Australian snooker scene, such as it was, came along to wish us luck. The reception was absolutely fantastic and my best man, Peter Wake, did me proud on the day. For one thing, he made sure I turned up on time and was immaculate, which was no mean feat. We used to call Peter 'The Mathematician' because he headed a betting syndicate called the Legal Eagles, a group of lawyers who placed huge bets and won fortunes on the horses. Now this group were highly sophisticated in their approach to gambling. They even had access to a computer at the university, which they used to collate and analyse the form on races. They were way ahead of their time. No wonder I was friends with them. They were a great bunch, as were all Cara's friends. What I liked most was that they were all successful in their own right. I became just another one of the crowd. That gave me a degree of anonymity, which I enjoyed.

The plan was for us to head straight off on honeymoon to

the Great Barrier Reef, directly after the reception, but as we were about to leave Peter Wake happened to mention that The Who were having a huge party in the hotel where we were staying that night. The whole band was there, launching the rock musical movie *Tommy*. I was a big fan of the band and couldn't resist the opportunity of meeting them. So we got in the car and drove over to the Sebel Townhouse hotel in the King's Cross area of Sydney. When we got there we were astounded – the boys had turned the place into a huge pinball arcade. It was truly amazing and, even better, the champagne and beer were still flowing when we arrived. We just walked into the party and Roger Daltrey made sure that we were well looked after. It would be reasonable to assume that the two of us stood out like sore thumbs at this rock and roll party. After all, Cara was still in her wedding dress and I was fully kitted out in my wedding suit, hardly cutting-edge rebellion in 1975, but the truth is we fitted right in.

The place was full of acrobats, stilt-walkers, fire-eaters and those people who paint themselves all over and pretend to be statues. There were even fully fledged transvestites, which was unusual in Australia in those days. Cara in her wedding dress and me in my wedding suit just blended in. I don't think many people gave us a second look. Who knows, maybe days later when people were talking about it, someone may have said, 'Did you see the lady-boys and the stilt-walkers? Weren't they great? And what about that couple who came as Alex Higgins and wife. Struth, man! He even spoke like the Hurricane.'

The one drink we intended to stay for turned into many and we ended up postponing the Barrier Reef by a day while the boys made us guests of honour. Elton John was there, and Keith Moon, who made a big fuss of us, but I never met Elton at that hotel. I met him years later at a concert at Wembley. When Cara and I eventually did get away, almost twenty-four hours later than planned, we had a great honeymoon. We went up the coast to a ranch owned by one of Cara's uncles. The days were spent riding round the outback and in the evenings we drank fine wines – we both loved the Australian Cabernet Shiraz and Chardonnay – argued, debated and generally egged each other on. It was all good fun and we enjoyed the making-up part most of all. That was how we were together – volatile but happy. We returned to Sydney because my career beckoned and I needed to travel back to the UK. Cara stayed behind, and for the next two years or so that's how it was. I would fly to the UK and Cara would come over when she could get away from the salon. We would have a great time for a few weeks, then the rot would set in and we'd end up having a huge row. This usually ended up with me going to stay with someone or Cara going off to friends in London, or even back home to Australia. I did love Cara with all my heart, she is a great girl, but maybe I didn't love her quite enough to make it work. Who knows? I believe the real reason we eventually split was because of pure logistics. Our jobs meant that we had to spend a lot of time apart, so when we were together, the pressure on us was intense. We felt we had to have a good time, all the time, to make the most of those days and weeks. That's not real life and it can't sustain a relationship forever. I often think that if Australia had had a proper snooker circuit in those days, Cara and I might still be husband and wife.

A child was born during the marriage, but I am not certain I am the father, not that it would have mattered an iota one way or the other if Cara and I had stayed together. I'd have looked after her and loved her and the baby one hundred per cent. Why am I uncertain? Well, what with all the break-ups and being on different continents, there was a period, as far as I can recall, when we didn't share a bed for a few months. And then Cara was pregnant. Perhaps by yours truly, perhaps as a result of a silly fling in London. I just don't know. If it was the latter, I'm certainly not one to crib about that. I wasn't exactly an angel in that department myself. I have no contact with the child and I never paid any maintenance or anything of that nature. I've never been asked to. But I can honestly say that I wouldn't have shirked from my responsibilities. Hiding from things isn't exactly the Higgins way, is it?

We eventually agreed to part for good some time in 1977. It was probably the best thing for both of us. I did happen to see Cara and her child one day on a later trip to Australia. I was in Sydney, walking down the street, and spotted them on the other side of the road. I noticed that the youngster had lovely natural sandy hair, just like I had as a kid. Cara is a brunette, so who knows, maybe I am her father. Cara is now happily married again to a lovely fella, Bertie Webster, who is a very successful bookie in Australia. We used to go to his beach parties. They were very exclusive, but we were part of the in-crowd and always got invited. She's had a better life since we parted than I have had, so good luck to her and her family. I wish them nothing but the best.

It was during one of the roughest spells of our relationship, just as we were finally realising that enough was enough for both of us, that I met the next Mrs Higgins. It was in a wine bar in Manchester, called Oscars, co-owned by George Best. Lynn Avison was her name and I immediately knew that something special was about to happen in my life. From that moment on, she has played a more significant part in my story than anyone else has ever done, apart from my immediate family of course.

Lynn Avison and Alexander 'Hurricane' Higgins – it's a hell of a combination and story, which I'll recount in the full detail it deserves later. For now, I'll skip forward a few years to the mid 1980s, and the lovely Siobhan Kidd, 'the Blonde'.

Siobhan was so gorgeous and sexy. That's all the tabloids ever seemed to focus on. She was also a smart cookie and no mistake, obviously – she hooked me, didn't she, for a while anyway. I met Siobhan at a club called Brubaker's in Manchester at a time when things with Lynn were very much on-off. Well, more off than on, to be honest. So I began seeing a lot of Siobhan and I can honestly say I was in love with her big time, as I think she was with me. I wish I had her now. Not a day goes by when I don't think of her. She was studying psychology at the time and also working as a cocktail waitress plus occasionally serving behind the bar of the small VIP area where I used to sit. I was smitten from the first time I set eyes on her. I used to turn up there most nights just to be near her. I eventually asked her out on a date and to my delight she said, 'Yes.'

Shivvy, as I called her, had been good at art at school and so I helped her get a job working with a friend of mine, George Aird. George was the owner of Grove Galleries in Manchester. He bought and sold antiques and also restored paintings. Siobhan began with picture framing, but George soon taught her his secrets of art restoration, which involves mixing colours and oils together to get the original formula used by the artist. This is a very complicated process and takes years to master, but master it she did. She has gone on to become a great restorer, and I am proud that it was me who introduced her to the world of art. It was one of the best things I ever did for her.

Siobhan and I moved in together in 1987 after an incident outside Lynn's parents' house, which ended up with me spending the night in jail. It was the day after that that Siobhan suggested we live together at her place in Fallowfield. She knew what she was getting into. I got arrested again that summer – that second time for a blazing row I had with Lynn at Manchester airport. Lynn had already left me by this stage – for good, as it turned out – and Siobhan and I would divide our time together between her place and mine, where I was living on my own. It was an arrangement that suited us both because we liked our own space. When I was alone in the house I occupied my time with snooker and music, both of which I love with a passion. My house, Delveron, was my dream home, but my finances were looking rocky and I realised I would have to sell it. Moving in with Siobhan seemed like the best idea for my heart and my bank balance.

Siobhan was thirteen years younger than I was, and a real beauty – still is, no doubt. We had some amazing times together, but my God was it a roller-coaster! I totally accept I sometimes have a short fuse, but Siobhan was more than capable of standing up for herself. She was a fiery one and no mistake. Our relationship sort of reflected my whole life, I suppose: huge highs and terrible lows. A troublesome ongoing situation with my management company at the time, led by Howard Kruger, didn't help matters, and put a lot of pressure on me. I sometimes think that if it hadn't been for the fall-out with that company, Siobhan Kidd might have become Siobhan Higgins. I would have proposed to her I'm certain, but she might have said no. I'll never know for sure.

We certainly had our moments, Siobhan and I, and we packed a lot of them into 1988. One such event that resulted in lurid headlines was Siobhan's supposed suicide attempt. I say 'supposed' because I don't believe she really was trying to take her own life. I don't even think it was a cry for help, as some suicide attempts are categorised.

Why would Siobhan try such a thing? I was madly in love with her. She knew that. I've heard it said that she took an overdose because she thought I was trying to get back with Lynn. What rubbish. I certainly wasn't looking for a reconciliation with Lynn. I had no intention of leaving Siobhan and she knew that. A couple of days after she got out of hospital, we went together to a tournament – hardly the actions of a couple whose relationship was supposedly in freefall. So what would have been the point? Added to that, Siobhan was far too strong a character to try to kill herself, and it would have been against her personal beliefs. I believe the overdose of pills was a mistake, pure and simple – almost a tragic one, but a mistake none the less.

It is true that I was out when the supposed attempt took place, and I did find her unconscious on the floor and call an ambulance. It is also true that I didn't accompany her to the hospital but not because I didn't care. Far from it. I was too frightened to go with her. I was terrified that I might lose her. Forever. I couldn't face watching the doctors and nurses buzzing about her, sticking a tube down her throat or whatever it is they do to pump someone's stomach. No, I just couldn't do that. So I sat on my own, had a drink, and waited for news. Thank God it was good.

That summer, after Lynn and I had agreed to divorce, Lynn did a story with the *Star* newspaper in which she accused me of pretty much only being interested in wine, women and gambling. She was livid that I had said some very distasteful things about her, so she was getting her own back. Siobhan and I had a huge row over it all, and she threw me out of her flat, again. A few weeks later I went round to see her and she told me she had found someone else. I put the word round that I was looking for this guy. I am not sure if that did the trick or not, but that relationship seemed to fizzle out and I managed to win my way back into Siobhan's arms, although not for long. Towards the end of the year we had another blazing row. We are both passionate people and sometimes that passion boiled over – and on this occasion, it went too far. At some point I picked up an ashtray and threw it across the room. It hit the wall and shattered. I've heard it said that I threw the ashtray at Siobhan. I would never do such a dangerous thing as that. I threw it well away from her and at no time did I have any intention of using it as a weapon. I was arrested after a neighbour downstairs called the police. It ended with another night in the cells and later an appearance in court for breach of the peace, but I did manage to get back in with Siobhan before Christmas came along.

Another incident that everyone gets wrong is the one where I fell out the window of Siobhan's flat and broke lots of bones in my left foot. It was January 1989 and I had been out earlier that evening with snooker pro Tony Kearney. Like me, Tony loved to gamble, and he took me to a casino he knew well. I remember they used to entice punters in with a free steak dinner. I had four or five drinks only, so I wasn't drunk, and I certainly wasn't having any luck. I lost about £1,000 on the roulette tables, and decided to cut my losses and leave after about three hours. I went back to the flat with Tony and we had a drink. Only problem was, Siobhan wasn't too keen on Tony, so he left after the drink. Siobhan was well pissed off because I'd brought Tony back with me. She went and had a bath to try to calm down, but only after locking the front door – locking me in, in effect. I walked into the kitchen to get the post. I still had my full-length trench-coat on and I leaned on the window frame as I read my letters. To my joy there was a cheque for £2,000 in one, but my delight almost immediately turned to fear, when the window I was leaning on suddenly swung open and I almost fell out, head first. I caught myself just in time, but it gave me an idea.

With the cheque in my pocket, I was keen to return to the casino and win back my grand – getting out of the flat was the problem. I looked out of the window to see how far it was down, and calculated about 30 feet. We were on the second floor. I figured that if I landed on both feet and bent my legs on impact, then rolled, just as I learned to do when riding – or not riding to be more precise – I could escape. Out I climbed and dropped like a paratrooper – until the wind caught my coat like a sail, and unbalanced me. All my weight crashed down on one foot. I fell forward and bashed my head into the bargain, knocking myself unconscious. I was out for a few minutes and when I tried to get up, I just crumbled into a heap. As I lay there, I saw Siobhan looking out of the window at me. She raced to my rescue and I went to hospital for an X-ray, although I still wanted to go to the casino. I had broken numerous bones and would be off my feet for weeks, maybe months. I couldn't even have a cast on my foot because it would have stopped the bones knitting properly. All I had was an open cast on my lower leg. I had to laugh at the article in the paper the next day reporting a cop saying, 'Mr Higgins was not seriously injured; luckily enough he landed on his head.'

The injury didn't bring me enough sympathy to win my way back into Siobhan's good books, however, and I stayed with a great friend of mine, Sean Naughton, while I was recuperating. I hobbled around for a few days but soon got bored. Fortunately, Sean had a pool table and I thought I'd give it a go, although I didn't think there was any real chance I could play, what with crutches and my foot in such a bad way, but I was wrong. I found that if I put my weight on the hand that was on the table, rather than on my foot, I could line up my shots perfectly well. The next night I went with Sean to a local tennis club that had a full-sized snooker table, and gave it a go. It was exhausting, but it worked and I realised at that point that I wouldn't have to break my appointment with the European Open in France, which was only days away. That was important to me because I desperately needed the ranking points.

I turned up at the tournament still on crutches and had to endure a string of terrible jokes about Long John Silver. Someone even asked me if John Parrott was going to do pantomime with me that year. Even hopping around and sweating like there was no tomorrow, I still managed to win my first match, beating Les Dodd 5–2. Always the entertainer, I knew the show had to go on, until Willie Thorne beat me in the next round that is. It was a monumental effort for one world ranking point.

Although I was out of the tournament I was fairly happy with the way I'd played, even with my foot in plaster. When I'm up against it, that's when I am most dangerous. The Irish Masters was only a couple of weeks away and, although I didn't hold out any realistic hopes of winning, I wanted to be sure I gave myself the best possible chance, even though I'd still be on crutches. I was booked for a couple of exhibition matches against Willie Thorne and Cliff Thorburn and, although I lost them (the pockets were just too generous I felt, so my better play didn't give me the advantage it should have), I knew by the way that I was striking the ball that things were coming together. Given everything that was going on, I'm not sure how.

I don't just mean my foot. Siobhan and I were on much better terms again but my finances weren't. I was stressed, in effect bankrupt, and in trouble. Quite how I held it all together I don't know. Especially when, a couple of days before the Masters, I was approached by some very dodgy-looking blokes outside the Crown Bar in Belfast, and offered £10,000 to lose in the first round. There was just a moment when that sounded a tempting offer. A guaranteed £10k would have relieved some of the financial pressures, but the Hurricane always plays to win and plays honestly, so I refused. Thank God I did. It was the last major tournament I won, and for me personally it proved to be a very precious victory, for reasons I will go into later. Hobbling and still on crutches, I twice came back from being several frames down, first against John Parrott (no jokes this time), and then in the final against Stephen Hendry. The cheque for £32,500 was most welcome, even though it all went off to the official receiver, in whose hands I remained.

What was less welcome, however, was the throng of press interviews that followed my 9–8 victory. It wasn't that I didn't want to do them. I was more than happy to explain at length to a captive audience just how great I'd been. No, the problem was how long it all took. You see, in 1989, with the way things were going for me, and after the Irish Masters victory, I just knew I was going to win the World Championship, but I needed to qualify and my match was the next day in Blackpool. By the time I turned up to face Darren Morgan, I was knackered. Half-asleep, I tried my damnedest to win, but Darren held firm. I lost 10–8 and missed my chance to conquer the world again.

My long-running affair with Siobhan continued to go downhill after we had a blazing row while I was competing in the Hong Kong Open in 1989 and I threw her out of our hotel room, naked. Fortunately for her she had managed to snatch some underwear just as I grabbed her arm and marched her out the door. Dressed in what she had on, she called reception and got another room. I left the next day but I did pay for both rooms. It was the least I could do . . .

A little while later we rowed again and I, to my shame, went a bit mad. I ended up throwing a table across the room and whacking Siobhan with a hairdryer and bruising her cheek. Unforgivable, I know. I ended up in court again and was fined with costs.

That incident proved the final nail in the coffin of our

relationship, although we did try to patch things up. By this stage we were living in a lovely cottage in Holcombe Brook. It was in Siobhan's name but I paid for it. I'd come to an arrangement with the official receiver whereby I could put the money I made from exhibitions into the purchase and that meant I didn't get any help in paying rent. Fair all round.

As I said, we were trying to patch things up between us, but it wasn't working. We had a terrible row again – over what, I can't remember – and it ended up with us pushing and shoving each other. I really wanted to make things work so I suggested Siobhan call her mother, Sheila, and ask her to come round to act as a sort of arbitrator. I got on very well with Sheila. I'd met her very soon after Siobhan and I got together and we clicked. She was very keen on Siobhan and I making our relationship work so she was the ideal person to talk sense into us and defuse the tension. We both calmed down to the point that we decided to go for a walk, to talk things through, or so I thought.

We climbed a hill near the cottage and when we got to the top, Siobhan turned to me and said, quite simply, 'Shag me.' I was quite startled but more than happy to oblige. I threw the long sheepskin coat that I was wearing on to the ground and we tumbled on top of it, all arms, legs and passion.

'Now that is the way to be forgiven,' I thought, as we made our way back home. But within half an hour, Siobhan had packed a few things into a bag and was gone.

I tried to get in touch with her over the following weeks, but she was having none of it. She'd come to the end of her tether and there was nothing I could do about it. I had to accept the situation and try to move on. I agreed to sell the cottage and that Siobhan could keep the proceeds. The place sold in no time at all. I remember my very last visit there, packing up the last of my possessions, closing the front door for the last time. I stood there reflecting on what I had hoped was going to be a happy home for Siobhan and me, and how it had all fallen apart. In my frustration I picked up a stone and threw it through a window. Shattered dreams and shattered glass. But by that stage, I'd already met my next serious partner.

It must have been about three or four days after Siobhan and I had officially split. I'd been at my solicitors, sorting out the paperwork on the cottage, and he dropped me back in Manchester, in St Ann's Square. I walked into a wine bar there and met a very attractive woman, Holly Haise. As I later learned, Holly was a twenty-six-year-old high-class escort girl and she earned a fortune. She was also the mistress of a wine and champagne merchant who looked after her very well. I never paid for sex with Holly, nor indeed with anyone. I really liked Holly when I met her. She was bouncy and fun to be with, but I can't with all honesty say that I ever loved her, just the sex really. I had a tempestuous affair with Holly for over eight years and lived with her on and off for most of it.

The first time I stayed with her was the same day I put the stone through the window of the cottage at Holcombe Brook. The press were desperate to find out what I was up to and they had me tailed to Holly's place, where I was dropped off by my solicitor. I had to stay there for two days. There was no way out if I didn't want my photograph plastered all over every tabloid in the country, and I'd had more than enough of that. I eventually did have to leave, however, and so, after darkness on the second night, I slipped out the back, crawled commando style across the lawn, quietly scaled the fence and disappeared up a hill into the night – and straight into two bloody enormous Alsatians. I nearly shit myself. It was like bumping into the Hound of the Baskervilles. Double. Fortunately, their owner was with them and he recognised me. 'Come on, Alex, let's go to my place. The press have been driving me nuts hanging around all this time. I'm not surprised you want shot of them. Come in and have a drink and afterwards I can take you to wherever you need to go. No one will see you leave.' I'd made the perfect escape. In view of what happened later, I should have kept running.

Without doubt, 1997 was the most memorable year in my relationship with Holly. So much happened, I almost don't know where to begin. This was the year that Holly tried to commit suicide by walking into a local reservoir. I wasn't there at the time so I don't know what happened, but I suspect that it might have had something to do with the drink that Holly was knocking back around then. I also think she might have been on some medication but things were beginning to spiral out of control for her at that stage. Her head must have been really fucked up, poor girl. She might not even have realised what she was doing. I don't know.

It almost goes without saying, but things between us were extremely volatile around then. She came round to my flat one time when I was out and put my TV in the bath and sliced up my clothes. We'd have rows, then make up. Sometimes she would lock the front door of her place and hide the keys so I couldn't get out. There were more bolts on her door than they have at Fort Knox and all the windows were locked. That would lead to more shouting matches.

One night I'd been out with some friends and came back to find the front door locked and bolted from the inside. I had very little cash on me, and the keys to my flat were inside the house. I had nowhere else to go so I spent the night in her brother's caravan, which stood in her driveway. In the morning, bleary eyed and unshaven – there was no hot water in the caravan – I emerged down the steps to be met by a paparazzi snapper, stood right in my face and clicking away. I was furious and tried to throw something at him – a shopping trolley or some such thing, I can't quite remember – and stormed off. I think the whole thing might have been a set-up. Holly was always being contacted by the press, looking for stories and offering to pay. I don't know for sure but I think she succumbed that time. Why else would the photographer have been there in the morning on that one day I was forced to sleep in the caravan? It didn't really matter, I suppose, but the headline the next day – 'The Hurricane is down and out living in a caravan' – hurt and created the impression that that was where I spent most of my days. Total nonsense but the rumour stuck for a while.

Next stop in the 'glorious' year of 1997 is August. What a month that turned out to be! It kicked off with an exhibition in Ireland, which I did for Tommy McCarthy, and then it was on to Devon to play in a qualifying match for one of the thirty-two places on the main circuit – I was ranked 156th at the time. I wasn't feeling in the best of moods at the Plymouth Pavilions, and so when I lost 5–1 to a little-known professional, Neil Mosley, I started kicking off back stage. The argument was about the referees and how they always seemed to crowd me, even though I asked them not to. I ended up being pushed out of the players' lounge, because I refused to take off my baseball cap, and the argument carried on in the hall. Minutes later the police arrived and told me that, if I didn't shift myself, I would be spending the night in the cells.

I took their advice, moved on to a few pubs and had calmed down a bit when some snooker fans asked me to join them for a drink. We ended up in a nightclub, where I got into an argument. I decided to call it a night, but as I walked out, I was hit by some bloke. He was a big fella and I wasn't even going to try to get him back. I just left and was walking down the road, glad to be away from there, when this bloke appeared out of nowhere. I think it was the same guy from the nightclub, but I can't be sure. Anyway, he was suddenly in front of me and started whacking my legs with an iron bar, the dirty coward. I ended up crawling a few hundred yards, but the pain in my legs was so bad, I passed out.

I came round as a group of people started to gather. One fella was trying to turn me over on my side. 'Lay still, mate, you'll be OK. I've called an ambulance,' he said. It later turned out that my helper, Steve Graham, was a bouncer from the club. He had heard the commotion and came down to see what was happening. I don't think I ever thanked him properly, so if you are reading this, Steve, I hope you realise that I am most grateful to you. You may have even saved my life that night. I ended up in hospital for the few hours that were left of the night, and then discharged my sore body when the doctor came round to see me. They wanted me to stay in for a few days for observation, but I just wanted to get back to Manchester and Holly. I hobbled out of there, my shoe unbuckled because of the severe swelling, in a very distressed state.

I believe I was set up and that the attack was pre-planned. I don't know why, but I do know that the attack was so severe that it stopped me playing my scheduled match the following day. Perhaps someone didn't want me qualifying. I'll never know. The guy very specifically kept on whacking the iron bar on my ankle, as if to make sure proper damage was done, and no money was stolen. I noticed him jumping into a yellow-and-black taxi before I passed out and the police tracked him down. It turned out he was a soldier – the sort of bloke who knew what he was doing. I'd hoped that he might get done, but the incident never went to court. I don't know why.

I was recuperating a couple of weeks later at Holly's when we had an argument to end all arguments. It also nearly ended my life. There has been a lot of speculation about what happened that night, stories that I was drunk, aggressive and barged my way into her home. Well, this is what really happened. It all started innocuously. I was sitting in the living room reading. Holly was in the kitchen. That's often how things were. We didn't exactly communicate. I never understood why Holly preferred to sit on the hard kitchen chairs when there was a perfectly comfortable sofa in the next room. Anyway, I kept shouting through to her, 'Why don't you come through and sit with me?' and she said the opposite – 'Why don't *you* come through and sit here?' That's all there was to it but by 1 a.m. we were at each other's throats – almost literally. We'd both had a few drinks by that stage, but neither of us was drunk. At some point she reckons that I hit her. I don't remember that at all. She picked up the phone to dial 999. I told her I would pull the plug out of the wall so she put the phone down.

The next thing I know, at around 5 a.m., the police are breaking down the door. I don't know who called them. Holly perhaps when I was out of the room. I calmly spoke to them outside and explained that we were having a domestic and that everything was fine, but they wanted to make sure for themselves and insisted on seeing Holly. They found her hiding under the kitchen table – why, I don't know – and after they spoke to her, they left. She'd refused to make a complaint. The situation was not that serious. I watched them drive off and went back to the house. There was Holly pouring herself another drink and as soon as I walked in she started on me again. I wasn't going to keep taking all this abuse and gave her back some of my own.

This went on for about three hours and, as the morning light was beginning to break through the kitchen window, Holly grabbed two sharp knives, a small one and a large one. It was like something out of a martial arts film. She stabbed me in the right arm and as I reeled back she stabbed me again in the arm and then in the stomach. I was cut quite badly and kept shouting at her that I was bleeding. She didn't care and threatened to finish me off. Well, I know when I'm outgunned and I was starting to think that I was in serious trouble.

I staggered out of the house in a wild panic, ran round the corner and dived over a bush into someone's front garden, where I lay in silence for a good few minutes. I was afraid she had followed me. I had never seen anyone in such a strop. Fearing for my life and bleeding badly, I tried to get to a friend's place about two hundred yards away, but in my panic and confusion I ended up at somebody else's house. The owner took me in and rang for an ambulance.

At the hospital we were greeted by a barrage of press and I was quickly taken into a booth to be seen by the doctor. I was sitting in the booth later that morning when the police came in to see me. 'This is serious, Alex. Do you want to tell us what happened?' They kept going on at me, as if I was the guilty party and I just go so fed up I said, 'Fuck off the lot of you. I'm not pressing any charges. I just want out of here.' I knew that if I refused to make a statement, they wouldn't have any evidence to bring a charge. That seemed to do the trick and I agreed to come to the cop shop later and sign a disclaimer or something. I never did. Holly was arrested and spent the afternoon being interviewed, but as I hadn't made a complaint or a statement they bailed her to appear back there in a few weeks' time. She did end up in court, but the case was eventually dropped due to lack of evidence. A terrible thing happened to Holly only a few days after the stabbing. She was brutally attacked in her own home by two thugs. They punched her and kicked her. It was an awful incident. I don't know if the police ever found out who was responsible.

I left the hospital by sneaking out the back way, got into a taxi and went to a pub. It wasn't quite opening time, but the landlord let me in anyway. I sat in there on my own, still in my bloodied clothes, and had a couple of Guinnesses. Then a mate arrived to take me to his place and clean me up. I'd had a lucky escape and I had to laugh it off. The next day I got a call from Dublin on my mobile phone. It was Louis Copeland, my tailor friend.

'Alex, I've just heard that you've been stabbed. Are you all right? Is there anything I can do?'

'I'm fine, Louis,' I said. 'It didn't hurt at all. I've been stabbed in the back so many times in the past.' Louis laughed at that one and knew I would be OK.

I have hardly seen Holly since that day. I did have a conversation with her over a year later, when I was recovering from my cancer operation. Well, to call it a 'conversation' would be overstating it. I told her in no uncertain terms how I felt. She'd been doing interviews in the press, saying how much she wanted to see me and to patch things up because she thought I might be dying. She kept saying she was going to nurse me better. What a joke! This is the woman who stabbed me, for God's sake. Then she let it leak that I was staying with my sister Jean in Belfast after the operation, which wasn't true anyway. My family know only too well how I love my independence, so Anne had arranged a flat for me. I told Holly to 'keep quiet or else' and that one phone call about the stabbing could put her behind bars. I didn't really mean that, of course, but I was angry. I wanted her to stay out of my life. I did miss her lovely daughter, Sam, though. I'd been like a father to the girl for the eight years her mother and I were together. Sam was pregnant at the time of the stabbing and I'd been asked to be the baby's godfather, but after what Holly did, that became impossible. I hope Sam and her daughter are doing well.

Holly was one hell of a wild woman and I knew there was no

way I would go back to her after what she did. She was so unpredictable that she even kept a voodoo doll of me in her flat – pretty well from the first day we met, or so I heard. I've never actually seen it. Apparently, any time we had a row or fell out, she would stick pins in it. It never worried me until the pins became kitchen knives.

I did see Holly one more time, about three years after our phone conversation, actually twice more and on the same evening. I was very low in spirits and money. I was staying in a hotel in Clifton, near where she was living, and I thought she might be able to cheer me up, even help me out a bit – a bad idea, I know. I should have stayed well clear. She wouldn't open the door to me and so a row broke out, inevitably. I left but, quite unfairly, her reaction really got to me. After a couple more drinks I went round again, to try to reason with her – not a likely scenario. This time she did answer the door but almost immediately things sparked off and we were yelling at each other. I might have grabbed her for a moment or two, around the neck, to try to shut her up. I had a scarf in my hand and quickly realised how threatening that might look to her. I meant absolutely no harm, but I knew I had to go, so off I stormed. Someone called the police and when they caught up with me an hour or so later they cautioned me and said I would be arrested if I returned to the flat. I had no intention of doing that. It was yet another domestic between Holly and me, and the police treated it as such. This time I was determined to make it the last one and in that at least I succeeded.

7

On the road and off the rails

•

I never really thought about what my life would be like after winning the world title. In fact, there wasn't an awful lot of change – not immediately anyway. Later that very night I was being driven by my great friend Peter Madden for hours and hours – from Sheffield to Brecon Beacons in Wales – to fulfil an exhibition engagement that had been booked six weeks previously. The club said the next day that they would have totally understood if I'd cancelled, but that wasn't my style. I'd made a commitment and I was going to stick to it. So this small club, miles away from anywhere – or that's what it felt like– got the first gig with World Champion Hurricane Higgins. And boy did we enjoy ourselves. What a party everyone had.

The money I could command did start to increase, of course, but I didn't seriously consider that I would ever become a rich man by playing snooker. I was determined just to enjoy it all while it lasted. I was the youngest player to win the title, I was arrogant and I thought I was a sporting superman who couldn't be beaten. But like the original Superman, I had my own Kryptonite – my mood swings.

About two months after taking the title from John Spencer, he beat me 13–10 in a special tournament, and not only did he take the winner's cheque of £150, he also won a private bet with me and took most of my runner-up money as well. Easy come, easy go. The truth is I was starting to get lots of work by then, although that may sound a strange word to use. Sports people tend to look at what they do as work. We have to. I travelled all over the British Isles and Ireland, which for me was hard at times, because I couldn't drive and couldn't afford a chauffeur. I had to use public transport and that isn't always reliable, as you will no doubt know – certainly not in the 1970s. Many a long wait I had, shivering on station platforms, wondering what the hell I was doing. David Beckhamesque my life certainly wasn't, regardless of the impact I'd made when I was crowned world champion.

I changed managers, having been approached by London company Snooker Promotions, which was run by broadcaster Peter West, his business partner Pat Nally and a really nice bloke called Simon Weaver. They helped organise my first trip to Australia, in 1973, which was when I met Cara and a few other lovely Australian girls. I enjoyed my time there . . .

That first time, I travelled with John Pulman to play in a televised tournament, and on the way we stopped off in Singapore. This was a whole new world for the back-street boy from Northern Ireland. I was on my way to international stardom.

I liked Singapore. They did things differently there. We played one game in the middle of a packed shopping mall called the People's Palace. We were up on a raised stage in this ultra-modern indoor complex. I'd never seen anything like it. We played a game called hexapool, on a six-sided table. That was a first. In those days, all sorts of gimmicks were being introduced as part of the snooker revolution that was slowly creeping across the continents. We stayed for five days and John and I took in all the wonderful sights that Singapore has to offer. And there were some sights to see, I can tell you.

John was something of a ladies' man in his day. He always

The boy who would be king... Three years old celebrating the Queen's coronation.

19 years old and on my way to winning the Northern Ireland Amateur Snooker Championship.

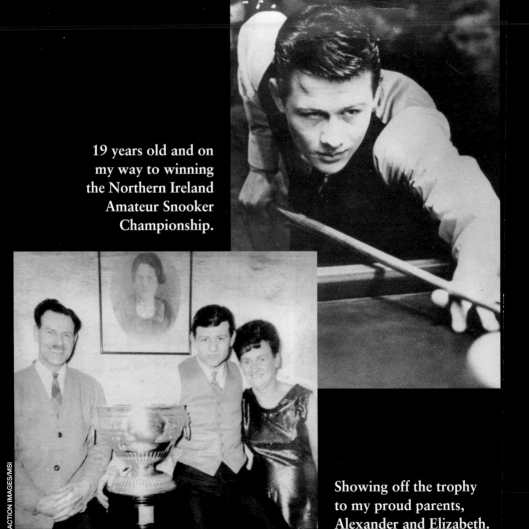

Showing off the trophy to my proud parents, Alexander and Elizabeth.

Mum, all dressed up and looking fabulous.

Dad outshining his son in the dapper dresser department.

Mum and Dad, always happy together.

My three wonderful sisters. Still looking after me. Jean, Isobel and Anne.

I knew how to dress in the early 70s alright. Blousy sleeves, tank tops and bow ties. No wonder I was such a hit with the ladies...

Forgiven by Lynn after being cleared of assault in the 'Spitfire Girl' incident.

5 January 1980. The wedding tha almost didn't take place. We had great day but not a great marriage

Lauren, just two weeks. I was the happiest man on the planet.

'You'll play for United one day, my beautiful boy.'

The 1982 World Champion.

WELCOME
HOME-
WORLD
CHAMPION

dressed fabulously, as I've mentioned previously, and he certainly had a way with the girls. Well, one evening when we were out drinking in a swanky club, John was in full flow, impressing a gorgeous girl, and I was loving every minute of watching the master at work. We were with a group of other players and one of them lent over to whisper something in my ear. I had to ask him to repeat it – not because the club was noisy, but because I couldn't believe what I was hearing. He confirmed what I thought I'd heard, and we concocted a plan immediately.

We knew that John would soon be escorting the girl back to his room and we were determined to get there first. We bribed one of the chambermaids to let us in and I hid in the closet while the bloke who had spilled the beans crept out on to the balcony. We didn't have to wait long. About twenty minutes later we heard John's key in the lock and, sure enough, he wasn't alone. We watched as he smoothly offered her a drink from the mini bar, poured out two whiskies on the rocks and sat next to her on the sofa. We watched with growing anticipation as their small-talk became more amorous. They kissed, John's hands were roaming all over her stunning body, and slowly up her long legs . . . and up and up . . . until with that fabulous shriek that John always had, 'Ya ya ya yeah!' he leapt a mile off the sofa. His girlfriend was a lady-boy. Neither John nor I had ever heard of such a thing. I thought I was going to wet myself with laughter as I tumbled out of the closet and our mate burst in from the balcony. John was a good guy and took it all in the right spirit. He gave the 'girl' some cash for her time and to get a cab home, and we settled in to finish off the whisky.

John and I had many great times together. I loved sitting having a drink with him and listening to his stories about some of the old greats, like Joe Davis. I miss him terribly. Rest in peace JP. Even though we got on really well and I enjoyed travelling with him, inevitably, when you spend time in close proximity with someone, small tensions can come to the surface – as they did one evening when I broke his finger. We were playing a game called spoof. Everyone holds up to three coins in their closed fist and you all have to guess the total number of coins that everyone is holding. If you guess correctly, you are out. The loser – and the person who has to buy the next round – is the last one in. We loved the game and used to play it a lot – and it could become very competitive. One night John was winning every round and as he sat back with a smug smile on his face, having once again guessed correctly, he kept wagging his finger at me. He was beginning to bug me so I simply told him that, if he did it again, I'd snap his finger. He did . . . and so did I. He complained for a bit after that but forgave me. I'd given him fair warning after all.

Snooker in Australia was dominated at that time by a man I later came to know very well. We called him 'Steady Eddie' Charlton and I believe he stunted the growth of the game in Australia by his own greed. From what I heard, sponsors might have been willing to offer a prize fund of Aus$10,000 if Charlton had helped to organise a tournament, but instead he'd suggest a series of exhibition matches for the same amount – and, of course, he would be the star performer, pocketing the largest slice. He was a good player, mind you, with great consistency, but I always thought of him as being a bit boring. He did beat me in our first clash against each other, though, 19–17.

Australia was my kind of place, full of great characters, great women (not least Cara) and great opportunities. I still love the place. I met some very lovable larrikins (as the Australians would call them) in Oz and, like some of my friends in London, they were gangsters, underworld figures. Gambling is huge in Australia and as such is a magnet for the criminal elements. One of the most notorious club owners in Sydney was a gentleman by the name of Joe Taylor, whom I met one night in an illegal gambling club he operated, called Carlisle House.

Joe was the Godfather in those parts and my friendship with him didn't exactly get off to the best of starts. In fact, I inadvertently insulted him and was thrown out of his club. I was in there playing a few frames for money – fairly big money – against a guy whom I felt was a bit of a bandit. In other words, he lied about how good he was so I'd receive a major handicap. I think I ended up giving him a 40 or 50 point lead. I was getting creamed and was becoming increasingly pissed off. Eventually, I'd had enough – I hate cheats – and turned to him and said, 'You're a rotten bastard and I'm cutting.' Joe had been watching (not that I knew who he was at the time) and said something to me. I didn't catch it but I was in no mood to be polite and ask him to repeat himself. 'And you can shut the fuck up as well,' was my parting shot as I headed towards the bar. I wasn't there for long. Out of nowhere two huge bouncers picked me up like I was a piece of paper and the next thing I knew, I was in the alleyway. On my arse. I honestly didn't know what I had done, not until I asked the doorman to explain. When he told me the person I'd upset, I knew I was in real trouble. Falling out with Joe meant falling out with half the city. Not my slickest move ever.

I realised I had to make amends quickly and wrote an apology on a napkin, which I handed over to the doorman and asked him to deliver for me. About ten minutes later I was 'escorted' once again – this time back into the club, where I explained to Joe why I had reacted in the manner I had. I told him I certainly hadn't intended any offence. Joe accepted my side of the story, told me he'd misjudged me and we shook hands. We remained firm friends till his death years later. Joe told me later that night that he liked my cockiness and self-belief. He always admired a man who could do what he said he could do. He detested bullshitters.

I was back and forth to Australia a few times after I won the World Championship. On one occasion my trip back took me via India. It was an expenses-only trip but Simon Weaver assured me I would love the place. 'It has such culture, warmth and history,' he said. I was excited at the prospect of seeing another way of life, but I was in for a shock. I was picked up at the airport at 5 a.m., just off a flight from Perth, by a gang of what I would now describe as bandits. I mean that in the nicest possible way. They were real characters. There were five of them waiting for me as I came through the arrivals hallway, and when they said they had an Ambassador car waiting for us, I was rather impressed. I imagined some sort of fancy limo waiting to sweep us to the hotel in some style. How wrong I was! Instead of the lap of luxury, the six of us (plus my luggage and cue case) squeezed into the equivalent of a Morris Minor.

We motored along – and we motored and we motored. The hotel wasn't far from the airport but as my 'limo' sounded like a souped-up hairdryer and didn't go above 25 mph, the journey took forever.

To say I was pleased when we finally arrived at the woeful-looking hotel would be an understatement, but I had no way of knowing what was to come. Beggars camping out in the reception area asked me for money as I made my way to the desk. I'd never seen anything like it. Having checked in, we all made our way up to my room. Being a well-brought-up Belfast lad, my first question to my hosts was, 'So, lads, what do you fancy to drink?' Coke or Pepsi was the response. There was nothing else in the room, so I had to settle for a warm bottle of Mateus Rosé that I'd brought with me from Australia. The wine was the height of sophistication in the early seventies. After an hour or so, my welcoming party left and I decided I needed to grab a couple of hours' kip. But first I had to get rid of an unwelcome visitor.

Just as I had been about to climb into bed, I'd noticed the biggest cockroach in history crawling under my door. Quite frankly, I was terrified. This thing looked like it could eat me alive. I had to take drastic action. It was him or me. I eventually won, thanks to the assistance of a rather thick telephone book and three or four mighty whacks. 'Welcome to Bombay, Alex,' I thought. 'How the hell am I going to get to sleep now? What if he wasn't alone . . .' I climbed into bed, tucked the bedspread tight around me so that nothing could get in while I lay there, knocked back the rest of the Rosé and prayed I didn't hear the scuttling of tiny feet across the floor.

I awoke a few hours later, still in one piece and having showered and dressed – I checked my shoes very carefully for any lurking monsters – I was just imagining how I could kill my managers, painfully, and get away with it, when a knock on my door pulled me back to reality. It was Wilson Jones, a real gent and a former Indian amateur billiards champion. He just popped by to introduce himself and to give me the rundown on the following day's activities, which would take place in front of a Bombay Gymkhana crowd, most of whom, as you can imagine, were very wealthy men. I thought that was very good of him, making sure I knew what to expect.

My first match was against the Indian champion snooker player, and the hall was packed to the roof. The heat was unbearable, there was no air conditioning and my shirt was soaked through. I was wearing an outfit designed by the Savile Row tailor, Tom Gilbey – designer certainly, but not designed for those temperatures. All I wanted to do was get the frame over and go outside to cool off. I made a break of 107 to crucify this guy, and as I sat down a smartly dressed businessman came over to me and said he would give me 3,000 rupees if I could make a 100 break.

I looked at him in astonishment and said something along the lines of, 'I've just done a 100+ break, are you fucking blind or what?' He looked at me as if I was from outer space. 'What's the point of me coming for free, if you are then going to offer me money to do something I've just done? You should have said it before.' I didn't need this crap. After all, I was the world champion and felt I should be treated as such. Very quickly, I'd had enough.

I undid a couple of buttons on my shirt. Well, I was sweltering, wasn't I? If Tom Jones had done that at Caesar's Palace, it would have taken three weeks to dig him out of the mountain of knickers the women would have thrown at him, but by no stretch of the imagination could I be described as Tom Jones. Vegas might have loved it, but Bombay certainly didn't. I had just innocently insulted their ways. I played another five or six frames – and didn't make another century, so didn't even pick up the 3,000 rupees – and as I hit each ball, I sweated off another eight ounces in weight. I hadn't eaten anything because I kept thinking that some creature with a million legs had crawled over it, so with the heat and not eating I was wasting away, fast.

After the match, I was approached by a local dignitary. I thought at first he was going to give me a large cheque, but all I got was a pewter cup; it wasn't even silver plated. That was the moment when I finally woke up from the nightmare and decided to have some drinks on my hosts. After a few too many, I asked to be taken back to the airport and, to my surprise, they didn't argue with me. When I got there, I was met by my (then) girlfriend, and unofficial fiancée, Liz Kendall, who had just flown in to be with me. I told Liz all about it as she walked with me to the ticket desk, where I gratefully paid £350 each for a ticket right back home.

The next day in the *Times of India* newspaper an article read that I had been sent home, having insulted the country, the culture and the people of India. Supposedly I had behaved in a 'disgraceful manner'. Nonsense, in my view. I didn't insult the people, the culture or the country. What I did do was put all those pompous, jumped-up businessmen in their place.

While the real people scraped together a few pennies each day to make a living, these colonial throwbacks were basking in their own form of colonialism. The poverty surrounding the outrageously rich was the real insult as far as I was concerned, and I had been happy to tell them that – admittedly after a few drinks. But I should have realised I wasn't going to win this one. Influential people can always manipulate the press and that's what I felt happened here. Stories came out and I was made to look the bad guy. I was just happy to be going back home with Liz.

Liz was a woman after my own heart. We shared a love of horses and she was a point-to-point star in her days on that circuit. She stabled her two horses with a small trainer in Epsom, and I remember on one particular day we rode across the Downs and tied the horses at a pub on the course called the Rubbing House. You weren't supposed to ride across but two horses, a beautiful woman and a pub at the end of the journey were too much to resist.

I met Liz when she was working in Churchill's nightclub in London. She was a really great lass and I thought we might be able to make it work but, like most of the women in my life, Liz finally had enough one day and we parted company. I think she always had a soft spot for Higgie, though. In October 1988, Siobhan and I were staying in a hotel near the Hexagon Theatre in Reading, while I was playing in the Rothmans Grand Prix (Steve Davis beat me in the final). We were having a lie-in when the phone rang. I picked it up and it was Liz. I hadn't spoken to her in years, but I recognised her voice instantly.

'Hello, Alex. Long time no see. I'm getting married today and I'm very happy. But before I tie the knot I just wanted to call to wish you all the luck in the world. I still think about you a lot. Take care of yourself.' And with that she was gone. I thought it was so sweet of her, although Siobhan looked at me rather suspiciously for the rest of the day. I haven't heard from Liz since. I hope she is very happy.

Back in England, in the early seventies, snooker was beginning to gather momentum and fans – and not just conservative types, but fans from all walks of life, including women, which was almost unheard-of back then. With television providing immediate access, and without the need to suffer stadiums stinking of pee or dingy smoke-filled halls, females were turning their interest towards the sport, and snooker was the beneficiary. I was, too, if I'm honest. The BBC had been the sport's best friend but now everyone wanted a slice of the action. I am credited with having been the catalyst for this huge leap in the game's popularity but, although that may be true to some extent, other factors and other people were also stoking the fires of progress.

I took the sport to the people and they loved me for it. While others were trying to sanitise it, I was unconventional. The powers that be were trying to make snooker into a sport of kings, like horse racing, but the fans were cultural rebels and they wanted to be part of the sport, not excluded from it. When the snooker authorities and the BBC banned me from television, or fined me for 'behaviour unbecoming', all that did was to make me even more popular. All they managed to achieve was to alienate themselves.

On the road and off the rails

My former manager John McLaughlin was filmed describing me as, 'only having three vices, drinking, women and gambling, and not necessarily in that order'. That didn't do me any harm. But it was a combination of efforts that made me, and the sport, so popular. Those efforts were not coordinated. In fact, they were all over the place. There were two camps in the early seventies – those for the sport and those who sought to see bad in everything new. Let's call them Luddites. In my view, the Luddites form the section of the press who have little talent or foresight; they are jealous of the quality writers so they basically take the piss out of anything new or popular. Unfortunately, they still exist today. One camp was saying it was a great sport, with access to the people, for the people. Anyone could participate for the few quid needed to buy the equipment and, unlike with tennis or horse riding, snooker clubs and associations were easy to join. They weren't selective, snobby or inaccessible.

In the other camp, you had programme makers and newspaper journalists reporting on the seedy and sleazy side of the sport, going out of their way to portray snooker as being played by low lifes. In one documentary someone said of me, 'He essentially inhabits a world that is shoddy and tinselly.' They even filmed me at one club in the north and showed the green moss and mildew growing on the outside wall. These types don't have the talent to make interesting films or write interesting articles, so they play up to a minority of other cynics and pass it off as entertainment. I must have been a godsend to them and they made the most of it.

By the start of the 1973 season, snooker was getting its first taste of the future and sponsorship. First on the scene were Park Drive cigarettes. They put up £8,000 and got a million pounds-worth of publicity for it – not a bad deal. I shouldn't be cynical, I know, but I am because it's my natural way. Just twelve months had passed since I became world champion, but they didn't have a ranking system in those dark days, so I was portrayed as the No.1 with Spencer No.2 and Reardon No.3. The prize money for the outright winner of the World Championship was now £1,500, and every player, right from the first frame, got something just for qualifying, starting at £100.

The defence of my world title kicked off in April at the Manchester City Exhibition Hall and was played over a concentrated thirteen-day period, which was a far cry from the previous year's set-up, when the tournament stretched over a number of months and venues. The game was crawling, however slowly, into the modern age. My management company, Snooker Promotions, had arranged this new format. They wanted to make it look properly professional so they brought in an eight-table arena. One main table in the centre was reserved for the highest ranking players and was the focus of TV coverage, while the other players used the remaining seven tables around it.

I drew Pat Houlihan first (in what was actually the second round proper as I got a bye in the first) and won the first session 7–1. I was wearing a pair of white Oxford bags that day, to the disapproval of the officials. They seemed to want my blood from the minute I walked in the place. I was late arriving for my match because I'd got chalk on my trousers and had to sponge them off and dry myself. When I eventually got out into the arena, I immediately felt an atmosphere, and as I walked to the table, the crowd started booing me. Pat was looking at me with a face like a hangman, and the referee asked me to explain the delay. I tried but got nowhere and he docked me a frame, so I just got on with it. Officialdom and Alex Higgins never did see eye to eye.

My break in the ninth frame was 78, which I made in record time. From that moment the crowd went from mumblings of disquiet to nods of approval and support. I'd won them round by living up to my name. Within those few minutes I was forgiven for the lateness by the now grateful crowd. Pat just shook his head in despair as I sat down, lit a cigarette, sipped a drink and lay back in my chair, trying not to look at the crowd. I ended the night as the winner of my first round 16–3, and the crowd, the commentators, the referees, the officials and the security people went home fully satisfied at what they had seen that day.

In the quarter-finals I was playing the legendary Fred Davis and between us we managed to bring about a first in snooker – 'Rain stops play'. It was hilarious to say the least. The day session had gone without a hitch, but as Fred started the evening's play, the roof sprung a leak, and because of the netting that had been put in place above the table to stop anything falling on the baize, the water came down like a fine rain. Play was stopped, the position of the balls marked, the table covered and we went off for a drink until the leak was fixed. I guess they should have anticipated such a problem – after all, neither Manchester nor Alex Higgins are exactly famous for being dry. Playing Davis was hard work. I underestimated him and the old man of the baize took me to the hilt of the round, which I won by taking the thirtieth frame.

I had reached the semi-finals and was playing Steady Eddie, but my game just disappeared and I lost 23–9. I was interviewed afterwards and blamed my new-found lifestyle of wine, women and horses. Honesty is always the best policy, after all. Only thing is I don't think I was being completely honest when I said that.

The real reason I didn't retain my title, I believe, is that I wasn't practising enough, and that wasn't as a result of the wine, women and song that many people believed was my downfall, although they didn't help. I wasn't practising enough because I was touring the country too much.

In those days, only two tournaments offered anything like significant prize money. In order to make ends meet – and remember, I couldn't drive so I often had to employ a driver to take me places, which was another expense – I had to play in exhibition matches the length and breadth of Britain. I loved doing it, don't get me wrong. I met so many fascinating and friendly people in the clubs. I'd turn up, take on the best players that particular area had to offer, then go for a few drinks and a chat afterwards. I believe that was one of the reasons I was so popular. People respected the fact that I didn't try to hide behind my fame. But it came at a cost. If I wasn't being driven, I would be on the train, and you can't practise in the back of a car or in a dingy British Rail carriage.

One of the key things about my snooker was that I was an innovative player. I was forever inventing new shots, finding new angles. I was always trying to improve my game but new approaches took hours of practice to develop and refine, and because I wasn't putting in the necessary six or seven hours a day, I was standing still. And it cost me my world crown.

I might no longer be the world champ, but what the hell, I thought, there is always next year. Only problem was, things were beginning to unravel. Up to then I hadn't really been living the high life. Sure, I'd go to nightclubs, but they tended to close at around midnight back then. I'd often be back in my bed by one in the morning. I knew I had the skill to keep winning, but that skill needed to be nourished. I wasn't practising, so the nourishment wasn't happening and I found myself in a downward spiral. I wasn't playing as well as I knew I could, and so, to compensate, I started to stay out too late partying. I thought I could beat the system but I was wrong. While the other competitors got their sleep and practised on the tables for the next day's sessions, I was out on the piss, chatting up birds and generally having a good time. Is it any wonder I let myself down in matches? To top it all off, the WPBSA (World Professional Billiards and Snooker Association) fined me for being late for the Houlihan match and wearing clothes unbecoming of a professional. They were such a pathetic bunch at times it's no wonder we fell out.

I went from one defeat to the next and just couldn't seem to stop the rot. I wouldn't admit to myself that my lifestyle was to blame. I was like a man possessed as I continued to get into fights in clubs, fights with girlfriends and, worst of all, drink-fuelled fights with the press. Simon Weaver took me to lunch one day and read me the riot act. He wasn't impressed that I was getting into too many bad situations. 'If you don't start toeing the line, Alex, the Association will ban you from playing,' he told me. I sat there and listened, but I was angry at it all.

He said if I didn't start to comply with convention, his company would dump me, and then I would have no management at all. 'If that happens, Alex, no one else will take you on. Then who will fight your corner?' I didn't really feel that anyone did. I still didn't see the sense in it. I was still an arrogant little guy from the back streets of Belfast and I wasn't going to let anyone tell me how to conduct my life. We ended the lunch with me apologising for it all and promising to try harder, but Simon wasn't convinced. Who can blame him?

I was becoming very inconsistent in my behaviour as the year drew to a close. I failed to turn up at a club in Wales one night but that was because I got my dates confused, and that is the truth. Another hefty fine was winging its way towards me, but I was given a reprieve when I offered to pay all their out-of-pocket expenses and play another night for free a few weeks later, which I honoured. I also got a standing ovation, and a letter of appreciation went off to my managers when I did a night of snooker at the B & K club in Watford. My snooker was brought alight by the warm crowd and I played my heart out. Simon said afterwards that there was hope for me yet. At least I ended the year on a high because I was soon off to Australia to see my on-off girlfriend Cara. Everyone said she would be the making of me and maybe she could have been . . . if I'd let her.

8

What goes around, comes around

•

Australia in early 1974 was both good and bad for me. I was loving spending time with Cara – she was a very refined lady, with a strong will, a great sense of fun and a wild streak that suited me perfectly. As I've mentioned previously, through her I got to know a lot of Sydney's most influential people, including the Legal Eagles. They all treated me very well – even when I did get into a few daft scrapes and rows when we were out and I drank a bit too much.

There was nothing too serious about these incidents, but I was gaining something of a reputation. Fortunately for me, and for the Aussies, before anything got out of hand I had to come back to the UK, to enter the 1974 World Championship. This time I was determined to win it and show them all that I was the best player of all time.

Once again I received a bye in the first round, and so I found myself taking up arms against Bernard Bennett in round two. I saw him off fairly easily, 15–4, and was confident I was playing well. So much so that when I met Fred Davis in the next round – the quarter-finals – and found myself 13–9 up, I felt I could breeze my way through to the final, not least because sixty-year-old Fred was recovering from a heart operation. The Higgins nostrils flared and scented victory. Fred, whom I greatly admired, wiped the floor with me in the next two frames. Frame 25 was next and that's when I lost my cool and any chance of victory. I was leading by 32 when referee Jim Thorpe called a foul on the blue ball. Fred saw it and took a pause to give me time to protest. Thorpe insisted I had performed a push-shot and I knew I hadn't. 'That's no foul,' I informed him, politely of course . . . He was adamant and dismissed any protest on my part. I looked around and every face I saw had a neutral look on it. No one knew what to make of the incident, or my reaction.

Then the nostrils flared again. My blood temperature rose to boiling point and I blew it, big time. With a wrath never seen before or since at a championship, I let loose at Thorpe. 'You should read the fucking rule book!' I exclaimed. Even as I opened my mouth I could imagine the WPBSA spending the money they were about to fine me. Thorpe, and most of the watching world, heard every word of my outburst. The incident put me off my stride and I ended up losing 15–14. Fair play to Fred Davis. To hold it together after that disruption was a hell of a thing to do. Thorpe was reprimanded for a similar decision at the 1981 championship, when he ruled against Dennis Taylor, and was taken off any further matches by the promoter, Mike Watterson. Dennis later said his shot was more a shove than a push, which virtually vindicated Thorpe because that is a pretty thin line of distinction. The authorities obviously agreed because Thorpe went on to referee the 1984 World Championship final.

After that fiasco of a match, I was doing a press conference in the players' room, slagging off Jim Thorpe and his decision, and as usual a reporter started winding me up. I gave him a real mouthful, swearing and shouting in front of everyone – not a smart move and another black mark, but I have to say that I believe every row or scuffle I ever had with a tabloid 'journalist' was justified, although not everybody would agree with me on that one.

That incident proved to be the final nail in my coffin as far as my managers were concerned. They dumped me and I ended up being taken on by Maurice Hayes, who ran a company called Q Promotions Ltd. In the stable with me was Graham Mills. The company also looked after two up-and-coming amateurs, Willie Thorne and John Virgo.

My relationship with Maurice got off to a flying start when, in late December 1974, I won the Watneys Open at the Northern Snooker centre in Leeds and banked the £1,000 first prize, but not before another controversial incident involving a referee and a marker. In the semi-final against Reardon, there was a dispute about a 20-point gap in the scoring. The marker and the ref were both replaced, but I still won the round and then the final, which clearly came as something of a surprise to Maurice. He'd booked me to play in a club in Essex on the night of the final, presumably because he had no belief that his latest signing would make it that far in the tournament. That cost me £965 in compensation for not showing up. Cheers, Maurice.

He might have cost me some money that night, but Maurice had a big impact on snooker. It was Maurice who was responsible for securing sponsorship from W.D. & H.O. Wills, the tobacco company, for the 1976 World Championship. From that point onwards, the prize money, the competition, the entertainment value and the quality of players rose to new heights. And so the Embassy World Championship was born. The fact that he was being kept so busy putting together sponsorship deals for his players and the game in general, had a spin-off effect on me in that he didn't give me too much hassle about my behaviour. In retrospect, I'm not sure that was a good thing, however.

Maurice had good connections in Canada and so in 1975 he arranged my first visit to that country. I was looking forward to a new beginning and a career boost to get me back on top. Cara went back to Australia and I went off to the Rockies – well, Toronto and Ottawa to be precise. It was a great trip snooker-wise. I won the Canadian Open, which was my first significant win since the World Championship. I was under strict instructions not to 'Drink Canada Dry' as the ginger ale advert suggested. Unfortunately, leopards don't change their spots. They never do. And this one was no exception.

I was trying to forget all the hassle I had been getting from the WPBSA, but I am my own worst enemy at the best of times, and my rebellious streak often gets the better of me. In the previous year or so, I felt I had been fined and spoken to like a naughty schoolboy by the Association, so I'd fought back by trying to wind them up. I turned up at one tournament wearing a green suit and I also refused to wear a bow-tie all the time. Not exactly *Rebel Without a Cause* you might think, but then I overstepped the mark once again. At a match in Ilfracombe I was baited by a heckler, lost it big time and threw my cue at him, spear fashion. That didn't go down too well and I was duly 'escorted' from the table.

All these incidents were reported to the WPBSA and I was fined and fined, then fined again. They hated me for my cavalier ways. They wanted to bring some decorum to the sport, but they didn't seem to realise that it was my outrageous style of play that brought people into exhibitions and tournaments. I was putting bums on seats, not them, and I was in no mood to compromise.

I had even been barred from ever playing on the TV programme *Pot Black* again. The show had started in the late sixties and was originally put out in black and white. Before winning the championship in 1972, I had been on a few times and had made some comments they didn't like. The show was a kind of tournament on air, based on a round-robin format, with each 'match' consisting of playing one frame, for which you got points if you won. At the end of the season, the top players would have a play-off for a trophy of a silver salver, but typical of the tight-fisted BBC, no prize money. I complained too much and was eventually banned – well, not banned so much as not asked to play any more. There is a subtle difference. I think.

One of the final indignations for the show's organisers – for that read 'Ted Lowe' – was the now famous pissing in the sink incident in the studio. I was in the changing rooms getting ready and fancied a pee. Now, if you've been to the Pebble Mill studios in Birmingham, you will know that the toilets are a fair walk from the changing rooms. So I pissed in the sink – with the tap running, I hasten to add – and got found out. That wasn't the only time I got into trouble for being caught short, but I'll get to that other incident later.

I did eventually get back on to *Pot Black* in 1978 when Ted Lowe realised that it was me who attracted the viewers. I think people tuned in just to see if I would kick off and many a time I didn't disappoint them. My view on the whole affair was that it was a shite programme. It took forever to play your frame – stop, start, stop, start – because of the filming I presume, so there was no rhythm to the play. And it was hot as hell in the studio. The lights they used threw off so much heat that the studio audience was either in a trance or half asleep. The atmosphere wasn't helped by the fact that they filmed the show a few days after Christmas, when everyone – players and fans – was already worn out by the seasonal festivities. They paid us £100 a day to sit around while they frigged about with the cameras and lighting, then just as they got it right, the union tea break would come along. We played one frame, under those circumstances, to determine the best player. How the hell does that equate to a sporting challenge? I really couldn't have given a damn whether I played in it or not.

Ted Lowe is a nice enough fella who enjoyed a drink, that's for sure, but he didn't like me and told me so many times. I wasn't exactly a fan of his, either, so the feeling was quite mutual. When it came to the brave new world of snooker that was happening all around him, in my view he had his head in the sand most of the time, and up his own arse the rest of it. It seemed to me that he and the others involved just wanted to drag snooker back into the dark ages, while players such as Reardon, Spencer, me and all the others were keeping it interesting and bringing in new blood, both fans and players.

So, against that background, the trip to Canada went well enough. Let's just say I was as outspoken as usual, but it all ended to my benefit when I walked off with $5,000 in prize money for winning the Open. It was a busy year for travelling. The 1975 World Championship was held in Melbourne, at the Nunawading Basketball Centre. That suited me fine. I was going to Australia anyway to play and to get married to Cara. My ex-managers, Peter West and Pat Nally, who had organised the previous year's tournament, were getting a bit bored with all the competition in the sport, and Eddie Charlton, who had his own promotions company, was bidding for the opportunity to put the championship on in his home country. When he got it, in my view he proceeded to make it difficult for 'competition' to feature in the event. For instance, I wasn't invited to play, but I wasn't going to let that stop me. I entered anyway, to his dismay. Likewise, the draw was done to Eddie Charlton's rules, which were in fact contrary to the WPBSA's own rule book. The result was that Eddie didn't have to play Spencer, Reardon or me in the opening rounds.

Personally, I thought that Charlton's behaviour in the whole affair was not only biased, but unsportsmanlike, which is even more shocking when you consider that Charlton was a surfing, athletics, cricketing and boxing champion as well. He even carried the Olympic torch for the 1956 games in Melbourne. He'd put the world's three best players in the half of the draw that didn't include himself, presumably in order to give himself an unfair advantage – in a tournament that, as the organiser, he shouldn't even have entered. If you read the rules of any competition, it always excludes employees, and sometimes their direct relatives, from entering. Somehow the WPBSA let him get away with it, which only adds credence to my belief that some of the people who ran snooker were not generally acting in the best interests of the people they were supposed to represent, the players. Ray Reardon beat me in the semi-finals, 19–14. Ray, to his credit, went on to play a spectacular final against the home favourite, Charlton, beating him fair and square, 31–30.

I had other things on my mind after the tournament – my wedding to Cara and our honeymoon. After that, it was time to return to the UK. By then Maurice Hayes had also signed up Cliff Thorburn, Taylor and Spencer, so I should have been in great company, but I'm afraid the only real company I was keeping, apart from Cara's, was my own. My behaviour was making me increasingly unpopular with the establishment, perhaps with good reason. One incident in particular always comes to mind when I think back on this period of my life.

Terry Griffiths was an amateur player in 1975. He continued to work for an insurance company and enjoyed his status as Welsh snooker champion in the valleys of his home country. Being an enterprising chap, he once used his local popularity to organise an evening of snooker with me, at a cinema in Llanelli. Although it was all quite amateurish – the table was set up on the stage where the screen would have been, and all the drinks were served in plastic cups – to give Terry his due, he sold the place out in a matter of days. My reputation can't have harmed ticket sales, mind you. He even got some sponsorship from a local brewery. I, rather arrogantly, didn't give him enough respect, thinking I would just play it out. I planned to let him take a few frames and then clean up, so as to make him look good and me even better. I arrived early to practise, but I also started on the free drinks.

By the interval, I was getting pretty pissed off with the whole affair and decided to nip out for a quick drink from a proper glass. So a Welsh mate of mine and I sneaked off to the nearest pub. We walked in, fought our way through to the bar, which was surprisingly busy, and stopped in utter amazement. The reason for the place's popularity was staring me in the face – a smiling, attractive and well-endowed topless barmaid. Unbeknown to us, we'd walked into the first legalised topless bar in Britain. I nearly toppled over backwards, but ended up pissing myself with laughter at the absurdity of the evening. Mind you, that was the last good thing that happened that day.

Terry played well that night, and I played poorly. When Terry potted the last ball to win, I turned to the referee and stuck two fingers up at him. I felt that he had been biased against me all night. As always, I had told him not to crowd me. 'Stand at least six feet away,' I instructed him, but he just ignored me. Still, that is no excuse for bad behaviour. I am a professional and should have acted like one. The crowd booed me and I walked off, my feelings hurt at being beaten. In the hospitality room, the sponsors were there with their wives and kids. They wanted their money's worth, so I signed autographs and posed for pictures.

I was sitting having a vodka and orange when I spotted a lovely girl across the crowded room. Our eyes met, you know the scenario. She came over and introduced herself. 'Hello, Alex,' she said in a very sexy Welsh accent. 'I'm Terry's sister-in-law.' She pointed to a man standing talking nearby, and said, 'That's my husband.' I didn't catch his name. I wasn't interested.

I was, shall we say, a little over-familiar with her and the husband took offence. I wasn't trying to pull her at all. Getting involved with other men's wives or girlfriends is a total no-no for me. I was just showing off, to try to re-establish myself after getting beaten. The next thing I know I'm throwing a punch at this huge Welshman. Thanks to the drink, I missed. However, I did end up smacking the guy beside him, and all hell broke loose. I could feel I was on to a loser and so I stupidly picked up a bottle to wave around at anyone who thought I was fair game. Shouting abuse and threats, I went into back-street Belfast mode, inviting anyone and everyone to take their chances. Terry just rushed me and disarmed me in one move. I left while I was still winning, so to speak.

I was sitting in the lounge of a club a few miles away the next day, reading the *Racing Post* as usual, when Terry came in. I was feeling a bit ashamed and embarrassed at what I had done but when I'm in the wrong I won't admit it or show remorse, it's just not my nature. He stood there for a minute waiting for an apology, which he still hasn't got to this day. I want to put my house in order, so I'll publicly make it now: 'Terry, I am truly sorry for the way I behaved that night, not only to your family, but to the many friends and supporters who came along to watch us both play.' I hope Terry will accept it, even though it has been a long time coming.

The year went by and I was determined that 1976 was going to be a refreshing new start for me. Cara and I were getting on well, when we were together, and I had taken up golf, which helped me to relax. I was practising snooker up to ten hours a day and getting into a fairly fixed routine. It started to pay off and my consistency improved.

In February I was playing Willie Thorne at an exhibition in the Leicester YMCA, and whitewashed him 10–0 in the afternoon session. I started off at a furious pace and Willie never caught up. I broke his spirit in about the fourth frame with a break of 149. Yes, 149. A world record, I think – and pure genius, if I say so myself. Let me explain. It started off with Willie committing a foul off his break and in so doing, snookering me. I took brown as my free ball and green as my choice of colour. I knocked in the fifteen reds with thirteen blacks and two pinks. Then went on to clear the table of all the colours – 149 break.

The exhibition was meant to be the best of nineteen frames – ten in the afternoon and the remainder that evening – but it was all over before the evening session could start. I thought about heading home but I didn't want to disappoint the spectators. So I suggested to Willie that we start from scratch for the second session, provided he could find some more money to play for. My original fee was securely in my pocket by then. Willie and his mates raised a further £250 and, within a couple of hours, that too was mine. I won seven frames on the trot. Willie eventually took the final two frames but, of course, by then I didn't care. That was a good day's work, and still time for a couple of drinks with Willie and his mates in the pub next door. The best part of it all was that my old enemies were queuing up to praise me and my performances in the press. The Hurricane was back with a vengeance. I was ready to blow away all and any competition at the forthcoming World Championship. I was determined to carry off the trophy, and the record-breaking £6,000 prize money.

I reached the final against Reardon and I was so relaxed and confident that Ray and I even went out together the night before the match to celebrate. We were with my mates from Manchester United but Ray didn't drink as much as I did, or stay as late. What did I care? I was invincible, wasn't I? I had seen off all the other big boys already – Thorburn, Spencer and Charlton. All I needed to do now was add Reardon to the list.

What goes around, comes around

The first day's play was quite painful for me, and I mean that in a physical sense. I had the mother of all hangovers and the bright illumination of the venue, plus the additional TV lights, weren't exactly helping. Even Reardon complained about them. The day finished with Ray up 8–5. My school report that night would have read: 'Higgins is a slacker, must do better in class and pay attention more.' I was very subdued, which no doubt had something to do with the after-effects of the vodka the night before.

The second day was going better for me. I'd fought my way back and was leading 10–9. Ray was still in combative mode, though, and quite rightly demonstrated it with the organisers when he complained about the table, which they duly adjusted. I've heard it said that this is what put me off in that final, and that I lost my concentration because of Ray's complaint. That is total rubbish. I had no problem whatsoever with Ray's comments. They were justified and he was right to raise them.

No, the reason I lost the final was because I made a grave error just around this stage in the match. Instead of using the rest for a tricky shot, I decided to play with my left hand. I'd obviously done so many times before – but the World Championship final was not the place. I missed the shot, and the frame turned from me coasting with a 50 or 60 point lead to Ray stealing it. With that, he was on a roll and built up a lead that I just couldn't claw back.

With the score standing at 15–11 to Ray, referee Bill Timms made a bad call – and I think that did throw me. Quite a fuss was made over the call and Timms was actually replaced by John Williams. I am not sure why. I've heard suggestions that it was because he and Ray had a separate argument at the break but I doubt that. Ray isn't that sort of character. I think there is every chance that Timms retired himself from the match. He was a very proud man – obstinate even – and I think he would have felt slighted by the complaint about his decision and that will have been enough for him to pack his bags. Anyway, we finished the day 24–15 in Ray's favour, and three frames into the final day, it was all over. I actually conceded the match a frame early by mistake. Being the gent that I am, when I found out my mistake I didn't feel that I had the right to play on.

I'd failed at the final hurdle, but at no point did I think that my late nights out, my troubled marriage and my mood swings had contributed to that failure. I still wasn't prepared to take responsibility. I hated being second best but hadn't yet realised what I needed to do to be top of the world again. Then, to cap it all, my management company fell apart. They had made too many mistakes, all of them too costly, and their involvement in the World Championship proved a bridge too far. Not only were they falling apart, but it transpired that they'd been taking bookings for exhibitions for the players and not always telling us. So guess who got a reputation for not turning up to events? No manager, a bad name and no world crown. Not good.

9

A circus tent and a magician

•

It was 1976 and my life was rapidly going down the same hill as my marriage. Both were competing to see which one would get there first to drive me insane. A psychologist once said of me, 'Higgins is the nearest you will get to a sane man bordering on insanity,' and he was probably right. I did get some revenge for the Reardon defeat, though, when I later beat him in the finals of the Canadian Club, but it was scant consolation.

I went back to Australia to try to patch things up with Cara and also to play some matches there. I wanted to see if my marriage could be salvaged. It couldn't, but Cara and I had a good time regardless. That was the way we were. We couldn't stay husband and wife but we loved each other and got on fantastically well. We were in Canberra for the World Professional Matchplay championship, staying at the Canberra Rex Hotel, which had a swimming pool. It was very cold, unusually so for that time of year, and one afternoon a guy bet me Aus$1,000 that Cara and I would not strip naked and stay in the swimming pool for twenty minutes. 'Put your money down,' I said, and asked Cara if she'd do it. 'No problem, baby.' We jumped in the pool bollock naked and twenty minutes later we won the bet. Easiest $1,000 ever, rounded off with two hot whiskies, one bottle of Dom Perignon and some great sex.

I was still a big crowd puller, despite my lack of discipline. I played in the Winfield Masters for Channel 9 in Sydney and also a match in Melbourne. I was reasonably happy with my form in both, but when the big one came along – the Matchplay – I crashed out early. The whole tournament was a bit of a fiasco, to be honest. Eddie Charlton had been given permission to promote it as a world championship tournament, but how the hell can there be two world championship events? Charlton just seemed to be in it for the money, not for the good of the sport. The cheeky bastard even wrote to me and told me to behave myself while I was in Australia. Like I was going to listen to him! I got into a bit of bother while I was out there – the usual stuff – and although Cara did come to Canberra to support me, we both knew we were over. She'd had enough of all the hassles, and I agreed with her.

Charlton went on to win the tournament by beating Ray Reardon in the final, and to everyone's dismay the Aussies started to call him the world champion. To be fair to them, it was billed as a world championship tournament and he had not only won the final, but defeated the reigning world champion, so it was logical to think that the crown now belonged to Australia. Some people in England even started to call him the world champ. It was a sorry affair and I blame the WPBSA for it all, a shambles run by a shambles.

As for me, I went back to my lonely flat in Manchester with my marriage all but over. I did have some luck around that time though. Del Simmons, who ran the International Snooker Agency (ISA) along with Spencer, came to see me and signed me up. I had high hopes of becoming my former self as a player, because this time Del would keep me in line and out of trouble. Like a cat, I was using up my lives and I needed to have strong, reliable management to guide me.

I was travelling so much around the UK, earning a living, that

I hardly noticed the weeks going by, and soon it was 1977. I was always playing snooker in either a tournament or an exhibition, living in cheap hotels. It was a bloody lonely existence, I can tell you. Yes, I was surrounded by fans and admirers, but I was still lonely.

I played in the Benson & Hedges Masters in London, and started off fine, reaching the semi-finals. But by then I had tasted the nightlife of the Big Smoke and succumbed to my bad habits of late nights and too much booze. I was beaten fair and square by the new kid on the block, Doug Mountjoy, another Welshman. With the World Championship only weeks away, I needed to get my game back on par if I was to make any impact.

I wasn't relishing returning to Manchester. There seemed little to fire me up there but back I went all the same. I was on a real low but just as I was sliding even further down that slope of despondency, hope for the future arrived, sitting in a bar and ignoring me. That was when I met the beautiful woman who was to become my second wife, Lynn Avison.

Everything seemed to click for me at a Benson & Hedges event at Leopardstown in Ireland, a place I was very familiar with. There's a racecourse there, after all, and the tournament was held under the stands. Perhaps it was because I'd met Lynn. Who knows? She was a good influence on me, that's for sure, because I stayed pretty sober most of the time and my game just got better and better, too good for Taylor and Reardon. I had to play Dennis in the semi-finals and in the final frame he tried to demoralise me with an opening break of 57, but I was sharp that day, very sharp. Taylor got too cocky and he looked at me with a smirk, as if to say, 'It's all over, Hurricane, you're blown out.' Then he missed a red, a simple shot that he hit too hard. I was straight in with a 70 break to win the frame and a place in the final. As I potted the black, I smirked back at him, but he wasn't giving anything away and remained his usual po-faced self.

Lynn came to watch me play Reardon in the final. Her flight was late and I hadn't had a chance to embrace her when she arrived as the match was in full swing. She found herself sat close to where Ray was seated during play. Now Ray has a roving eye like the best of them and between frames and shots he started to chat up my girlfriend, not that he knew her as such then. I was across the table from them and said nothing. I was determined to let the result do my talking for me – and it did. Reardon 3, Higgins 5. To Reardon's further dismay, I walked over to Lynn and gave her a peck on the cheek. The trophy, the cheque and the girl were mine. I led Lynn off to the sponsor's room for a glass of champagne and I could feel Reardon's eyes burrowing into my back. I loved it. When I potted that final ball I remember the crowd went mad. Most of them were from the Republic, of course, but to them it didn't matter which part I was from. They still considered that a paddy had won it for Ireland. I was now confident of victory in the forthcoming World Championship, which this year was being held for the first time at the Crucible in Sheffield. The enterprising Mike Watterson was responsible for getting it moved to the theatre after his wife had seen a play there and suggested it to him in passing. He'd even got the prize money up to a staggering £17,000 for the winner, and this year I was determined it would be my name on that cheque.

As history has already recorded, my 1977 World Championship bid came to nothing when I lost in the first round to Doug Mountjoy. I was devastated. I'd blown it again. I was surprised at the press reports, though, which were virtually saying that now I was out, the public interest would dwindle. How wrong they were. My getting knocked out at such an early stage created such a furore in the press that interest in snooker, and specifically the World Championship, rose dramatically. Just for the record, I went out 13–12 to Mountjoy after he potted a long black that could have gone either way, and Spencer won his third championship against Thorburn, 25–21.

More travelling by train and hitching lifts from all and sundry was the order of the day after that. I ended the snooker year at Pontins holiday camp in Prestatyn, Wales. Pontins were getting in on the popularity of the sport and they ran a tournament that encompassed two competitions, one of which you could enter only if you had appeared on *Pot Black* that year. I'd been snubbed by the programme so that route wasn't open to me. However, the other was an open competition. Any professional or amateur could enter, but the pros had to give a 14 point start per frame to any amateurs. The scoring was unusual as well. The qualifying sheets, as the rounds were called, consisted of a two-frame match with an aggregate score. This meant that, in effect, the pros were giving the amateurs 28 points per match.

There were some very good amateurs that year, some playing to a professional standard. It was nice to see good players coming along and playing their sporting heroes. If I had been one of them, I would have felt privileged to have been able to say to my grandchildren, 'I was there. I played the Hurricane and nearly beat him.' I say that tongue-in-cheek, by the way. I whizzed through the prelims and ended up in the final of the qualifying rounds, playing an amateur from Manchester called Billy Kelly, who was left-handed, a distinct advantage to me.

After the first game, taking in Billy's lead of 14, I found myself 104 points behind with 12 or 13 reds left. The table was awful – which meant that a lot of the advantage my superior play should have given me was negated. The highest break I made was 28. It looked as though it was all over for me but I clawed my way back into the game, requiring something like seven snookers to have a chance. I eventually won by potting the last three colours, blue, pink and black. People were astounded. I had done the impossible.

Around 800 amateurs and pros had entered the open competition, and I was one of four who made it downstairs to the main arena to play in the final rounds against the winning *Pot Black* pros. During the two weeks I was at Pontins I was playing every day in the tournament, and then taking on all-comers for cash at night. My play was razor sharp. Lynn and her sister came up from Manchester for the last three days and they saw me win the competition by beating Terry Griffiths in the final. He was still an amateur at that time and so received his 14 point lead, but he was also the Welsh and English amateur champion. He won the first two frames but then I settled down and played ruthless snooker to win 7–4. That match was watched by over 2,000 snooker fans, that is 1,300 more than get to see the World Championship live, although of course millions watch it on TV. I gained a lot of new fans at that competition and was grateful for the support.

The next day Lynn, her sister Carol, Con Dunne, who is a friend of Jimmy White's, and I all headed back to Manchester. The journey took a lot longer than it should have done because Con wanted to stop at every other pub, not that I was complaining. What did annoy me, however, was the state of the bloody car. It kept stalling on us and had to be push-started. I swear to God I pushed that car ten or fifteen miles that day. Time was getting on a bit and I was gasping for another drink. We'd just passed Manchester airport when the car conked out once gain, fortunately only a few hundred yards from a watering hole I knew quite well. It was a sign, I told myself, that I had earned a glass or two. So I stepped out of the car, straight into a foot-deep puddle of water. It was the last straw. I was tired and pissed off. Con could see that my sense of humour was rapidly disappearing, and thought it was probably a good time to offer to help push the car as well, so I pushed from the back, while he pushed from the front passenger door. The car jolted, lurched forward and he fell face first into that bloody puddle. I loved it. I said to Lynn and Carol, 'Pick him up. I'll see you in the pub.' I enjoyed those couple of drinks. I was knackered but elated after the exertions of the previous two to three weeks. I had won something the real snooker players and fans enjoyed, and I had done it the hard way.

I went back to Canada after winning the Pontins competition to compete in the 1977 Canadian Open. The tournament had always been played at the Canadian National Exhibition, a sort of World's Fair style event that is held at Exhibition Place in Toronto. The venue that had been used previously had been booked up, so some bright spark had the hugely innovative idea of staging the tournament in a big top, rented from a visiting circus. There was sufficient room for six tables. We ended up playing in temperatures of 90° without any air conditioning, which was reminiscent of my visit to India, complete with elephants thrown in. The elephants were performing in the next-door circus, as was a brass band and a ringmaster with a suitably carrying voice. Tents don't have sound-proofing . . . Actually, as it turned out, the conditions weren't that bad and it was far better to stage the tournament than to cancel it.

I went through that tournament like my nickname. I blew Thorburn away 9–6 in the quarters and Reardon in the semis 9–7. Then came the final between Spencer and me. Spencer, you have to remember, was part of my management company, so he tried to talk me down from my high with some advice on decorum. We ended up having a huge row, which soured the final for me a bit.

I wasn't going to let him get to me though, so I kept off the drink the night beforehand and it worked. I beat him 17–14, but

I was later to pay for it when he put in a bad report to Del Simmons about me.

The Toronto Blue Jays baseball team have their stadium next to where we were playing, and that week Diana Ross was appearing there. After my quarter-final win I bought six tickets and went along with Tony Meo, Tony Knowles, Kirk Stevens and a couple of other friends. It was a great concert. Afterwards we went to one of the bars in the ground, had a few drinks and then went back to the Sheraton in the city centre. While I was there I met an old acquaintance, the actor David Hemmings. He was filming in Toronto at the time. I had met him via Oliver Reed in London some time earlier. He came along later in the week to watch me play in the semi and afterwards we went for a few beers in one of his favourite watering holes, an English-style pub called Her Majesty's in Yonge Street.

After I had won the tournament, David asked me to stay on to play in a video-linked game of darts between Her Majesty's and a pub of the same name somewhere near London. He was very insistent and said he would pay for my flight back. How could I refuse, especially when he explained he had a huge suite at the hotel and there was more than enough room for us both. So I moved in.

David spent the majority of his time plastered, as far as I could see – he liked his booze did our David – and the director of the movie was at his wits' end. On about my second day there David was out cold by mid afternoon. The director was on the line, going bananas because David was due to film a scene. Action was required. I got a car to take me to Chinatown where I bought about $50 worth of Chinese food. When I got back with it, David was still sprawled out on the bed. I filled a champagne bucket with ice-cold water and just gave him it flush on the face and chest – that did the trick. I got him a bath-robe and asked him if he was hungry. 'I'm fucking famished.' You should have seen the look of delight on his face when he saw all the take-away containers strewn across the dining table.

The phone rang again and sure enough it was the director. I explained that, 'Mr Hemmings is having a bite to eat and he will be ready for the shoot in about one hour.' Doctor Hurricane had done a good job. I went with David to watch the filming, and they required only about four takes of his scene before it was a wrap.

Later on that night I was still awake in the suite, watching some late-night TV, when the phone rang. David was already crashed out so I answered. It was Donald Sutherland. I recognised his voice instantly. He asked me who I was and I replied, 'The Hurricane,' and asked what message I should give to David. 'It's not important, Mr Hurricane,' he said. I liked Sutherland as an actor and I was quite chuffed with that little chat. David filmed again the next day and that night we played the darts match. I can tell you that Her Majesty's won, but don't ask me which one. We were all pissed as farts and I can't remember. I'm pretty sure we didn't even know on the night.

When I got back to the UK, I was once again invited to play on *Pot Black*, which was to be filmed over the Christmas period. Del Simmons, who had struck the deal for me, told me I was skating on thin ice with ISA and the BBC, so if I wanted to make my comeback, I'd have to keep my head down, my temper under control and my big mouth shut. That promise I made under duress and knew I would have a problem keeping it.

Next stop was Blackpool and the first UK Championship in late November. The tournament was later played in Preston, Bournemouth and York. I reached the semi-finals before my luck ran out. I was trailing Doug Mountjoy 6–2 in the ninth frame when a whingeing spectator kept complaining that he couldn't see the table properly. I tried to ignore him, but it just put me off and I went on to lose 9–2.

My relationship with Lynn was keeping me in a fairly good mood, most of the time. Being in love tends to do that for me. I was looking forward to the future and doing my best to regain my world title. This time I would do it for Lynn to show her I wasn't a loser. Just before Christmas, I reached the final of the Dry Blackthorn Cup at Wembley. Patsy Fagan beat me 4–2 but it was a pretty good way to end the year.

I kept my hot streak going by regaining the Irish Professional Championship in Belfast early in 1978, a title I'd last won in 1972. I must admit I was delighted to beat my old adversary Dennis Taylor 21–7 to take the trophy.

I was on a roll and I was going to make the best of it. I needed the money to keep up my lifestyle, so Lynn would continually be impressed with me. Next, at the beginning of February, came the Benson & Hedges Masters in London, which I won in good style. The press were heralding my return to the top, and my rivals were shaking their heads in disbelief. I think most of them had been hoping I would give up the ghost and retire from playing, but I hadn't even started yet.

So, snooker good – behaviour less so. I got myself into a lot of trouble with the WPBSA and Del Simmons during the J.W. Lees Trophy pro-am competition. It was held at the Potters club in Salford, where I used to practise, six miles from where Lynn and I would live. I reached the semis and was pitched against a good amateur, John Hargreaves. Since it was a pro-am, I had to concede a 14-point lead and from the start he was playing superbly. I asked for the balls to be changed, but Jim Thorpe, the referee, wasn't having any of it.

'What's the problem, Alex?' he asked.

'The balls are sweating,' I replied.

A circus tent and a magician

The heating at the club had not been turned on until after the match started, which is why the balls were reacting as we were playing. Normally, the temperature is set at a consistent level at least six hours before a match gets under way to avoid this problem. Thorpe asked Hargreaves if he was happy with the balls and he said he was. I was annoyed by that and ripped into Hargreaves, telling him that he was the amateur and I was the pro. I told him he knew nothing about the game. Thorpe told me that the balls were staying and to stop complaining. So I let rip at him, too. Toys duly thrown out of pram, I refused to play any more until the situation was sorted. All a bit childish, and yes, embarrassing now, when I think back.

Thorpe and Hargreaves eventually compromised with me and allowed me to put the balls in a tray, and leave them on the radiator while we took our break. Hargreaves beat me 5–3 and went on to win the final against John Virgo 5–2.

I might not have been setting the world alight in the pro-am, but I was confident that when it came to the big one in Sheffield, I was on song. My form when it mattered, most notably at the Benson & Hedges, was good. So what happened? I got dumped out in the first round for the second year in a row. It was some match. I lost to Patsy Fagan on the pink in the twenty-fifth frame. I should have won easily. I had more than enough chances to stretch too far ahead, but over-confidence crept into my play. I went for some big, showboating shots, missed them and Patsy plugged away at me until he snatched victory. I was shattered at this kick in the balls to my comeback. Lynn put it down to wild living, which I didn't think was fair, and she warned me that if I didn't start to conform, we would be parting company. I didn't want to lose Lynn so I tried harder to be a good boy. Honest I did. My gambling habit was also beginning to bother Lynn. She wanted me to start saving some of my earnings, but I took no notice and continued to gamble, on the horses mainly, but also in casinos and on football.

It was around about this time that I first started encountering another new kid on the block, an upstart from the Romford stable of entrepreneur and snooker-hall owner Barry Hearn. 'This is Steve Davis,' I was told one day, and in front of me stood a skinny, badly dressed, ginger-headed boy from London, with a cue. In 1974 Barry became chairman of Lucania Snooker Clubs, a company that ran a number of halls. A couple of years later he was taking up-and-coming amateur and professional players under his wing, giving them the opportunity to show what they could do. Davis was one of those players. Hearn used to get professional players, including Spencer, Taylor, me and the other usual suspects, to come down to Romford to play exhibitions at his clubs against Davis. The clubs themselves were pretty dingy places on the whole. I don't think it would be an exaggeration to say that the Jampot was more hygienic – and that was way back in the mid sixties. I remember noticing that a layer of grimy ash covered almost every surface of the establishments, apart from the tables. Regardless of the state of the places, Barry was doing a good job in promoting himself and Davis, or the 'Ginger Magician' as he liked to call him, and it paid off for him. He sold the snooker halls in 1982 and went on to develop the game, and many players, around the world.

Next stop was Canada to defend my Open title, this time in the usual venue. I started off playing really well, even in practice where I got another 147 break to add to the few others I already had under my belt. It's great when a 147 is witnessed, though, especially by the press. In the quarter-finals I came up against Davis, one of the first times we'd played each other in a major tournament. I was on top form and beat him 9–8 to secure a place in the semis, where I would be facing another Londoner,

Tony Meo. I'd first encountered Tony three years previously at Pontins holiday camp, when he and another scalliwag pal – Jimmy White – followed me around for days during my exhibition matches. Tony must have picked up a good few tips because he beat me 9–7 and fair play to him. He deserved his place in the final and I was rooting for him, but it wasn't to be his year and he lost to Cliff Thorburn 19–17.

Back in the UK, the *Daily Mirror* wanted to get in on the act, as snooker's popularity continued to grow. In typical *Mirror* style, they wanted to go one better then anyone else. They called their competition Champion of Champions, and commissioned boxing promoter Mike Barrett to organise it for them at Wembley. It was a four-man tournament, and those considered by the *Mirror* to be champions were Reardon, Mountjoy, Fagan and myself.

The final was between me and Reardon and we fought a great fight. I was ahead, then Reardon went ahead, then I got the better of him and then out of nowhere, Ray would play superb snooker. It was a joy to play him and a joy to watch him. He beat me 11–9, which was far from a disgrace for me. After all, I did get to the final and was only beaten by a better player on the day. I played some of my best snooker in that match, mostly because of the way Ray played. He was pure competition and that is what fires me up to turn it on.

The UK Snooker Championship was in its second year in 1978 and was being sponsored by Corals the bookmakers. I travelled to Preston Guild Hall at the end of November to take part. In a quarter-final against Fred Davis, I took the first five frames and thought I had him whooped, but Fred came back bravely at me. After the tenth frame I had reassessed my position and was 8–2 up. I wasn't going to blow it from there, and didn't. I played David Taylor in the semi-finals and he went for the kill from the first frame. By the time the interval came round he was 7–1 up.

I tried to come back at him after the break, but he wasn't for beating that day and played some great shots to beat me to the final with a score of 9–5. Doug Mountjoy took the title that Taylor so deserved to win, the two of them battling through twenty-four frames before Mountjoy was declared the winner and new title holder. I was actually quite pleased for Doug because he'd missed out the previous year.

Early in the new year, I won the Castle Open in Southampton, taking Fred Davis for a 5–1 victory in the final. The Benson & Hedges Masters was next on the agenda and I had a good feeling about retaining my title in the tournament. Held in Wembley's conference centre, the competition started off well for me. I was keeping my promise to Lynn to lay off the booze and the wild nights. To be honest, I had to, certainly on those occasions when Lynn took me to tournaments. I reached the final and came face to face with South African Perrie Mans, a very tricky opponent who played in much the same way as I did. He took my title off me by 8–4 and was a worthy winner. He smashed his way through the frames by taking long shots and risky pots and it paid off for him.

After that, I thought I had to prepare for the World Professional Matchplay Championship in Australia – only I didn't. To my annoyance, Eddie Charlton banned me from entering, I suppose because he disliked me and was frightened of good players. He even got the WPBSA to agree to the ban. In my view, this amounted to my own association agreeing to an unfair and illegal ban that they should have had nothing to do with – isn't that the equivalent of a union stopping a member from getting a job? That can't be the correct way to support your members.

A circus tent and a magician

I was about to appeal against the WPBSA and that Matchplay decision when I heard the best news I'd had in years. The competition wouldn't be going ahead that year because the sponsorship money had failed to materialise. Revenge was sweet, especially as I didn't need to lift a finger.

10

Cracks beginning to show

•

On 5 January 1980, a sunny but coldish day, I became a husband again, but only just. The wedding very nearly didn't take place because I was having serious second thoughts. Well, you would if the night before you'd been sleeping with another woman.

In the run-up to the wedding – which Lynn had organised entirely, I just wrote the cheques – I kept asking myself, 'Why am I getting married? Do I truly love Lynn? Or is it just because I don't like to be lonely?' Perhaps every groom-to-be has similar concerns, and perhaps every groom-to-be goes out for a few drinks the night before he gives up his 'freedom' – but I doubt every groom-to-be has those few drinks with a beautiful woman who is not about to become his wife, and whom he knows is special, having been seeing her for a couple of months prior to getting married. And I'm damn sure not every groom-to-be goes to bed with that other woman just a matter of hours before he walks down the aisle. But this groom-to-be did all that.

It was the last time I slept with this lady, but I guess I should have read the neon signs that were flashing at me – 'Higgins, you are not ready to be married again. If you can have a relationship with another woman while your bride-to-be is planning the rest of her life with you, then you are being unfair on everyone. Don't do it. Don't do it.' But I didn't read those signs and Lynn Avison became Lynn Higgins. When I look back now, I wish I had stayed with the woman I spent the night with, and left Lynn at the altar, but I didn't have the courage to do that. So I broke my own heart by saying, 'I do,' that day. I know that sounds harsh – and I love the fact that Lynn gave me two beautiful children – but I think both Lynn and I would have had happier, more contented, lives if we hadn't married.

I arrived with my best man, Geoff Lomas, in a Rolls-Royce – not the Rolls-Royce that I left my house in because that broke down halfway to the church. Fortunately for us, a good friend, Mick Baker, was following close behind and he gave us a lift in his brand new Roller. It may not have been quite as old and classic as the first one, but it was a damn sight more reliable.

At the church we were met by a crowd of photographers. This was meant to be our special day and to my mind they were ruining it. So in traditional Hurricane fashion, I set about them with a vengeance, trying to get rid of them, as the village looked on. Perhaps I should have taken the breakdown of my car, and the fact that moments before I became a husband again I was involved in scuffles and a row with the media, as signs of things to come as far as the wedding was concerned, but never mind that now. The rest of the day went well, even if the marriage ultimately didn't.

Being married again, being in love, being looked after and feeling good about myself meant that I was sure I was on my way to getting my hands on that World Championship trophy again. I was convinced that this was the year I would break my spell of bad luck. My earning potential was getting better, we had a nice house and I was at last beginning to feel like a champion. I had everything I needed to have a great year. Lynn was busy house-hunting for a bigger place.

The snooker started off well enough and, although I was in hospital for a few days with an ear infection, I managed to win the Padmore/Super Crystalate International at West Bromwich, beating Perrie Mans 4–2 in the final. I lost the final of the Wilson's Classic in Manchester to John Spencer, during which I got into another row with Jim Thorpe over one of his decisions. Guess what? I was fined again. All in all, though, I was playing better and staying sober most of the time.

I was doing really well in the Benson & Hedges Masters, wiping the opposition out in good, old-fashioned Hurricane style. I finished up in the final against Terry Griffiths and was convinced that my form was such that I'd certainly regain the trophy I'd relinquished the year before. But it was Terry who walked off with the prize, winning 9–5. I have to give him his due in that match, he won with a 131 break in the final frame. That's good snooker.

Next came the Irish Masters held at Goffs in Kildare. The tables were set up in the horse auction arena, which always made me smile, but I was beaten in the semi-finals by Doug Mountjoy, who played some great frames. Terry Griffiths won it that year 9–8. He was on a hot streak, that's for sure, but I was pretty warm as well – and was about to overheat.

I am not a big beer drinker. I do like my Guinness, but I don't really drink bitter or real ales. However, I'm told one of the finest real-ale brewers is an old established East Anglia-based company, Tolly Cobbold. In 1980 they sponsored a tournament for the second year, and I went down there to compete for the £1,500 first prize. I liked East Anglia. It's a friendly, peaceful place – or it was until I got there. I managed to get myself into some more trouble and Del Simmons went ballistic at me for it. Del was at the time fighting the WPBSA on a number of issues, not all to do with me, and the last thing he needed was for them to be able to hit back at him by fining me once again.

The trouble started during the fifth frame of the final between Dennis and myself. Nobby Clarke was the referee and he ruled against me on a foul shot he claimed I committed. I protested at the decision in my own way, quietly . . . at first. Clarke insisted I had fouled the shot, hitting the red and black at the same time. I appealed to Dennis to back me up, but he claimed he didn't see it. 'I was drinking some water and missed it, Alex,' he smugly said. I appealed to the audience, who seemed split over it, and Clarke told me to accept the decision and sit down. Terry Griffiths was there watching and so I even appealed to him to intervene, but he just shrugged his shoulders and said something along the lines of 'I'm not getting involved.' Fair enough, I suppose.

Clarke made the matter worse by giving Dennis a free ball a few minutes later in another controversial decision. Del went mad when he heard about my behaviour because he knew the match was being televised all over the region and that the Tolly Cobbold family would be watching it, either in the hall or on the TV.

I always have a problem with referees who will not consider changing a decision. Anyone who knows me will tell you that I am the most considerate and honest player in the business. If I make a mistake and no one else sees it, I will always own up. The reason is that I play the sport for the love and competitiveness of it. I am a competitive person and, like my friend Ollie Reed, I love a challenge. There is no point in competing in a sport to see who the best player is if the rules you are playing to aren't evenly applied. I know most referees don't like me and that's fine, but I still expect them to be professional. They should be honest enough and unbiased enough to make the right decisions, and accept when they've made the wrong ones, so that the two combatants are facing each other on equal terms. That's the sort of fair-play attitude I adopt and I expect it from others, but I don't always get it. The fact that referees aren't ex-players doesn't help, either – they just don't understand the finer points and technical aspects of the game, which again can lead to incorrect decisions being made. Players know when a foul has been committed by the noise and the way the balls move among other things. Referees all too often miss that.

I was already two frames down to Dennis and I considered that he should have stuck up for me. If the roles had been reversed, I would have certainly backed him up, if of course I'd seen the shot and it was not a foul or even borderline. I was livid with the way I'd been treated, so when Dennis next missed a pot and sat down, I rose from my seat, walked past him eyeing up my play and just said, 'Bloody cheats.' It was loud enough for him to make out, but hopefully not enough for everyone else to hear.

I wasn't playing a psychological gambit and my intention was not to even up the play by unsettling him. I was merely expressing my thoughts and, in fact, my remark wasn't aimed so much at him as at Nobby Clarke and referees in general.

I finished up the winner by a very narrow score of 5–4, and Dennis later said that the remark had hit a nerve and put him off his stroke, so to speak. Perhaps he was feeling guilty about not owning up to the fact that he knew it wasn't a foul. I don't know. One last note on the foul-shot incident. Anglia Television got a lot of calls about it and when they played it back on *Points East* (a kind of *Points of View* programme), I was vindicated.

By April I had won a few tournaments, including a plump prize for the inaugural British Gold Cup, which followed directly on from the Tolly Cobbold. Although I lost a few too, the money was coming in fast and furious, and I later also won the Pontins Professional at Camber Sands. It was a good haul for the year. Lynn was driving me to some of the tournaments and exhibitions that were close to home, and at last I was starting to enjoy the fruits of my labour, just as Steve Davis was. Barry Hearn really looked after his players, especially Steve. There was no standing about on cold windy platforms for them, no coming home as the cock was crowing. No, he made sure they were all driven to the venues, or had a car to get there.

As the World Championship approached, Lynn announced that I would a father before the year was out. I was already buzzing about my form and this was the icing on the cake. I can't remember a time when I was more confident as we left home for Sheffield and the Crucible. I started off playing Jimmy White's old mate, Tony Meo. It was tight and he played a mean game, but I got there in the end, 10–9. Perrie Mans was next and I saw him off with a respectable 13–6 score. I could smell victory, or so I thought. It might just have been the new floor cleaner they used.

Barry Hearn was there watching over his new boy, Davis, and I was happy to wipe the smile off his face when I gave Steve what for in the quarter-finals. Steve had played a fine game against Terry Griffiths, beating him 13–10, and I knew he would be a handful, but I wasn't nervous – even when he recorded a 136 break in the third frame. The first day's play went on to produce some superb snooker from us both. I nearly got a 147 on the last frame of the first session, making the score 4–4, and we left the arena at the end of the day with the score at 9–7 to me.

I went in for the kill the next day. I was totally concentrated, confident, happy and sober – not a common state of affairs, I must admit. The Hurricane blew well that day and took Davis out of the competition 13–9. I shook the Ginger Magician's hand and said, 'Never mind, Steve, maybe next year.' He nodded his head in agreement and smiled at me. As for Hearn, well, I confess I did feel a little smug that I'd stopped his boy getting his hands on the trophy – for that year anyway. Steve, of course, went on to be crowned six times over the following decade. You've got to admire that consistency.

Next on the hit list was another favourite of mine, Kirk

Stevens. I always liked Kirk, but business was business and I had to go for the throat with him. It all ended in tears for Kirk when I finished up the 16–13 winner to claim my place in the final against Cliff Thorburn. It had been four years since I was last in a final, but I wasn't married to Lynn then, I wasn't happy then, I wasn't going to be a daddy then. I felt good, the time felt right and as we went to bed the night before the final, Lynn cuddled me and said she was so happy for me. I was happy for us both and for our little baby growing inside her. 'I'm doing this for you, babe,' I said through tears of joy and she squeezed me tighter. I felt safe in her arms, confident that I would win the title.

The next day I started off well enough. The crowd was willing me to win, and I began to feed off their confidence in me to do it. That was what eventually made me start to play a different game. I stormed into a 5–1 lead and sustained that four-frame advantage up to 9–5, but by then I had abandoned the strategically sound attack-and-defence approach and started simply to attack, attack, attack, almost as if I was at an exhib-ition, playing long shots to impress them. Cliff may have been nicknamed 'The Grinder' but normally I was a better tactician – I knew when to play safe and I knew when to go for the jugular, but not in this match. He pulled it back to 9–9.

My confidence was still sky-high on the resumption of play the following day. The crowd once again was buzzing and their support was predominantly in my favour. But the unforced errors that had plagued me in the last few frames of the previous day had not disappeared. The adrenalin was flowing through me and I don't think I respected Cliff sufficiently. When you do that, invariably the gods of snooker turn their back and the balls stop running for you. I lost my momentum and Cliff kept clawing his way back, doing nothing more special than 25 or 30 breaks and leaving the cue ball safe on the cushion. It was enough and we found ourselves 16 all in the best of a 35-frame final. Both of us were shattered, physically and mentally. Now was going to be the time to sort the men from the boys.

Cliff approached the table and I sat there, ready to pounce as soon as he missed a shot – and I sat there and I sat there. Cliff just kept putting them away and after he passed 80, I thought, 'Never mind, two frames left. All I need to do is take them both. I can do that.' But I never got the chance. Cliff played the finest game of his life to take the trophy. I was gutted for sure, but there was no animosity. Cliff and I shook hands and I congratulated him. He'd played well and the crowd gave him a warm round of applause, but I sensed they were disappointed with the outcome.

It was no consolation, of course, but it had been a great match. I might not have won, but once again the Hurricane had delivered in the entertainment stakes. And I learned an important lesson over those two days, on how to win. I knew now that I had to be stricter with myself. I still wanted to please the public but not to the detriment of how I played.

Some six to seven weeks later I travelled to Montreal to play Thorburn again, this time in a challenge match. It took place in a venue that housed an Olympic swimming pool, so held a huge audience – some 8,000 people watched us over the two sessions. That's near enough 7,000 more than were at the Crucible for the final. The crowd were incredible. On paper Cliff was the home favourite but that day I swear they were all rooting for me. It felt like Sheffield – only better. I was determined not to get carried away and make the same mistakes I'd made in the World Championship, and concentrated hard on my game. Revenge is a great motivator. And I succeeded, beating Cliff 11–5. The noise in the arena when the final ball dropped was astounding, probably the loudest I've ever heard at a snooker match. The victory was sweet, but it certainly didn't satisfy my hunger for another world crown.

Although things were going well, I could feel pressure building inside me – slowly perhaps, but building. I was under constant instructions to keep my head down and my nose clean from my management team, while at the same time they were putting me in for more and more exhibitions. I found myself booked to play in all corners of the country, with no thought given to the distance between shows. It would be one night Newcastle, the next night Bristol, for four, five or six days on the spin. It was exhausting and I was becoming more and more frustrated. Were my management team really looking out for me? Or were they happy to take the bookings and their percentage, whatever the cost to Alex Higgins? In my mind, which side of the fence they stood on was quite clear.

I was also under constant pressure from Lynn to slow down and get home more. She wasn't coming to matches so much now because of her pregnancy, which meant we were spending more and more time apart. Even though I was just doing my job, being so often separated is not good for anyone just starting out in a new marriage.

The problem was, I allowed myself to get sucked into a very unhealthy mindset. I might have been well-intentioned, but I wasn't very self-aware. I always wanted to please the fans so I would play extra frames when I didn't need to, and then I'd spend hours after matches signing autographs and posing for pictures, having a couple of drinks, while Taylor, Spencer, Davis and the rest were doing the sensible thing – fifteen minutes with the fans and then back home or to the hotel. I couldn't do that. I always felt that the people who came to see me play, and to support me, deserved some recognition for it. It was expected and I duly obliged. It was all part and parcel of being the Hurricane. These were my own kind of people, from my kind of background. I wasn't dubbed 'the people's champion' for nothing. It was a title bestowed on me in honour of the way I treated my army of followers.

So the legend began to grow. 'Higgins is amazing,' the fans would say. 'He's out on the town and still playing the best snooker around. He's superhuman.' I knew I wasn't super-human, of course, and the late nights and booze did take its toll, but because I was hyperactive and imaginative I found I could sometimes win matches even if I didn't feel well within myself. And so I let the gradual slide continue. Looking back now, I can see that I allowed that social aspect of my relationship with the public go a little too far, to my detriment.

The Coral UK Professional Championship in Preston in November was another spectacular tournament in which I ended up in the final. I hit a 134 clearance against Willie Thorne and my game was just getting better. I saw off Fred Davis in the quarters, Reardon in the semis, and then I hit the wall. Lynn was due any day and what with the disruption that understandably causes, together with the year I'd had finally catching up with me, I ran out of steam. Steve Davis annihilated me 16–6. It was his first major win. When I went over to congratulate him, I wondered whether I was shaking hands with the future of snooker. If I was, I was determined I wasn't going to make it easy for him over the years to come.

If losing so comprehensively to Davis was a bitter pill to swallow, a few days later I couldn't give a damn about it. On 2 December my beautiful baby daughter Lauren was born and I was the happiest man on the planet.

11

Lynn Avison

●

A lot has been written and said about Lynn and me over the years, by both of us, and by many others. Much of it has been speculation, fantasy and elaboration. I've been a part of some of that, I know. I like to tell a good tale. Well, here is what really happened between the two of us, as I remember it, having lived through it all.

As mentioned previously, we met in Oscars, the wine bar that George Best and his friends owned in Manchester. It was 1977 and I had just come back from the Benson & Hedges Masters in London, having returned from Australia not long before that. I was going to have a few weeks off and had decided to go out on the town to try to cheer myself up. That particular evening I was wearing a big Stetson-like hat, although there were no corks, as has been reported in some places. As I walked in I spotted a friend, Bernadette, whom I used to see from time to time. She was with a couple of other girls, one a smallish blonde – Lynn. I fancied her immediately and so made a beeline for Bernadette, but it was Lynn who was in my sights. It's been said in the past that I asked Lynn to buy me a drink and that I followed her and her mates out of Oscars when they left to go to a disco. The truth is I was playing it cool. I was Alex Higgins after all, and this was my patch. I knew George and I knew I'd get my girl. I was looking good in hat and coat (which Lynn later said she thought looked scruffy! Me, scruffy! Never!) and I was confident the Higgins charm would work its usual wonders.

Only it didn't. Not immediately. We chatted in the group for a while. I offered to buy her a drink. The usual stuff. But for some reason she wasn't reacting as I hoped. I was intrigued. I had my own plans for the evening and so I let them head off to the club they wanted to go to, but before they went I managed to get out of Bernadette that Lynn worked for Servisair at Manchester airport. She might have tried to give me the brush-off, but I was far from out for the count.

As I lay in bed that night, unable to sleep, all I could think about was Lynn. Cara and I had realised by that stage that our marriage couldn't be fixed. I was feeling sorry for myself and pretty low. Lynn had come into my life when I was feeling vulnerable, so it was probably a combination of those mixed feelings that led me to fall in love with her so quickly and so decisively. But I wasn't going to show my hand too quickly. I left it a week or so before I called her at work. In fact, I rang a number of times because each time I made the call, the response was always the same. She would pick up the phone, then, as soon as she heard my voice, she would tell me to get lost and slam it down. Now I really was hooked. This was not what I had expected at all.

As I was a frequent air traveller and I also banked at the airport branch, I 'accidentally' bumped into her at the airport one day and eventually I got my date. Lynn told me later that every-one she mentioned me to told her to avoid me like the plague. Her mum knew all about my wild ways, fighting, drinking and carrying on with women. 'Lynn, this man is on self-destruct and it will only end in tears,' was the advice she gave her daughter, and so after our first date I knew the way to her heart was through her mum. If I could win her over, I would win Lynn over.

That first date was nearly our last. At the time we were both separated from our marriage partners and I suppose we were both quite cynical about relationships. Lynn's husband was a computer technician who liked to hang around with musicians and play guitar in his spare time, whereas Lynn liked to go clubbing from time to time and so they drifted apart. It wasn't easy getting to know her. I used to impress women with my worldly knowledge of music, food and other things, but Lynn was so different and argumentative. She wasn't taken in by me and I loved that about her.

'OK. I will go to dinner with you, but I'm not promising anything else,' she said.

'Great,' I replied, and before I could say another word she said, 'Pick me up at eight. Do you have a pen to write down my address?'

'Sorry, babe, I don't drive. Never had the need to. I'm playing tonight at the Potters snooker centre, I'll send a cab for you.'

The line went very quiet for a minute and then she said, 'Don't worry about it. I'll pick you up at the snooker centre.'

I had been playing most of the afternoon and by 8 o'clock I was ready to quit for the day. I was about to pot a ball when I noticed everyone around me looking towards the door. Something had obviously caught their attention. I took the shot, missed, and as I turned round to see what the fuss was all about I noticed the deathly silence. Then I saw Lynn standing in the entrance. There she was, this lovely woman in the most gorgeous dress, her short hair perfectly framing her small face and glowing smile.

'You look great, babe,' I said, and putting my cue away I walked over to her.

'Alex,' she whispered, 'you're not even changed yet.'

'Babe, this is it,' I replied. I had no intention of changing. I wore formal gear all the time when I played in tournaments and exhibitions, so when I was socialising, I hated getting dressed up. I had a jacket to slip on, which I felt transformed my look from casual (for practising) to smart casual (for going out). She wasn't impressed.

'I'm not going out with you dressed like that. Goodnight.'

I took her arm and apologised as though my life depended on it. Luckily enough, she was sufficiently intrigued and we went out to Charlie Chan's restaurant for dinner.

We had a great time. She even played me along as I tried to impress her with my knowledge of Chinese cuisine, little knowing that Lynn was a big expert on the subject. After dinner we still had so much to talk about that we went on to a club for a final glass or two. Neither of us wanted the evening to end but as Lynn had work the next day the witching hour became 2.30 a.m. and she dropped me off at home.

We stood outside my flat and I gave her a light kiss on the lips and we cuddled. As I held her for the first time I could feel the warmth from her slim body. I could also smell the lingering aroma of her perfume and as our heads rested together, I felt a great weight had been lifted from me. I did love Cara very much and missed her a lot, but the constant arguing and fights made it impossible for us to have a happy marriage. I knew as I held Lynn in the early hours of that morning that a new phase of my life was about to begin, and as she disappeared off in her car I made it through my front door, collapsed with exhaustion on to the settee and slept peacefully for twelve straight hours.

The next day I called her house and spoke to her father.

'Mr Avison,' I said, jokingly, 'I'm in love with your daughter, sir, and I want to marry her one day.' I'm not sure he got the joke, though. The truth is I'm not sure Mr Avison ever got my jokes, or got me. We were always perfectly civil to each other, but never friends.

In many ways we were diametric opposites. For instance, I liked to throw my money around, buying presents, drinks for everyone, while he was much less profligate. Nothing wrong with that of course, but it illustrates how different our characters were. In fact, I wish I'd been a bit more prudent over the years. One of my (many) faults in life is that I give too much away. All the money I was earning playing snooker went as quickly as it came. Easy come, easy go. Anyway, after I'd delivered my line there was a deathly silence and eventually, after what seemed like an eternity, he answered, 'Well, Alex, I think you'd better come round. We should probably meet first, don't you think?'

We did meet later that day, as I was waiting for Lynn to get back from work so we could go out again. Lynn's mother, Betty, was there. I became very fond of Betty. She was a very quiet, unobtrusive woman, and very house-proud. She kept their bungalow in pristine condition. Every time I was there she seemed to be forever polishing and cleaning. And it wasn't too long before I was there a lot, as a lodger in their spare room, thanks to my flat being burgled.

This was the flat that I was sub-letting off Alex Stepney. Some people had moved in next door and there was a lot of painting and decorating going on. One particular evening I was at home and I heard the bloke from next door out in the hallway, working on his front door. I popped my head out my flat and said, 'Hello, I should introduce myself. I'm Alex. You're hard at it. Fancy a beer?' He came in. We got chatting and I never thought anything of it, but I reckon he was looking around, totting up what was in the place and waiting for his chance. I can't prove it, of course, and it doesn't matter anyway as the bloke is dead now.

About two to three weeks' later I was down in London for a match or a series of exhibitions, and I became involved in a fracas. Although Lynn and I were dating, I decided I fancied going to see an old flame of mine, a lovely Welsh girl I'd met on a train a few months earlier, when Cara was back in Australia. That was quite a journey I can tell you. Sex in a British Rail toilet is not easy but it is great fun – especially twice.

It was an inter-city train, I think heading to London – one of those ones with individual compartments. There was this girl, two old biddies and me, sitting quietly, all minding our own business, but not for long. The girl was a stunner and we soon got chatting over a glass or two of BR's finest wine. The chatting soon became flirting, which soon became out and out lust. One look between us and we both knew what we wanted. We excused ourselves politely from the carriage, tore up the aisle to the nearest vacant toilet, fell through the door, unbuttoning and unzipping as we went and proceeded to engage in what can only be described as a quick 'knee-trembler'. Business over, we tidied ourselves up and headed back to our seats, trying to be as cool as cucumbers. I don't think we succeeded, not given the look the two old dears gave us as we sat back down. I suppose our actions may have been less suspicious if we'd headed towards the buffet car. That might have provided a legitimate excuse for our departure together, but as we had clearly gone in the opposite direction, I am pretty sure the game was up.

We settled back down but I wasn't happy. While satisfying up to a point, the sex had been rushed, frantic and, frankly, not up to my usual standard – too much Hurricane speed and not enough Higgins flair. I was determined to put that right.

I was fiddling with an Aero wrapper when I had an idea. I whispered to my new friend, 'Listen, babe, I'd love to do that again. With a little more time to show you what I can really do. But I don't want to embarrass you in front of Miss Marple and her friend. If you're up for it, here's what we'll do. I'll excuse myself and head towards the buffet car. Five minutes later, you follow. And keep an eye out for this chocolate wrapper sticking out from a toilet door. That's where you'll find me. See you soon, I hope.' The plan worked to perfection.

Given our first encounter, it was little wonder I was keen to see her again. She lived somewhere around Aldgate but she wasn't in when I knocked on the door of her flat. 'No problem,' I thought. I'll pop next door to the pub for a drink, or two, or three – quite a lot, in fact. Having downed more than my fair share, I went back across the road and was delighted to see a light on in her living room. I was less happy, however, when she answered the door and a brute of an Australian bloke was standing next to her. I had absolutely no right to be annoyed, but I was. I fired off a few verbals and headed back to the pub. Not smart, Alex. I sat, brooded on the supposed injustice of it all, had a couple more drinks and decided to have it out with my rival.

Needless to say, they didn't answer my knock – so I kicked the door in. I was halfway up the stairs when I was confronted by this giant fella and some blows were exchanged. There was only one winner and it wasn't me. The police were called and I was arrested, charged and locked up for three or four hours to sober up. Then they let me go, telling me to report to Old Street police station a week or so later.

I finished my business in London and headed back up on the train to Manchester. I went straight to my flat and that's when I found the door ajar and my place stripped of all meaningful possessions, and I mean stripped. Everything, including my cooker, was gone, apart from the three-piece suite, for some reason. Must have been too difficult to get it through the door.

I was really upset, not about the possessions, although they cost me a small fortune because I wasn't insured, but about the personal stuff – pictures, trophies, engraved silverware that I would never be able to replace. I called the police and they sent along a sergeant and a forensic team. After the officer had interviewed me about the details of how long I'd been away and what was missing, and the scene of crime guys had done their bit, I thought I was done for the day, but far from it.

'I'm sorry about this, Alex,' the sergeant said to me, 'but I have some other bad news. You're under arrest.' I nearly fainted.

'What for?'

I'd forgotten about the appointment at Old Street and the Met police had called Manchester to pull me in. They took me to the nick and put me in a cell. It must have been around 3 o'clock in the afternoon. I was to be taken down to London in the morning. I asked to see a detective I knew well and said to him, 'Listen, surely you can't lock me up here until tomorrow. At least get some of the guys and ask them if they will take me out for a few drinks. All on me.' They agreed, and off we went to a few pubs where the coppers drank and I started to buy the boys anything they wanted. They were drinking half milds, while yours truly got stuck into the brandy. This was a serious crisis after all.

After a while, one of the coppers asked me what I, the felon, would like. 'A large brandy and soda, thank-you.' Another copper asked me if I wanted a drink and I ordered another brandy and soda. And so it went on for a while until my policeman friend cottoned on to what was happening. 'Alex, you're an expensive guy to arrest. The boys are all on halves and you, you bugger, order a brandy!' With that, he said their shift was about to end and took me back to the cell. I thanked them all for their hospitality, ate a cheese sandwich and slept like a top.

The next morning I was picked up by two idiots who were to escort me to London – in cuffs. I couldn't even buy a cup of tea on the train. Those two bastards seemed to think I was a mass murderer. When we arrived at Euston, the escort was changed to

London CID, who were much more amiable and removed my cuffs. They were hardly taking a great risk, were they? These were sensible guys, as my court appearance wasn't until 2.30 p.m. they said we had time for a quick one in a lovely local pub, and gave me the run-down on the huge press interest that my appearance had stirred.

After a couple of pints I was taken through the back door of the court. I had about one hour to wait before I faced the magistrates and the outcome was that I was given a conditional discharge. I had to pay legal costs plus the cost of the door. There was still quite a posse of press waiting for me to appear, at both the back and front of the building, so one of the officers suggested a way to bamboozle the press. God bless him. He was looking out for me. He and one of his colleagues led me up flight after flight of stairs to the roof of the building. We climbed out and one of them turned to me and asked, 'You don't suffer from vertigo, do you, Alex?'

'No,' I replied.

'Good, but I'll go first anyway. So I'll be there to catch you.'

I didn't realise what he was talking about until he took a run and jumped the four-foot gap between our building and the next. The other officer and I followed with no hesitation. I guess he had done it many times before and as I knew I could jump better than most of the horses I'd ridden, I wasn't scared.

We escaped through a skylight and down some stairs, and I found myself in the nearest pub. It was one of those classic London jobs, with private booths. Perfect. The media boys were running around like headless chickens looking for me and I was yards away, sipping quietly on a pint of Guinness. It was one of the most enjoyable days of my life. I am forever grateful to my two saviours for their sense of fair play. Lynn was none too pleased that I'd been to court but as I didn't feel the need to explain that the whole incident had come about because I had fancied catching up with an ex, she forgave me, and I moved into her house. During the next few months I travelled all over the country, using Lynn's family home as my base. Travelling around the country, and indeed around the world, is a wonderful opportunity, a privilege you could say. Wherever you go, lots of people, fans, want be with you, to shake your hand and buy you a drink. You have to entertain them and the better you do that, the more they want to be in your company. It is very tiring. Being in love is one thing, but absence doesn't make the heart grow fonder. It just makes it wander.

I loved Lynn and at first I had no problem turning down the offers I received to share more than a quiet drink. In our first year together Lynn did try her best to come to as many matches as she could, but she was never a real fan of the game. I had to suggest quietly that she go to the lounge for a drink during one exhibition match when she wouldn't stop talking to her cousin Bernadette, whom she had brought with her for company. She was none too pleased with me. It was clear to the audience what was going on and as Lynn marched off, she gave me one of those ice queen looks. I had to go after her and calm her down. I explained that there was a certain etiquette to the proceedings and that seemed to do the trick.

I must admit, however, that when Lynn wasn't with me, I wasn't entirely faithful to the relationship, and often when I was at the other end of the country, I would pull a girl for a one-night stand and move on to the next town. However, I am sure that Lynn stayed faithful to me throughout.

I started to become quite romantic in my old age and one day I just said, 'Let's go to Paris, babe.'

'When?' she asked.

'Tonight, after the exhibition.'

I was due to play in Scunthorpe that night and then I was free for a good few days. I phoned some friends of mine, Geoff and Helen Lomas, and they agreed to come along. I had bought a second-hand Daimler that day – I had been doing quite well – and I thought they could share the driving with Lynn.

The show was a long drawn-out charity affair. After the exhibition I had to officiate at a fund-raising auction and, as these things always do, it all took much longer than anticipated. So it was later than we would have liked when we headed off in grand style towards Dover. Lynn drove at first and I was navigator, in the front passenger seat. We drove through the night with various changes behind the wheel but I remained in charge of the route. It was exhausting for everyone and we were mighty relieved on reaching Dover. We drove the car on to the boat and went to the bar/restaurant for refreshments.

On reaching France the tricky part was to make sure we got on the right road to Paris. Well, we failed. Geoff did anyway. He was driving and ignored my instructions when he saw what he thought was a sign for Paris. I told him it was the wrong way. If we had stuck to my original route, it would have saved us three hours on the road. Once we were going Geoff's way, though, we were stuck with it. It was pissing down with rain and as Geoff – in fact none of them – were used to driving on the wrong side of the road, I had to keep sticking my head out the window to say whether or not it was safe to change lanes. By the time we reached the outskirts of Paris we'd been driving for three and a half hours and, having had my head stuck out of the window for most of that time, needless to say I was cold. And angry. So angry, in fact, that I'd had enough of the bloody navigating – they hadn't listened to me anyway. I demanded they stop the car and I jumped out and stomped off up a back street. They could find their own way to the hotel. Well, they made a meal of that.

I'd calmed down a bit and got back into the car but by the time we found a car park it was half a mile from the hotel and I was so tired I refused to move. I was happy to stay where I was. The atmosphere wasn't exactly all set for a jolly holiday. To my mind, there were three wankers in my Daimler. I'm sure if the Daimler was a dog it would have bitten them.

Lynn went straight to her room and refused to go to a bar with Geoff, Helen and me. The three of us had made up by then and we were determined to have a good time. Not so Lynn, however, so I decided to give her some shock treatment. Geoff and Helen said they were sure they could change her mind and we arranged to meet in a place called the Cockney Pride. I headed off down the Boulevard Gare du Nord, which is where all the hookers hang out, and spotted a tall, black-haired Moroccan girl. My French isn't very good but I managed to get across that I wanted her to come to a bar with me for a few drinks and I'd pay her 300 francs, no strings attached. She was a little apprehensive but she came and when the two of us walked into the pub, Geoff and Helen nearly collapsed. They said that Lynn would be there in five minutes. That suited me fine. I wanted to teach her a lesson for going off in a strop. You can't hustle a hustler.

When she eventually turned up, she sat with Geoff and Helen and I left with the hooker. I paid the girl her money and she asked me if I was sure I didn't want sex. I gave her a peck on the cheek, shook her hand and said, 'Good luck.' She smiled and I returned to the bar.

'That was quick,' Geoff commented.

'I took her to the Daimler and had a blow job, just to christen it so to speak,' I replied. Lynn got up and left in a huff, which was exactly what I'd hoped for. I appreciate I wasn't being very fair but I was annoyed. I'd been awake for hours – the others had been kipping when they weren't driving – I'd been ignored, chilled to the bone and Lynn had shouted at me for ruining the trip when I'd refused to get out of the car. I was being childish, I accept, but to my mind, at that point in the trip, it was Alex and the Daimler 1, Geoff, Helen and Lynn 0.

Despite this setback, the rest of the weekend went well and it certainly didn't put me off wanting to spend time with Lynn on holiday. Some time later I got a booking to play a series of exhibition games in Trinidad and I wanted her to join me.

One of my first matches was in a place called San Fernando, about forty miles from Port of Spain. It was right in the jungle and I was booked to play there for two nights. On the first night the table was set in the middle of a kind of bandstand, in a clearing in the centre of the village. The people were so enthusiastic and I played great snooker that night, especially when you consider that moths and all kinds of flying insects were attracted to the light of the table. It was like bloody Heathrow at the height of the holiday season with insects landing and taking off. I felt like Zorro with a cue instead of a foil, I was taking so many swipes at them, but everyone was having a good time. They were drinking the local rum and coconut water, made from freshly cut green coconuts – now that's a great drink – and afterwards I was singing and dancing with the locals. Wonderful fun!

The second night I played at quite a large villa. About forty people were crammed into a snooker room along with a multitude of insects. The atmosphere was very smoky but I was used to that type of thing from my teens in the Jampot. Well, not the insects perhaps, although they had their fair share of blood-suckers there, too. The table was very slow with the humidity, and the pockets were as tight as vestal . . . well, let's just say they were tight. I played out of this world that night. I had a host of breaks over 80 and 90 and then I crafted a most beautiful 146 clearance of 14 blacks, 1 pink and the colours. I was buzzing after the game and was invited to join the audience for a drink or two. They offered me a drop of whisky and I said that I couldn't drink it neat but that coconut water would be the perfect mixer. Straightaway, a guy picked up a machete and went outside. I followed, intrigued, and as I watched he scaled a coconut tree and hacked off four or five coconuts. Hey presto! One whisky and coconut water. Not a bad drink at all.

The following day I went to another village to play and got my hands on a phone. I rang Lynn and told her I had paid for a ticket to Trinidad. Reluctantly, she came over. While I was there, I caught up with someone from the past – Wilson Jones, whom I'd met during my ill-fated Indian trip. He had moved to Trinidad and it was great to see him. I liked the man very much.

Lynn arrived a couple of days later. I was by then staying in the Farrell House Hotel at Claxton Bay. The Queen had stayed there apparently, but I'm not sure which one. Given the then dilapidated state of the place, I reckon it might have been Victoria. From our room – the one the Queen occupied, apparently – you had view of the bay . . . and the oil rigs. The place was a sorry sight after its days of splendour in the fifties.

We went to a local beach and met a Scottish guy who was very full of himself. He clearly fancied Lynn but I wasn't bothered. I agreed to play him in a game of squash at the local Texaco Oil Company sports club. He was about two hours late so Lynn and I had a game of badminton and sat down for a beer. He eventually bounced in, all fitness and biceps, at least that's what he thought. By that stage, I had begun to feel a bit queasy, what with running around the badminton court in the heat, but I agreed I'd still play him.

The squash court was about 250 yards from the main

clubhouse and just as we got there, I experienced a terrible knot in my stomach, like a severe cramp. I knew what it meant and I didn't have long to do something about it. I asked where the loo was and he said it was back at the main building. Too far. So, bent double, I scuttled behind some bushes by the edge of the lake. As I crouched down, backside facing the lake, shorts round my knees, I heard a thrashing noise in the water, and I looked round to see a crocodile making for my little arse! I ran like hell back to the squash court. Shaking, I said, 'Game over, I concede,' and walked back to the clubhouse with Lynn where I cleaned myself up. I told her what happened and she laughed as I gulped down a large brandy on the rocks.

From Claxton Bay we moved to Port of Spain for my last exhibition. We stayed at the Holiday Inn and we loved it. If you remember, some years ago Ian Botham supposedly had an affair while on tour with England in the Caribbean. The story went that while making love they broke the bed. Well, I think that Lynn and I may have weakened our bed a tad that trip!

Lynn and I had so many great times together, but in those first three years we drifted back and forth a fair bit. We used to row a lot because we were both feisty and independent. She didn't understand my needs – which were basically two meals a day and eight to ten hours of practice – and I wasn't listening to her when she complained I was away too much. But what was I meant to do? That was my job. I had to play in the matches and I had to practise. She thought I could just switch snooker off the minute I came home, but that was impossible. So the nagging started and the number of one-night stands increased. One of them hit the papers big time. It took Lynn a long time to forgive me.

It was around March 1978 and I was in Plymouth after playing a series of exhibition matches across the country. I hadn't been back to Manchester for a fortnight and so I hadn't seen Lynn, but the tour had been a success and I was in the mood to celebrate. That didn't last long.

I went for a couple of drinks in a local nightclub and got talking to a very attractive young woman. Actually, she got talking to me, but I didn't notice that at the time. I was happy for the company and together we went from the club to a casino. I lost the cash I had at the tables – cards and roulette – but felt Lady Luck must surely smile on me eventually. I cashed a cheque for £650 and went hard at it again, but that was soon gone and so was my good mood. The girl, Wendy Dring, just kept following me and I was too hassled and annoyed to tell her to fuck off.

We ended up back in my room at the Holiday Inn. All the way in the cab I kept thinking about how the night of gambling had gone, and the more I thought about it, the more I was sure I'd been stiffed. The turn of the cards, the roll of the ball, it didn't smell right. The minute I got into my room, I was on the blower, trying to cancel the cheque. In my mind, I hadn't lost that money fair and square.

As I was making my calls, my 'friend' started to undress and kept whispering in my ear about money, while stroking my back. I suddenly realised what she meant, or at least I thought I did, and I was having none of it. I am not interested in hookers, which is what I took her to be, whether she was or not. I offered her twenty quid for her trouble and asked her to leave. That did not go down well. Next thing I knew she was attacking me. I had no intention of hitting her but I had to defend myself. At one point I remember her grabbing a butter knife and coming at me with it. I grasped the blade as she waved it in front of me – it was blunt, thank God – wrenched it from her grasp, caught hold of her hair, and tossed her out of the room, throwing her jacket after her.

The police were called and the whole incident ended up in court. Ms Dring agreed with my brief that she could be a 'spitfire' sometimes and that was it as far as the tabloids were concerned. She became the 'Spitfire Girl' and they had a field day. It was hardly mentioned that I was cleared of assault.

Lynn may have forgiven me for the Spitfire Girl incident, but there was often tension between us, and not just over other women. I was in Sevenoaks one night, playing with John Virgo at a stag do in an exclusive club. We sat down to eat and then I played John over the best of five frames. After that, we invited members of the audience to take part. All sorts of side bets were going on each frame. The punters were really enjoying themselves, having a flutter, playing, drinking. They didn't want to stop and, as we were being well paid, John and I were happy to go along with it all. I'd asked Lynn to join me so that we could go from there the next day to London on a shopping spree. It was meant to be a surprise. I thought she'd love that. She didn't arrive until about 9.45 and as I hadn't realised it was a men-only event, she had to wait in the lounge. That pissed her off. I tried to explain that I was only doing my job, but she was having none of it. I wasn't even drinking that much. I was at the table all the time and when you're playing, you're too active. It's a sip here and a drag of your smoke there. But Lynn was livid, saying I'd brought her all the way down and now I was ignoring her. Off she went, back to the hotel in Sevenoaks, in a huff, and I carried on fulfilling my commitments.

The night eventually wound up and I headed back to our room, fully expecting to find her tucked up in bed. Instead, all I found was an empty room. She'd jumped in a cab and headed back home – so much for our fun couple of days in the capital. In my mind, Lynn had once again failed to recognise what I had to do to make a good living out of my profession.

One good thing came of the whole fiasco however. I won over a grand playing snooker against one of the blokes who had been at the event. He had very kindly given me a lift back to the hotel and had offered to take Lynn and me to the station in the morning. Only problem was, when he arrived to pick us up, Lynn was long gone and the London trip was off.

'No problem, Alex. If you're at a loose end, why don't you come and stay at mine? I've got a table and I'd love to challenge you to a few frames.' The offer sounded good so I took him up on it.

Now this boy had money, and liked to spend it. I remember opening one of the fridges in his kitchen, looking for something to eat, and being confronted by dozens of bottles of Dom Perignon. We made a dent in the contents of that fridge, I can tell you. He also had an account with a bookie. All I needed to do was call the bloke up, place my bet and hopefully wait until the cash rolled in. My host's credit was more than good enough. I didn't hold back.

We drank a lot, played a lot of snooker and placed a lot of bets over the two days. And I laughed a lot. He had probably the wildest cue action I'd ever seen. Every time he struck the ball I had no idea what was going to happen. With each frame we played, I was giving up a big handicap, of course, and what with that, the champagne, the tears of laughter and the fact that somehow or other, he potted balls, I found myself on a black ball finish with £1,700 riding on it. To this day I don't quite know how I let myself get into that position. I could ill afford to lose that sort of cash. Thank God I made the pot. I was already mentally deciding how to spend my windfall (on Lynn, of course) when we realised we hadn't checked on how good the horses had been to me. My £1,700 was quickly reduced to £1,100, which I more than gratefully received in cash. I decided not to tell Lynn the tale when we next spoke. I don't think she would have been amused that I might have been down £2,300 had I missed a black, especially as I hadn't even got round to telling her where I was for those two days.

I suppose deep down I knew that I could never really make Lynn happy. After all, she hated snooker and I loved it. It was my job but it took me away all the time. We couldn't have it both ways: either we made the sacrifice and had a good living or I gave it up and we stayed poor. Snooker was all I knew. I had reached the top and fallen, but I was still pulling them in. I was still the star attraction and I was still determined to regain my world crown. I needed Lynn at my side to achieve that. We talked about how we might make things work, given our differences, and we convinced ourselves we could. That's when we decided to get married.

12

That was my life, and my frame

•

I was buzzing after Lauren was born. I felt a whole new beginning was about to open up for me, even though I was still always on the road. I had no choice. Being away was part and parcel of the job. As I saw it, the job was playing snooker and I loved that. The travel was the sting in the tail.

At home I loved changing nappies and feeding my beautiful girl, I just hated the restrictions to going out on the tiles that having kids brought you. I needed that as a release. We hired a nanny, in fact two – unfortunately the first one didn't work out and had to be sacked. But Lynn always felt uneasy with leaving Lauren. I am not sure why we hired the nannies. We didn't really need them and I sometimes wish we'd never bothered, given what was to happen later. Lynn wasn't travelling with me and she had a support network close by, with her parents, sister and friends, but nannies we had. I hoped it might give us more time together, Lynn and I, but that proved a false hope. Not that I knew that at the beginning of 1981.

I was just getting over winning the second of my Benson & Hedges Masters titles against Terry Griffiths when the phone rang and I was asked if I would appear in *Pot Black* in London, to teach the singer Joe Brown how to play snooker. I had met him a year or so earlier at a book party so I agreed, and a few days later I headed down to the capital. As I got out of the car and entered the building, Eamonn Andrews appeared with that famous red book. 'Alex Higgins,' he said, 'you are well known internationally as the Hurricane for the express action you bring to the game. Tonight, this is your life.'

Suddenly a number of strange incidents that had occurred recently began to make sense. Del Simmons had been a bit elusive and I'd been booked to appear at a couple of events that were supposedly cancelled out of the blue, which was unusual. I realised at once that these incidents were probably various attempts to set up the evening that hadn't quite worked out. Until then, though, I hadn't twigged at all. I wasn't as sharp as I liked to think I was.

I have to confess, I was thrilled. I was a huge fan of the programme. Over the next hour or so they recorded my life story, complete with most of the people who had witnessed my triumphs and falls over the years. Both families were there, although they had been at war for weeks since Lauren had arrived in the world. There had been a bit of tension earlier in the day, I later heard, mainly involving Lynn and her sister and my three sisters. It was all about who was going to say what and about whom. There was only going to be one winner in that contest. The original Higgins girls triumphed.

A trail of people appeared, some of whom I even knew well! Cecil Mason, John Virgo, Steve Davis, John Spencer, Tony Meo, Jimmy White and Jackie Rea from my snooker world. From my celebrity world we had some Manchester United players, Emlyn Hughes from Liverpool (whom I'd met at a couple of charity golf events), Dickie Henderson, Suzi Quattro and many more. I can't remember them all right now. Suzi was there because I'd first met her a few years previously when I played her in a game of snooker arranged by the great rock promoter Mickie Most. She was a wild American chick and she shot a mean game of pool. We played in the Victoria Sporting Club in London, which was men-only in the snooker room. The fact that she appeared there created more publicity for her new record, which reached number one in the charts with a little help from the Hurricane. Mickie knew what he was doing all right. Unfortunately, neither his nor Suzi's chart magic rubbed off on me when I undertook a pop career a few years later.

The highlight for me was Ollie Reed. I couldn't wait to see him come on drunk, making a big fuss of me. He didn't disappoint, although he didn't actually appear in the studio. His contribution was pre-recorded because he was filming on location.

Ollie was drunk as usual and hamming it up, taking the piss. Wearing a very stressed waistcoat and a ripped shirt, his hair slicked back and holding a cue in one hand and a vase in the other, he fell down on to a stool and started to speak. 'You've caught me at a rather tense moment. Tonight I'm competing for this trophy, and you know how important they are to me.' He was trying to take me off, which most people in snooker try to do, lighting five cigarettes and doing my twitch, badly. He went on about how I had taught him a trick shot and beat him regularly at snooker at his home, but he had to get in that he always beat me in our drinking games.

He ended by doing a trick shot with the ball hitting a toy clown. The audience never quite got what that was all about, but I did. Ollie used to say that I acted like a clown but always bounced back. 'You can't keep a good man down,' he would say. The trick shot was his secret tribute to me – to both of us, in fact.

Despite the family row – which was a storm in a teacup compared to what was to come in the following years – it was a great night. The after-show party was terrific. I felt moved to have been singled out because it was a real privilege to be the subject, almost like the British equivalent of getting an Oscar or a gold medal. It meant you had arrived on the street of fame.

After appearing on *This Is Your Life* my popularity soared and bookings for exhibitions and personal appearances increased. So I told my management to up my exhibition fee to £750 per night. No one said boo. Del Simmons even set me up as a model for John Collier the menswear shop. I remember their advert song – 'John Collier, John Collier, the window to watch' – and there I was in that window as a cardboard cut-out.

As a consequence of all this, I wasn't spending much time at home and I hated the idea that I was missing Lauren growing up. I couldn't wait to get back after each match. I didn't want to miss her first steps. Lynn would constantly remind me that, despite being the daughter of the famous Hurricane Higgins, even Lauren wouldn't start walking till at least September, so I lived in hope. I wanted to spend more time at home, with my family, but needs must and both Lynn and I felt it was important that I earn money while I could. We agreed that the sacrifices we were both making would be worth it in the end. Looking back now, we were wrong.

Now I had the cash to look out for a bigger house in a more upmarket area. At that time we were living in Burnage, in the first house I'd ever bought. We'd been there for about two and a half years and it was the happiest place we ever had. I bought it for, I think, £21,000. It had previously been owned by an undertaker and he had built a large outdoor workshop. That was partly the reason I'd bought the place – I thought it could be converted into an excellent snooker room, but that never happened. We loved the house, but we wanted something bigger, now that we had started a family.

We eventually found our dream home in posh Cheadle, not far from the in-laws, the Masters snooker club in Stockport, and that old pal of mine Jackie Rea. When we first swung into the driveway, having picked up the particulars from the estate agent, I could feel the warmth of the house immediately. We both got out of the car and looked at each other with a smile. I think we fell in love with it at that moment, and no matter what the inside looked like, we were going to be moving in very soon. It was in a secluded spot, with a stream and only two other, very big, houses close by. Three bedrooms, living room, dining room, kitchen, triple garage and a room perfect for a snooker table – at no time in my childhood in the back streets of Belfast, did I ever think I would live in a house like that. Now here I was, a married man with a child, about to move into a house surrounded by rich, successful people. Yes, the Hurricane had arrived at last.

We called my solicitor and set the ball in motion, paying a little over £130,000 for 2 Bridge Drive, Cheadle, in Cheshire. We could imagine it being a happy family home, full of laughter and children. It would be our refuge from the rest of the world. Such high hopes we had, all eventually shattered. We did have some fun times there, like the Bonfire Night when I set off the fuse on a firework, stepped back to admire the imminent spectacle filling the skies only to suddenly be aware of a fizzing 'whoosh' as the faulty rocket (not my lighting of it obviously) screamed past my cheek and embedded itself in a neighbour's fence. Now this was a pretty posh part of the world, where people looked after their gardens and properties, to the point of regularly creosoting . . . and that doesn't mix well with an exploding firework, I can tell you. The fence went up like, well like a Catherine Wheel, and the whole affair cost me a couple of grand to fix. Did I say this was one of the fun times . . . The house, of course, was on a mortgage, which had to be paid every month, so I was committing myself to spending even more time away from the house of my dreams. Does that really make sense? I never quite figured it out.

It's been said of me often that around this time in my life – and indeed for the following twenty years or so – I was constantly out boozing and womanising. I want to put the record straight. Sure, I would have a few nights out. I was a successful and well-known personality and my job took me to clubs and bars. I was surrounded by booze, but I didn't always drink it. If I had, how could I have performed at the level I did, both in tournaments and on the lucrative exhibition circuit? That was where the money came from – but only if you delivered to the fans and the sponsors. So I had to work hard. I had to practise. I couldn't be, and wasn't, out on the piss every night, no matter what others might say. That's ludicrous. I wanted to be world champion again. I wanted to climb the property ladder, for God's sake. I sold the place in Burnage for about £25,000 and made virtually nothing on the deal. From there it was a big jump to £130,000 for Bridge Drive. I put down a deposit of £40,000. Where did that come from? Working hard.

I am not trying to reinvent history here. I did drink too much from time to time. I did get into scrapes. Stupid ones. I was foolish and sometimes unpleasant. I know that. Plenty of stories in this book prove it. All I am saying is that it wasn't every night – far from it – but all the quiet nights never make the papers, do they?

As for the womanising, again I'm not suggesting for a second I was an angel. I had flings. I had the odd one-night stand – perhaps more than the odd one. I am not proud of that. The temptations were there. After shows female fans would try to chat you up and occasionally I succumbed to their charms. But to suggest, as some would have it, that the moment I walked into any room, my skirt radar was on full alert is total bullshit.

On the snooker front, I was in serious need of catching up. Steve Davis won a host of tournaments in 1981, including the World Championship in which he knocked me out in the second round. I won one event. I knew I had to make sorting out my snooker room at home a priority. I needed to practise a lot more in my own environment, with my music and my own space, if I was to get the better of Davis and everyone else. I also didn't want to disturb Lynn and the baby, so I still practised seriously at the Masters Club in Stockport.

Another one of those new snooker tournaments that seemed to spring up out of nowhere with a sponsor's brand attached to the title, was the Langs Supreme Scottish Masters. That was one of the low lights of the year, a disaster from beginning to end. Since it was a new event, the BBC hadn't given it any scheduled time, so BBC Scotland took up the challenge. I made it to the semis, playing Cliff Thorburn. The fifth frame was going well enough and Cliff was at the table when I noticed that the score was wrong. The scoreboard was a very old-fashioned rollerboard and the scorer had made a mistake, a human error. The whole thing really was a bit of a shambles. Apparently, my score should have been four points more than the scoreboard showed. Of course, that drove me up the wall and I started shouting the odds.

I had a big row with the referee and just about all the officials. It upset my balance. I was forced to play for a snooker and ended up losing the round 6–2. I was later proved right by a TV rerun but the damage was done. I did get some satisfaction, though, when I saw a nineteen-year-old lad pick up his first major tournament trophy a few days later. Jimmy White was on his way and good luck to him. On the other hand, he was becoming another serious threat to the Hurricane for the World Championship title.

There was more drama to come that year between the Hearn camp and myself. I had agreed with Del that I would do a ten-day tour of the country with Steve Davis, playing exhibition matches against each other. The rows with Hearn started almost straightaway. He was the promoter of the whole event and, as such, he also had the rights to sell all and any merchandise. I got the hump when he started asking me to stay behind at the end of the evening to sign posters that he was selling. He didn't even offer me any extra money.

One night I went mad. I started throwing all the posters around the foyer and threatened to walk out of the rest of the tour. Hearn told me that I was contracted to complete it and he would 'sue my arse off' if I didn't comply. We eventually cooled down and came to a compromise. I would sign his posters but I could also separate ones of my own and keep the money. I spent the rest of the tour getting to the venues under my own steam and we all kept our distance when we were in the hotel. That didn't worry me. I am a natural loner, happiest in my own company.

Back at home, Lynn had been feeling pangs of loneliness throughout the year. Even when I was at home it was becoming increasingly fragile for us both. I needed to chill out and relax in peace for a few days after a road trip, but all Lynn wanted to do, not unreasonably, was catch up on lost time. I wasn't winning the big tournaments but I didn't have much time to sit and cry about that. I had to maintain my hectic schedule in order to pay the bills. I sometimes wonder how much Lynn thought about the pressure I was under to keep the money coming in. It was all taking its toll on me, physically. I was becoming exhausted – not helped by the late nights, I admit. I remember after Tony Meo knocked me out of the Coral UK Championship, I went back to the hotel, collapsed into bed and slept for nearly twelve hours.

I wanted to get back to the top of the snooker world as quickly as possible. My pride had been hurt by the defeats I'd suffered throughout the year. I wasn't going to let 1982 pan out in the same way. I had to change something – two things, in fact. First, I decided to look around for new management. I thought that if I squared it with Del Simmons, maybe Geoff Lomas's company, Sportsworld, would take me on. Del seemed to be more interested in sponsorship deals than in his players, anyway, so I just told Sportsworld that it was OK with him and, as it turned out, he wasn't bothered.

Next, I had to sort myself out. When I got back home after the Coral I told Lynn I had to do something about the state I was in. I was feeling so shitty all the time, I thought I might be on the verge of a nervous breakdown. I booked myself into the Highfield Nursing Home in Rochdale for a complete rest. For the first week I couldn't focus on getting better. I was just a wreck and going nowhere, but with help I managed to pull myself together in time to take on Steve Davis one last time that year. He beat me easily, almost inevitably, but for the first time in a long while, I felt good about myself. In my heart of hearts, I knew I could be back to my best. In an emotional statement to my fans after the Davis game, I made a promise that the Hurricane would return.

A fresh breath of confidence arrived with the new year. Lauren was now walking and communicating with me, father and daughter were bonding. On New Year's Day I was knocking a few balls round the table when she toddled in to see me. I picked her up and swung her round. She always liked that and giggled at me. I can still see her now with that huge loving smile that said, 'I love you, Daddy.' It brings tears to my eyes when I recall that look. I lifted her on to the table and she sat in the centre as I lined up the black. 'This one is for you, Lauren. Daddy is going to win the World Championship, just for you.' Then I potted the ball and threw my arms up in the air. Lauren got all excited as she sensed my own emotion and started giggling as she played with the other balls on the table.

I didn't want to blow myself out again that year so I made a promise to Lynn and Lauren that I would spend more time at home. I took it easy in terms of the tournaments I entered at the beginning of the year, although I did play in the Irish Professional, where I was disappointed to be beaten by Dennis Taylor 16–13 in the final. In the Benson & Hedges Irish Masters at Goffs I was playing well enough and made the semi-finals, only to be drawn against Davis, whom I had vowed to beat come what may.

As I have mentioned before, in the Republic of Ireland the fans get very loud at times, but they mean well. On this occasion they were one hundred per cent behind me. Davis went 3–1 up, but I was the one getting the support. In fact, the crowd was making me nervous as I tried to concentrate on cutting back the deficit, and I decided to do something about it. I got up, looked around at them and gesticulated with a 'calm down' motion with both arms, before putting my fingers to my lips to 'ssssh' them. The referee told me to behave myself. 'I'm going to report this to the Association,' he said, and he did. They fined me £1,000 for bringing the game into disrepute. Davis beat me anyway, 6–2, and loved every minute of it. So much for careful preparation for my assault on the world title.

Next on the list was the Highland Masters in Inverness where John Spencer won the semi against me 6–0. That didn't exactly please me, so I left the arena, hailed a cab and told the driver to take me to Manchester, where I was due to play in a pro-am the following morning. The taxi ended up costing me £350!

This was not the 'fresh breath of confidence' I was looking for. Again, something had to change – and I decided it was Geoff Lomas, who had been looking after me since I joined

Sportsworld. I called him in April, just before the start of the World Championship, and told him I wouldn't be needing his services any more. Then I called Harvey Lisberg, the managing director, and told him I was sacking them as my management team. I don't think he was too sorry to see me go.

I announced I was going to manage myself from then on – after approaching Barry Hearn, just to sound things out with Matchroom. We met in my suite in the Mountbatten Hotel in London, where we had a good chat. He explained that the other players in his organisation didn't want me to join and that was that. I was on my own as the biggest event of the year was upon me.

Being on my own also meant I represented myself at disciplinary committees. I was up in front of the next one for trying to quieten down the crowd at Goffs, along with a couple of other incidents I am sure. I decided to adopt a new tactic to try to reduce my punishment. It was a morning meeting and I appeared at the door with a trolley full of Moët & Chandon and orange juice. I remember Barry Hearn was on the committee and he just shook his head in resignation at my cheek. 'Right, lads,' I said to them all. 'We've all been here before. This time I thought we may as well enjoy ourselves. Tuck in and I'll wait outside for your decision.' I'm not convinced it worked – they did tuck in but my fine was as hefty as ever. I soon realised that I did need a manager after all, and called Del, with my tail ever so slightly between my legs. He agreed to look after me once again.

I might not have had the greatest build-up to the Crucible that year, but I was feeling good as I made my way to Sheffield. Lynn packed my bags and I threw in my lucky charms, including the now famous 'Lauren's Dummy', which I had taken to keeping in my waistcoat pocket. It made me feel closer to my daughter. I felt that if I had that with me at the table, then I also had Lauren there. Obviously, Lynn and Lauren couldn't come to every one of my matches over those two and a bit weeks, but they were there when they could be and always joined me in the players' lounge, so I very much felt part of the family unit.

I progressed to the semi-finals without too many problems, beating Jim Meadowcroft, Doug Mountjoy (did I say without too many problems – the score was 13–12) and Willie Thorne on the way to meeting my good friend Jimmy White in what turned out to be one of the greatest matches the Crucible has ever witnessed.

The only incident of major note along the way to the semi-final occurred late one night when I was practising in the arena after everyone else had gone. I was desperate for a piss but the toilets were miles away and I was in a groove in terms of my cuing action and I didn't want to stop. No one was about, or so I thought, and there was a handy flowerpot just there . . . I took advantage of the receptacle and carried on playing. Unfortunately, I was spotted by a security guard and reported. Pathetic really. It was hardly the worst crime in the world. I wasn't even being cruel to flowers. They were fake.

The semi-final was a back and forth affair. By frame thirty, I was one down at 15–14. I don't know what he was thinking, but Jimmy looked calm and confident. I do know that is exactly how I felt. He might have had youth, but I had experience. He had strung me along with some great snooker. This youngster whom I loved like a brother was making me work like a dog. I needed this frame to stay in the contest, and the one after it for a place in the final. The adrenalin was pumping but I wasn't feeling the strain. I play better under pressure. Those money games that I'd been playing over the previous fifteen years stood me in good stead. Whether it is for a shilling or a shot at the world crown, having something to play for is essential in my book. And I had more than personal glory at stake. I had promised Lauren that daddy would win the title this year, and that was one promise I intended to keep.

Jimmy broke and left on a long red. 'OK, kiddo,' I thought, 'here's your chance, take it.' The ball bounced out and my heart missed a beat. Jimmy took his chance – a red, then a black, then a red and a black and so on. I sat there watching the scoreboard ticking over, and my heart started to sink – 8, 16, 24, 32. When it hit 40, I really began to think that this might be the end for another year. He had been playing the two top pockets and had all the reds set up for a 147 break. The next red dropped and as he lined up for the black I looked away for a moment. A sudden gasp from the crowd told me what I needed to know – he'd missed.

I rose and surveyed the table. Jimmy didn't sit down, but stood swigging his water, perhaps assuming he'd be back to finish things off in a second or two. All the colours were on their spots except for the black Jimmy had missed, and this was sitting about a foot away from the brown. There were nine reds left, but seven of them were bunched together above the pink with the cue ball in among them. I walked round the top of the table, my mood slow and calm, yet my mind was racing. I stood there and crossed my arms as I tried to work out which red to pot and where to put the cue ball. I couldn't waste any colours; I needed the points. But there really was nothing on. I remember reminding myself of my own mantra as I stood there – 'Defence can be the best form of attack.'

I went for safety. I couldn't risk breaking up the pack of reds. That would have been suicidal. My decision nearly was. I left Jimmy half a shot, which he duly took into the middle pocket. It was a big gamble for him, but it worked. He dispatched the blue into the opposite pocket and then red and blue again. He was knocking them in like there was no tomorrow as the score crept up – 58, 59, then that gasp again. Jimmy's face sank. Another chance, but this time with the balls much better placed. I knew I had to clear the table to win. With five points on the board I decided to go for a risky black. I knew it was going to be the shot that determined the rest of the frame, and the match. It was risky because there was about eighteen inches between the cue ball and the black, but I made perfect connection. There was a slight judder in the jaws of the hole as the black disappeared into the top pocket, but I'd played it exactly as I wanted.

Jimmy was popular, but as that ball dropped, the reaction of the crowd suggested the people were back with the Hurricane. I was taking my time on every shot. What Jimmy was going through was anybody's guess. I asked the referee what the score was – 13. I couldn't afford to miss the next blue and I didn't. Three reds left before I started on the colours, all of which were on their spots. I had to get maximum points if I was to take the frame. Red, black, red, black, red, black. There was no room for error. I tried not to think of anything but winning.

With that last red I'd managed to bring the cue ball down to the other end of the table, and I was well positioned on the colours. The yellow dropped, then the green. The referee announced the score, '47'; brown, '51'; blue, '56'; pink, '62'. The black went in and the crowd erupted – '69'.

As I walked back to my chair I was totally oblivious of Jimmy. I looked up at the gallery and raised my index finger – 'Just one more.' I still had one more frame to play and win. I had an advantage over Jimmy on the final frame. He hadn't played for a good fifteen to twenty minutes and I was just off the table, feeling good, confident and full of the flow of play. I knew I had to keep up the pressure and try to weaken his resolve. I was, after all, playing one of the world's best players.

The thirty-first frame for a place in the final was played

minutes afterwards. I was fully recovered from the excitement of the last frame. I'd had a cigarette and was ready to take the next step towards regaining my title. The score was 6–0 to Jimmy when I went to the table to pot my first ball of the frame. Jimmy was back on the baize after my break ended on 59 and, to my surprise, he played a safety shot, bringing the cue ball back down between the yellow and brown.

It was a difficult table and I didn't want to open up the grouped reds for Jimmy, so I too played a safety shot. With 53 points in hand, I could afford to. I left Jimmy with a possible red to the top pocket when I tried to pot a long shot that bounced and settled near the pocket. He rose to the challenge and potted it, following with the blue. He had the chance to win the frame now. He went for a long shot, but missed. I went for the jugular. Lifting my right leg on to the table, I potted a lovely red in the top pocket, and a quick look at the scoreboard told me it was 60–12 to me. A potted black left four reds, but I missed my second to leave three. Jimmy missed again and I was back on. A pink followed a red then a black followed another red, and it was all over. I was into the final.

The feeling was immense. Jimmy came over to concede the game. I had taken away his moment of glory and in my joy I also felt his disappointment. I was almost sorry I'd beaten him. I couldn't just shake his hand. I had to hug him as if to say, 'Sorry, babe, but you'll have your day.' I wish for his sake I'd been right, but the gods don't give these things away easily and he never managed to take his rightful place as world champion.

13

The Whirlwind and the
one-armed man

•

I have made some great friends along the long road of my life in snooker. I have also met some of the world's most obnoxious, rudest and saddest people. They crop up throughout my story, I'm afraid. But here I want to take the opportunity to introduce a couple of the special people I have been privileged to get to know and call friends over the years.

The player I most associate with on the circuit these days, and the man whom I regard as one of my most faithful friends, is Jimmy White. The first time I laid on eyes on him was in the summer of 1975. I was at a Pontins holiday camp during one of the many exhibitions I was doing at the time. I'd noticed these two kids, one about sixteen and the other about twelve or thirteen, who had been hanging around wherever I went for days. As much as I'd tried to be friendly to them, they would get all embarrassed and run away laughing like a couple of schoolgirls.

One morning I was cooking myself some breakfast when I noticed them outside, with their snooker cues. So I got a loaf of bread and took all the knives from the cutlery draw. I went outside in my dressing gown and sat on the veranda, watching these two urchins out of the corner of my eye. I had noticed that there were always lots of seagulls circling the sky most of the day, looking for scraps to feed off, and so I sat there, pulling lumps of bread off the slices and throwing them at the birds. Then, when they came down, I threw the knives at them to scare them away.

Not everyday behaviour I know, but I reckoned that these two scallywags would be wondering what the hell the Hurricane was up to and hoped it would bring them out of their shell. Perhaps they would have the courage to speak to me at last. The little one finally emerged from round the corner and stood watching me in awe. The bigger one stood just behind him. All of a sudden, I heard a little voice saying, 'Oi! Mister! What the 'ell are you doing wiv those shitehawks?' I wanted to laugh at his accent, it was so Cockney and I've always loved that accent from my early days in London.

I had to look away in order not to laugh. Still throwing the bread and knives at the seagulls, and keeping my eyes fully focused on them, I replied, 'I'm getting my killer instinct so I can win this afternoon.' The little kid looked round at the big one and said, 'What'd 'e say?' and the big one said, 'Dunno mate, I fink 'e wants to kill someone. Let's go before he starts on us.' They both ran for it and I burst into fits of laughter and fell off the chair.

Of course, I hadn't realised it at the time, but the two lads were Jimmy White and his great mate, Tony Meo. Jimmy reminded me about that incident years later.

I met Jimmy again in 1976 when I was booked for an exhibition match with Terry Wittread, Willie Thorne, Geoff Foulds and Patsy Houlihan. Jimmy's dad, Tom, had booked us to play at his local working-men's club in Balham. Jimmy was just fourteen years old by then and had already got a bit of a reputation after regularly hitting breaks of 100.

The evening went well until I was asked if I would play the kid a frame. The little rascal beat me fair and square and it was then I realised he would not only become a great player, but a great friend. I was so impressed with Jimmy that before I left the club I asked Tom if it would be OK to bring Jimmy down to Southend in Essex on the following Sunday. I was playing another exhibition and thought it would be a good idea to use Jimmy to entertain the crowd while I took my breaks.

To be honest with you, I spent most of the breaks watching this young man doing a Higgins, and I loved it. Jimmy will tell you himself that he modelled his style on mine. I don't believe that. I think Jimmy is a very individual player with his own unique style, but I am grateful for the compliment. Since that time in 1976 we have become firm friends and have travelled the globe playing the game we both love. Unfortunately, we also have other traits in common that are not so good for us, namely drinking, gambling and smoking.

These days, though, Jimmy doesn't gamble so heavily, he is a smoke-free zone and drinks on rare occasions. I wish I had his willpower. I have stayed with him, and vice versa, over the decades and our adventures are still talked about by our former neighbours, local publicans and staff of the numerous betting shops we have frequented on legendary benders.

I was staying with Jimmy just after he'd moved to his new country house. We'd decided a few drinks were in order so Jimmy drove me and an old mate of ours, Peewee, to the nearest pub, about three miles away. We got to the end of the night and Jimmy decided to be a good boy and call for a taxi. He asked the landlord, who was another Londoner, to call one, but all he got in reply was a laugh. No one in the countryside, we were told, goes about in taxis.

'Well, what the hell are we going to do?'

'Try walking like the rest of us,' was the answer.

'Jimmy,' I said, 'what's the matter with you? We are three

strong men, let's walk it.' Out we went to be greeted by lashing rain and an empty car park.

'Sod that,' said Jimmy. 'If they can all drive home pissed, so can I.'

Peewee just shrugged his shoulders and the three of us got into the car. Peewee was in the back and I was in the front with Jimmy. Now Peewee was as pissed as we were, but he was still alert enough to put on his seat belt, which was very lucky for him when about five minutes later Jimmy decided to show us what it is like to travel inside a whirlwind. We couldn't see a thing with the rain, and I was carrying on with some witty story or something when all of a sudden we left the road, went up a steep bank and smashed into a brick wall.

Not having my seat belt on, I flew headfirst through the windscreen – actually not so much through it, as with it. We sort of left the car at the same time. Instinctively, I must have gone into jockey mode and tensed myself up, which is something you learn to do if you are ever unseated. I flew over the wall and rolled on the ground to break my fall, ending upright on my feet, completely unhurt, if a little disorientated. I found my way back to the car by following the headlights, and as I walked through the new gap in the wall I could see Jimmy wasn't too healthy. He had been smacked on the head by Peewee, and the steering wheel had had an argument with his chest. But apart from that, we were all OK. I stood on the remains of the wall and flinging my arms upwards I shouted to Jimmy, 'I am like a cat, James, I have nine lives and I think I have just used one of them up.'

'Get in the car now, you mad bastard,' he said. 'We've got to get away before the old bill get 'ere.'

Of course, he didn't realise that there are no old bill in the country, especially on a wet night like that one. So Jimmy reversed the car off the bank, taking the remains of the wall with us, and slowly drove the last mile to his house. He had left the garage door open so he drove the car straight in and stopped. As he did so the engine dropped out the bottom of the vehicle. Literally. The car lurched up and then back on the ground with a mighty thump. We looked at each other and just burst out laughing as the engine finally died in a hail of exhaust fumes and petrol vapour. We went inside the house and sat down in the kitchen as Peewee and Jimmy bathed their wounds. I poured us all a drink. Suddenly Jimmy leapt up saying, 'Oh, Christ, the bloody windscreen is still up there on the wall.'

'So what,' I said, 'it's no good now, Jimmy. The car's a fucking write-off.'

'I know that, you muppet,' he said, 'but the bleeding tax disc has the registration number on it. When the old bill find that, I'll get nicked. I'll have to go back for it.'

I thought he was mad but Jimmy rang a London taxi company and had them come all the way out to the house, pick him up, take him to the scene of the crime and retrieve the windscreen. By 4 a.m. Jimmy was back with the incriminating evidence.

The fun and games weren't quite over for the evening. With the knowledge that we'd had a brush with death, and escaped the wrath of the local police, I was feeling just dandy and challenged Jimmy to play me a frame of snooker for £300.

'I am invincible, I am the greatest,' I said, 'and I feel lucky.'

Jimmy grabbed the cue from my hand and threw it across the room. He then threw me out of the house. I was feeling on top of the world and full of vodka, so I went and knocked on the door of a nearby house and told the man that Jimmy White had just assaulted me and could he call the police and have him arrested. This man just looked at me and said something like, 'Oh dear, look, come in and I'll make you a cuppa.' The following conversation went along the lines of him persuading me not to involve the police as it would reflect badly on the whole village. I pretended to be swayed by his pleas.

He suggested that he run me to the railway station, but I was actually just winding him up so he would take me the whole way to Reading, where I was playing in a tournament. The only problem was that it was about a hundred miles away. But I guess he wanted rid of me, so at around 5 a.m., as the dawn began to break, I was being chauffeured to my next match by Jimmy's newest neighbour, who couldn't stand snooker but wanted a quiet life.

Our gambling exploits are as legendary as our drinking ones. One time we were in a small town in Ireland and decided to put a series of bets on at the bookies, then go to the local pub and watch the races on the telly. Unfortunately, as I'd done all those years ago in London, I wrote the series of bets out wrongly, so when we got to the pub Jimmy looked at the slips and realised I had made this huge mistake. We argued for about fifteen minutes and Jimmy really had the hump with me as we had put on about 250 punts. Then the first race came on. The outsider I had put on the slip romped home and we both did an Irish jig in the bar to the amazement of the locals, who by now were filling up this little village pub as word had gone round that the Whirlwind and the Hurricane were both in town.

We ended the afternoon over 2,500 punts up, as one after the other the 'wrong' horses won the races. We walked back to the betting shop to get our winnings and as we marched in we were met with a new sign that said 'No bets over 100 punts will be paid.' To say we went mad is an understatement. The crafty old fella who owned the bookies had realised just how much out of pocket he was, so he had changed the rules, but he had picked on the wrong punters to mess with. I threatened to climb over the counter and take our money but Jimmy pulled me back.

The Whirlwind and the one-armed man

Jimmy took control of the situation and demanded to know where the owner was. Needless to say, he'd scarpered – off to the golf course we were told. Had mobile phones been as popular then as they are now, he might have been warned and gone into hiding, but he didn't know we were on his path. We walked outside and asked one of the fellas in the now gathering crowd where the course was. He was more than happy to show us the way.

We walked for ages and eventually came to the gates of the golf course, where the crowd that had followed us stayed and watched from a safe distance. Our guide took us on to the course and, after talking to a few players, he pointed at a group of men and said, 'Dat's yer man der, wit the white cap on.' Now Jimmy was about ten paces ahead of me and as we got to this group of golfers he pointed at the bookie and said, 'Oi! You there, we want a word with you, mate.' The fella starts to shake as he realises who we are.

The golfers with him also recognised us, and they tried to shake our hands, but we just ignored them and confronted this fella.

'Now look, lads,' he said, 'let's be sensible about this. I'm sure we can come to an arrangement.'

'Give us our fucking money or I'll use you for a 7 iron,' I said.

'Yeah, cough up you conning old git,' said Jimmy. The bookie pulled a wad from his pocket and, shaking like a leaf, paid us out in full. The 'old git' knew all along exactly what we had won and why we were there. We took the money and as we marched through the gates the crowd gave us a cheer. It was one of our best days at the bookies.

Whenever I am in Dublin I often meet Tommy McCarthy, usually in the Lower Deck pub in Portabello on a Wednesday night. Tommy has had a very colourful life to say the least, but I have always admired him for his courage and determination. We have remained firm friends ever since we first met at the opening of the 147 snooker club in 1981.

At just sixteen years old he was involved in a bad motorcycle accident and lost his right arm above the elbow. Tommy had developed a liking for snooker at about the age of twelve, and the accident wasn't going to stop him playing. His love of the game led him later on to be the owner of many snooker halls in Ireland, and that's how I really got to know him. He would arrange for all the top players to come to his clubs and play, and he also arranged other exhibitions around the country.

I remember I was doing an exhibition match with Tommy at the Sally Longs pub in Galway, around 1997. Now, Tommy is well known by all the top players in and around the snooker circuit for his skill at the game. He has played and beaten many professionals, even though he only has one arm. He has a special tool that he attaches to his prosthetic arm, on the end of which is a snooker rest. He uses this and the cushion to play off. Tommy got talking to a guy at the bar, and the next thing I know we are committed to an exhibition of snooker at a day centre nearby for people with learning disabilities.

Tommy drove us the few hundred yards to the day centre the next morning and we met all the staff and people who used the centre. They seemed over the moon to have the Hurricane playing on their table. To be honest, it was one of the best days of playing that I can remember. They were all such fun to spend time with, and Tommy and I were being treated like gods.

At about 7 p.m. the guy in charge starts to organise getting everyone home, but before that they insist we have a photo to remember the day. So there we were, having individual pictures taken, when Tommy suggested that we should have a group photo with everyone, and I should be sitting on a chair at the end of the table, holding a cue.

So they all gathered round me, and on the table, while Tommy lines up the photo. All of a sudden I remembered that scene from *One Flew over the Cuckoo's Nest*, where Jack Nicholson is fishing off the boat, so I looked at Tommy and using the cue like a fishing rod I started to say, 'Cuckoo, cuckoo,' and then we were all saying it. The whole place was in bits laughing. It was the highlight of the afternoon.

The coaches arrived and most folk headed home. But someone had found a bottle of brandy and so we sat down with the remaining staff for the craic and a few jars. When it came to leave, we said our good-byes and walked to the car, only to find some bastard had smashed the back window and taken all our cases and about 2,000 punts in cash that we'd received for doing an exhibition a couple of days earlier.

We went back into the centre and told them what had happened. 'We don't even have a toothbrush or a change of clothes,' Tommy told them. They said not to worry and called a hotel to book us a room. Then they called the police while we all had some more brandy. The police arrived in the shape of two young rookies and an older sergeant; they were more interested in meeting me than solving the crime. Tommy was going mad at me to put out a spliff I had put together using some of the smelliest weed ever produced. It was huge. I am not exaggerating when I say it was about six inches long and smoking like a damp fire. I was just cracking up on the weed and brandy in between telling these two rookie guards what we had lost. All they kept saying was that they loved watching me playing on the telly.

They were totally oblivious to the smoking spliff and then Tommy started to crack up at them ignoring what I was doing. It was total mayhem. Anyway, they took the statement and I just kept saying to them, 'Listen, babes, I need those clothes back, Louis Copeland gave me them. And the money the fuckers have stolen from me, and here I am doing something for charity.'

'Now don't you be worrying, Mr Hurricane, we'll catch these fellas for yer,' they said and they were off.

One of the day-care people told us that behind the building was a halting site. Now for those of you who don't know, this is what the Irish call a travellers' site.

'Tommy, we have to go round there and see the big cheese,' I said.

'Fuck off with yourself, Alex,' he said. 'Are you mad? We won't be welcome. Let's tell the police and let them deal with it.'

But I was having none of it. I was convinced I could persuade them to give us back the stuff, assuming of course that they had actually nicked it in the first place.

We drove round there and as we entered the site the dogs and the kids came over to see who we were. I rolled down the window and said to a fella, 'Where's the head honcho, babe?' He just looked in the back of the car and said something totally incomprehensible. I got out of the car. With my top coat and a wide-brimmed hat, I must have looked like Clint Eastwood in a 'Dollar' film. That's what I like to think, anyway. The next thing I know I am being herded towards a caravan.

'Sure, will yer look at dat der. It's the fella from the telly now, Higgins,' I heard someone say.

'I need to see the head guy. Can you get him for me?'

'Ah sure I will now, come on and I'll show yer,' this kid said. He took me into a caravan and introduced me to the top man. Of course, he denied that anyone had taken our stuff.

'We get the blame for everything,' he kept telling me. So after a while I gave up and walked back to the car. As I got in there was Tommy laughing his socks off.

'What's so funny, Tommy? It isn't a joke you know.'

'Alex, I've just seen four blokes from the site taking an engine out of a car and they were all wearing Louis Copeland suits.' We both cracked up laughing and drove to the hotel.

The next morning was just as eventful. The incident was all over town. It was on the telly and the radio, the whole place was talking about it. As we had breakfast a procession of locals came by the table offering their commiserations and help. Then the police came in and told us that they had recovered our bags and clothes from the river. They were totally ruined and the money was, of course, gone. Fortunately, I always like to keep some cash on me so the bastards who nicked our stuff hadn't quite got away with everything. I had the equivalent of a few hundred quid in my pocket so I turned to Tommy and said, 'Let's go racing, babe. I feel lucky now!' Tommy just threw his hands up in the air and drove off towards the nearest track shaking his head at the cheek of me. We had a great day. People were buying us drinks and saying they were sorry to hear of the theft. We didn't let on about the cash we had, but the devil was around that day and we lost the lot.

14

Winner takes all

●

Just about everyone in the world who had a TV in 1982 watched me take that final frame to regain the World Championship. That's what it felt like anyway. I will certainly never forget it.

It was our thirty-third frame of the final and I was 17–15 up. All I had to do was win this frame and it was all over. I watched Ray Reardon go to the table first and sit down seconds later after potting the cue ball. Reardon was trying to play a safety game, but it had backfired on him. Now it was my moment. From the start of the frame I was totally focused, remembering that I had lost to Ray six years earlier. I wasn't trying to win this one in typical 'Hurricane' style either. I just wanted to win. Ray had left me with a long red to the top left-hand pocket, about eight feet away. I placed the cue ball in the 'D'. I wanted to make the shot completely straight and so I walked up the table to see exactly where I had to leave the cue ball to get on to the black. It was a dangerous and exacting shot. I had to leave the white ball on the precise spot that the red ball was sitting. If the shot was successful, with pinpoint accuracy, I could pot the black through a gap between two reds, just to the right of the cue ball.

I made the decision to commit fully to the shot, returned to the baulk and got down to line it up. It was a beautiful shot, the cue ball stopping stone dead. I hurried up the table to see if I'd engineered it exactly as I'd envisaged – 99.9 per cent accurate. I could now pot the black between the two reds. It was still a tricky shot, but it went down perfectly, and I proceeded to knock in the balls one after the other. All Ray could do was sit and watch – not that I was looking at him, or anyone else. When I got to 80 that was the final landmark I'd set myself and I gave a sigh of relief and smiled. Throughout the two days of the final I'd set myself certain targets, landmarks as I said, that would bring my dream closer and closer to reality. It was only when each one was achieved that I looked at the crowd. Other than those moments, I was totally focused throughout. I ended the frame with a flourish and as I knocked in the black for a break of 135, the crowd erupted into cheers and clapping. They were as happy as I was. I was, after all, the people's champion, and I had proved all the critics wrong. The public loved it.

I walked over to Ray and we hugged. The respect for each other was mutual. It had been an honour to have played him in that final and even in my moment of triumph I felt for him. He was such a quality professional, a gent and a great competitor. He had been so up for the match – that was why it had turned out to be one of the great sporting events.

At that moment I was still in Mr Adrenalin's grip. He's been with me throughout, but I hadn't let him dominate me. When he arrived on that first day of the final it was a bit like mounting a powerful horse, that I knew I had to live with for two days. Sometimes I controlled him, sometimes he tried to bolt, but I never let him get away from me. And by the end, Mr Adrenalin and the Hurricane were one. I'd needed him to get me through – him and Lauren, my inspiration. My love for her had driven me on during the whole tournament.

As they were trying to present me with the trophy and cheque, I only had eyes for Lauren and Lynn. With tears welling up, I beckoned them down. I took the cheque and held it, but still it meant nothing at that moment. I beckoned Lynn again. 'Come down, babe,' I whispered, and finally she did, with our baby, and the three of us hugged as if we were the only ones in the auditorium. I felt that even with all the practising, it was Lauren who helped me to win that title in some mystical way.

We celebrated that night with the officials and the players. I had a lot of press interviews to attend, plus there was a queue of fans wanting my autograph. This meant that Lynn was left on her own for parts of the evening, but there was nothing I could do about that. Those obligations had to be fulfilled. All sorts of stories have been written in the press about the after-match party, involving drugs, and Lynn and I rowing. It was a wild party – I'd just won the World Championship for God's sake – but the stories of snorting coke and having a slagging match are nonsense. Quite simply, it had been a long day and Lynn was tired. She had Lauren with her and it was quite understandable that she went to bed early. That's all there was to it.

I've also heard tell that she took Lauren on holiday to Portugal the next day without me. What crap. We weren't to-gether that day because I had to attend a disciplinary committee meeting, where I got fined something like £1,000. I can't even remember what the supposed offence was – it might have even been the pissing in the flowerpot incident, I'm not sure. After that I went back to Bridge Drive where Lynn's sister's husband, John Hough, had erected a huge banner – 'Welcome Home World Champion'. There are pictures of Lynn sitting on a wall next to it. That's clever photography if she was so furious with me that she took herself off to Portugal . . .

Lynn says I changed after winning the title in 1982, and began mixing with a different crowd, spending more time in London. She always says that it was from that moment on that we really began to be in trouble as a couple. Perhaps she's right, I'm not sure. I certainly wasn't going abroad as much after winning. I didn't need to. The engagements in the UK came in thick and fast. Maybe I was spending more time around the bright lights of the capital but the way I see it, I was working, in the course of which I was often away for five or six days on the trot. I guess it is understandable that Lynn felt unloved because she wasn't seeing much of me.

Whenever I was home from an exhibition or a tournament, I would find that Lynn would go to bed around 10 o'clock, but I wouldn't be tired. My body clock is clearly set differently from hers. So I would either end up watching TV on my own, or listening to a few albums in my snooker room, or I would occasionally pop into the Kenilworth, a pub about two miles away from Bridge Drive, for a pint or two and a game of darts. I got on well with the landlord and sometimes I'd order a Chinese takeaway to be delivered to the pub. He didn't mind. Was I avoiding going home on those occasions? I didn't think so at the time but when I look back now, perhaps I was deliberately staying out, even if unconsciously.

In the mornings I tended to get up around 10 or so, have a cup of tea, then head off to Stockport for practice. I liked to have a routine, and arrived at noon. That's where the quality players could be found. Some of the clientele were a bit rough and ready, but I got on with 99 per cent of them. The table I played on wasn't bad and the level of snooker could be very high. It is all very well playing a dozen or so games at an exhibition, but to stay sharp you need the best possible opposition. In Stockport, Warren King, some very good Canadians and talented amateurs would keep me on my toes. People think snooker players don't need to practise because we are always playing somewhere, but that isn't true. We need to hone our skills by trying out different and difficult shots. When you are playing a real frame, you can't take the risk of trying out a new shot because it could mean you losing the frame.

I liked the Masters Club and made some good friends there – especially my trusted referee Brian, who loved his pints of bitter. After playing snooker for hours, to unwind a number of us would sit and play cards. I enjoyed every minute of my time at the club – even the sight of some of the boys strutting their stuff at the Thursday night discos! Lynn was always invited, but never came. Can't say I blame her when I look back on some of the sights on that dance floor!

Lynn was often out by the time I was up, and then I'd get back late. She'd be off to bed soon . . . and so it went on. Married life with Lynn turned out not to be the life I wanted. Did I put the effort in? Probably not. I certainly have to take my share of the blame for the break-up, and accept the responsibility for my own actions.

One good thing that did happen around then was that Lynn announced she was pregnant again. We were both very pleased, but the same excitement between us wasn't there, and we both knew it.

One of the tours I undertook around then was particularly memorable, but for all the wrong reasons. A promoter arranged a trip around Northern Ireland for me to play a series of exhibition matches and take the World Championship trophy around to show to fans. The bloke asked whom I could get to come along with me to play each night and I called up Jimmy White, who jumped at the chance. Off we set in our tour bus. Well, I say 'tour bus' to make it sound flash, but in fact it was a simple motorhome with a few luxuries such as a chemical toilet and a camping-style cooker. It was all a bit amateurish but it was fun. We'd stop off en route to the various venues for a pint and Jimmy and I would happily while away the travelling hours playing cards. And all the time our promoter was collecting our appearance money from the events.

On day four, he just disappeared, taking all the gate money with him. Jimmy and I were staying in a hotel just outside Londonderry. Our driver was happy to spend the nights in the motorhome, guarding our gear – namely our cues and the trophy. In the morning, when we realised the bloke had done a runner, we all sat down to discuss what to do. Our next venue was supposed to be over a hundred miles away and we had no idea whether it was still on or not. We did a lot of phoning around, trying to find out what the hell was going on, and word of our plight must have leaked, because we heard that Conway, a snooker table company, had stepped in to save the last two nights' play. By noon it was all was sorted out, or so it seemed. We were ready for the off – apart from the fact that our driver had locked himself into the motorhome, and was refusing to open the door.

'What is your problem?' asked Jimmy.

'I haven't been paid and until I am, I'm holding on to all your gear, including the trophy. The law is on my side, mate,' he replied. I was livid, but Jimmy couldn't stop giggling.

'Open this bloody door!' I shouted at him. 'We haven't been paid either.'

'Bollocks. I don't care. You get me my money or we ain't going nowhere,' he shouted back.

I went back into the hotel and called the cops. Fifteen minutes later, a policeman turned up on a pushbike and tried to get the driver to open the door, with about as much luck as we'd had. I started to threaten the driver.

'Open this fucking door now,' I demanded. 'I want my bags, cues and the trophy.' I waited a few seconds, then turned to the copper and said, 'I'll shoot him. That'll be the easiest thing. Someone get me a gun.'

Jimmy was now in a state of complete hysterics. He was laughing so much he couldn't tell me that half the town had turned up to see the cabaret show. The cop looked at me and said, 'Now now, Alex, you can't threaten to shoot him.'

'No,' I said, 'don't be daft. I won't shoot him really. I'm a guest here. I'll have him shot.'

The cop knew I was joking and he told Jimmy and me to go inside the hotel while he spoke to his sergeant. So there we were, sitting at the table with some sandwiches and a pint. The next thing is a TV camera crew turns up, and the local radio station. It was like a bloody circus in that carpark.

Jimmy said, 'Look, Alex, he's got food and drink in there, and a toilet, he could hold out for a month, mate. Let's see what he'll take.'

In the end, the driver gave us all our bags, the trophy and our cues. It cost me £250 to appease him, but not before the army turned up as well. A passing patrol of heavily armed Paras had seen this group of people, complete with television crew, and had come to investigate. This was at a time when the Troubles were at their peak. We heard the posh commander radioing to his headquarters that they had averted a riot involving 'that snooker player chappie Alex Higgins'. We never did get our money off the promoter bloke, but we went to the next two events. We were given a lift to each one and they both went off without a hitch. It wasn't funny at the time, we were swindled, but Jimmy still cracks up whenever we talk about it.

There wasn't much that we would look back on in the following year that was going to crack me, or anyone else, up. There were two high spots and that was it.

15

Going downhill fast

•

The two high points in 1983? One came at the end of the year, but the most important one came in March, when my son Jordan was born. Before that, I was in trouble once again when my short temper went into overdrive at the Tolly Cobbold Classic in February.

I had drawn Dennis Taylor in the first round, and for some reason he was getting to me. I was niggled by him and that put me in a bad mood. I was determined to teach him a lesson by knocking him out of the competition. Unfortunately, it was me who went home early.

During the match it had been so hot in there that I had taken off my bow-tie. Just a few months earlier, the WPBSA had sent round a memo to all players to say that in future we had to abide by the 'stay smart' rule in order to maintain the sport's image as they wanted to portray it. At the time, there was a lot of nonsense said about the incident, but the referee Peter Koniotis had officially said that, due to the uncomfortable conditions, we could loosen our ties. No one in the WPBSA seemed to care about that, though.

I was so pissed off with the fuss about me being tieless that I stormed out and refused to do the usual photo call or meet the audience. It was all becoming so petty that I just had to get out. Later on I said to a reporter that I wasn't worried about being knocked out so early because the tournament was a 'Mickey Mouse affair anyway'. For that remark I am very sorry and apologise to Mickey for any offence I may have caused him.

The WPBSA were still at war with me, and obviously didn't like me being world champ. They thought they could use the champion to turn snooker into a posh sport, like polo. They never did get that it was a people's sport and I was the people's champion. I was fined over what happened at the Tolly Cobbold event even though the referee had given me permission to remove the tie. Taylor had complained to them that I had infringed the new ruling. It was all pathetic really, and childish.

I wasn't going to let the authorities get to me, though, and was determined to have the last word on the subject. So I went to see a specialist and he confirmed in writing that I suffered from a sweat rash that could be brought on by the wearing of a tie, any tie. The WPBSA insisted I see their own doctor and, to their dismay, he confirmed that I had a genuine complaint for which he recommended I get a special dispensation. It just goes to show that if you know you are in the right, stick up for yourself and you will win in the end. Pity I wasn't right all the time.

As the Tolly Cobbold ably demonstrates, my game had been suffering at the start of the year. That was due to a number of factors. First off, I had broken my favourite cue six months earlier. To a snooker player, this is a disaster. We get so used to a particular feel – our cues are like an extension of our own body. I had got hold of another Burwat and tried to adapt it, but I just couldn't get it right. On top of that, Lynn was getting cantankerous. She was heavily pregnant, and I am sure that had a lot to do with it. I was avoiding her, and staying away from home as much as I could. While that didn't mean I was out on the razzle every night, it also didn't mean I was living the life of an abstemious monk. That's hardly my style.

Going downhill fast

Looking back, I think my lack of ability to change my lifestyle radically was the main reason Barry Hearn decided not to take me on when I'd approached him previously. I am too stubborn and Barry was probably right to refuse me. I often wonder what might have happened if I had been regarded as 'Hearn' material. I had the talent and if Barry could have curbed the other bits, well, who knows. I guess that is one of the reasons I respect Steve Davis. He was 'Hearn' material. A lot has been written about my feelings towards Steve, but I have never said I hated him . . . well, I didn't say it and mean it. How could I? I hardly know him. We never mixed in the same social circles, and I have never got to know him personally. He has the talent, there's no doubt, but in my view it is to a large extent thanks to Barry's guidance that he has been so successful over the years. One thing I'm sure of, I would have been much better off if Hearn had been looking after me from the start.

Jordan was born on 30 March 1983. He was such a lovely baby and, as with Lauren, I was there at the birth. Lauren was the apple of my eye, and I loved Jordan just as much. Fathers tend to dote on their girls and mothers on their boys. It was like that in my family, but that isn't to say my dad didn't love me just as much as my sisters, just in a different way. The same was true for me and Jordan.

It was something I'd always dreamed of – having a son to share time with and take to Manchester United matches. I envisioned Jordan playing for them some day – fathers do that, don't they? Jordan has turned out to be quite an all-round sportsman and can hold his own in a number of disciplines, especially football. He has two good feet and is strong enough to make his presence felt on the pitch. I still believe he has the talent to be a professional, although age is not on his side.

I think it's true to say that Lynn and I harboured hopes that

Jordan's arrival might mark a change in the fortunes of our marriage. That I might settle down a bit and try and not travel quite so much. In fact, the problems escalated. Lynn was unhappy. I was unhappy. My family were unhappy and her parents were pissed off. At least, her dad was; her mother was always good to me.

I am not one to cry over spilt milk. That's not the Higgins way. What is done is done as far as Lynn and our relationship goes. Getting divorced was the best thing for both of us, but I believe I've kept a very strong bond with both my children. When they were growing up, before Lynn and I split, I spent a lot of time with them. Sure, I was away a lot, but when I was home, it was them and me. I'd carry them around, take them out, play with them in the garden. That creates a strong bond and it hasn't been broken over the years.

I think of them a lot, of course. I think of them in quiet moments, and tell stories about them to my friends. They call me every week at least, and I see them in Manchester whenever I'm there. Strange, the things that trigger off memories. Just the other day I hit my left hand on the side of the cooker and I felt a jolt of pain between my thumb and finger. I was immediately transported back to a moment when Jordan was about seven. We were playing football, which he excelled at, in the garden one autumn evening, just outside Lynn's house. We were already divorced by this time. I was goalkeeper and Jordan was shooting from about penalty range. The goalposts were two trees, and there was damp grass underfoot. I had told Jordan to send the ball in about chest high so I could catch it and quickly throw it back to him. Everything was going well, we were laughing and shouting – especially if he got one past me – when he sent a singing shot to my left. I moved to block the ball but I was wearing Italian leather shoes (always the natty dresser – even when playing football) and I slipped on the damp grass with my hand outstretched, all my fingers and thumb spread. As the ball hit my thumb, it stung like hell and I thought to myself, 'What strength my boy has in his feet!' But I soon realised that the ligament between my index finger and thumb, on my left hand, was torn. For a snooker player, that's pretty serious. Damage there can prevent you raising your thumb – which is exactly what you need to do to make a strong bridge and be able to put power into screw shots, which have always been a vital part of my armoury. It was a pure accident, of course, and it may have affected my snooker ever since, but that doesn't matter. Those moments, playing with your children, are more important.

I am very proud of both of my children and I hope they feel the same way about me.

The World Championship followed only a few weeks after Jordan was born. I wanted Lynn to come along to Sheffield to let the public and the press see that she was supporting me, that our marriage wasn't dead. Lynn told me to go it alone. She said she was too tired, what with looking after a new baby, Lauren, and running around after me. So that's what I did. I went off on my own, which just gave me the rope to hang myself.

Sheffield was being good to me that year. I was playing well and keeping to a good diet, with not too much drink. I even managed to get some early nights. The crowds were manic. It was one of the best-attended championships and a lot of people, including my fiercest critics, will tell you that it was because of me. No matter what anyone thought of my antics outside the arena, the response I used to get from the public when I was at the table was amazing. Electrifying. When I left, the sport seemed to die on its feet, as a result of a combination of things, not only me retiring. The main reason, as far as I'm concerned, was that the WPBSA was run by a lot of people who, in my view, had no interest in the sport.

I was defending my crown in the way a true champion should – with flair and ambition. I saw off Dean Reynolds, Willie Thorne and Bill Werbeniuk to reach a semi-final against Steve Davis. I think I admitted afterwards in an interview that I'd been 'stuffed' or 'crucified' or something like that. Can't remember exactly, and funnily enough, I don't recall much about the game itself. Davis won 16–5, with a session to spare. Enough said about that, I think. Steve deserved his place in the final, and indeed his victory over Cliff Thorburn.

I didn't go straight home, as perhaps I should have done, but instead stayed in Sheffield to drum up some potential overseas work with some businessmen who'd come to watch the championship. I also took the opportunity to catch up with an old friend I hadn't seen in a long time. After the disappointment of losing my crown, I needed some light relief, and I didn't think I'd find that at home.

Perhaps time together was what Lynn and I needed, away from the goldfish bowl that had become life in Britain. So when I received an invitation to the Winfield Masters in Australia, not long after the World Championship, I asked Lynn to join me. Lauren came along as well, and the nanny, but Jordan was too young and he stayed with his grandparents. The plan was to then go on a short holiday to Fiji. I did well in the tournament, reaching the quarter-finals, but that was as good as it got, apart from one evening which I'll come on to in a moment.

I was never comfortable with Eddie Charlton's involvement in the Masters competition. To me, being an organiser and a player was a conflict of interests. One night, when he came on the big tough guy and started lecturing me on how I had to behave when

I was in his country and at his tournament, I lost it and began shouting the odds about his involvement in the tournament. He warned me that if I didn't shut up and quieten down, he would 'knock my block off, mate'; I'd have liked to see him try it. I always thought there was something fishy about the way the tournament was run and I wasn't surprised to hear sometime later that someone involved in the organisation of it had been done for fiddling expenses. Among other scams, apparently, this person was putting players up in cheap hotels and then claiming far more expensive rooms for them from the sponsors.

One incident that happened when we were there probably reveals more about the state of my mind, and the state of my marriage, than anything else that happened on that trip. Lynn, Lauren, the nanny and I were staying in a suite in a plush hotel in Sydney. After the Winfield, I'd wanted to show Lynn the sights of that wonderful city, have a proper break, the two of us going off together while the nanny looked after Lauren. But Lynn wasn't interested. She, in effect, refused to leave the room. What was the point in bringing the nanny, at considerable expense, if we weren't going to use her? I became increasingly frustrated. I'd suggest dinner out, or a trip round the harbour – anything that might be fun and romantic – but no, I got no feedback. Eventually I'd had enough.

What sparked it off was a minor thing. The room had a mini bar, but it contained only a couple of cans of beer that I liked – Tooheys. I'd tried to suggest that we go out that evening but again I'd been rebuffed. We were sitting watching TV and I had the two tins from the fridge and then fancied something else. I'd picked up a very nice bottle of Hennessy VSOP in Singapore and decided that a brandy and soda would be just the thing. But the moment I poured it, that was it. I was pilloried by Lynn for being a drunk, for not caring. Everything under the sun. She said, or shouted, her piece, and then stormed off to her room, slamming the door.

For some reason, this didn't anger me. I just felt sad that it had come to this. We were on the other side of the world, with so many adventures to be had together, and as far as I was concerned, she wasn't interested. So I picked up the phone, called Cara, my ex-wife, and arranged to meet her in our favourite piano bar from all those years ago. We had a lovely two or three hours together. We danced, kissed, had a couple of drinks, reminisced about old times, walked along the harbour. And not once did I think of Lynn. It was as if she didn't even exist. And I was happy.

By the time I got back to Manchester I was at a very low ebb. The holiday to Fiji had not worked any magic and my marriage was clearly in tatters, I began to lose matches that I should have won easily and I was beginning to fall apart. Something had to give – and it was Lynn.

16

The beginning of the end

•

August 1983 proved to be a bad month in the Higgins household. Lynn always hated August anyway, because it heralded the beginning of the season, and she would complain that the pressure of the snooker world was getting worse every year. As the game was becoming more and more popular, and the rewards were getting bigger and bigger, there was a lot more pressure on the players to compete, compete, compete, and that had a knock-on effect on their families.

The cracks in our relationship that we had been trying to paper over since Jordan was born had become too deep following the trip to Australia and Fiji and so, one morning in early August, Lynn woke up, packed her and the kids' things, and went to stay at her parents' house.

I wasn't going to let Lynn go without a fight, though at first it was nice having the house to myself. I was actually quite domesticated. I could cook pretty well, having watched my mother prepare the family meals when I was a lad, and I could iron perfectly well. How I'm turned out has always been important to me. I've actually got a scar on my hand from ironing – that was my mother. At the age of about seven or eight I used to love standing at the ironing board, watching what she was doing. I remember once asking her what she was like as a young woman, what sort of things she did, and she got so distracted telling me about the Clark Gable films she loved to go to see, she ironed my hand! She was horrified when she realised what she'd done, but it was no big deal really. I could even sew to the point that I was capable of taking in a pair of trousers so that they fitted my slim frame just the way I wanted them to. Living alone wasn't a big problem for me.

Lynn and the kids were just a mile or two away at her parents' place and I missed them like mad, but I still didn't believe that I was to blame for this situation. At the time I was happy to blame Lynn and her attitude for it all, but I believed it could all be fixed. I am not a quitter and I certainly wasn't giving up on my marriage. I wanted us to be a family. I was seeing the kids from time to time, but I wasn't getting any 'quality' time with them. Lynn refused to come with them when I was about, but she sent the nanny to lurk in the background. It felt as though I wasn't trusted. That hurt. I didn't think there was any need for that.

I called Lynn regularly. At first she wouldn't speak to me. It was as if I was some terrible ogre, but I knew I wasn't. I admit I probably was drinking too much but it was only to help with the pain of being slighted, as I saw it. I only wanted what was best for us all. So I persevered.

Then came a breakthrough. Lynn called me up one day and just said, 'OK, Alex, I will give it one more try and go on holiday with you. But you must understand, this is it, no more chances. So make it good.'

I was over the moon. A few days earlier, I had asked Lynn to come to Majorca with me to sort things out and she said she would think about it. Jim and Betty weren't happy about it. That was probably because of what they were hearing about me. There are two sides to every story and they were hearing just the one presented by Lynn. I'm not saying I was an easy man to live with, but I wasn't the demon that some have made me out to be.

The beginning of the end

Lauren came with us while Jordan, once again, stayed with Jim and Betty. One child was enough to be dealing with. We were attempting reconciliation, after all. I didn't want to be staying at a hotel full of tourists who were going to be coming back pissed and singing at 4 a.m. every morning. I also didn't want to be bothered by autograph hunters while we sat round the pool. So I was delighted when a film director friend of mine suggested we stay in his lovely private villa. On the morning of the flight as I packed my bag, I remember that I almost forgot to pack my prescription of Mogadon sleeping tablets and some other anti-depression pills I was on at the time.

Sadly, our make-or-break holiday never really got going. Reconciliation was not in the air from the word go. It may sound harsh, but I felt Lynn was like a cold fish the whole time we were there. We never held hands, she didn't want to do this, or that, or indeed anything. Even when we did stop for a drink somewhere, I'd hardly have a sip, and we were off again. I had envisaged lazy afternoons sitting in a quiet bar, watching the world go by, chatting, getting to know each other again, with Lauren snoozing in her pushchair next to us, but that never happened. Lynn just didn't seem interested at all. I wondered why she'd agreed to come at all.

So I spent a lot of time running about after Lauren, especially when we were out eating. She and I loved to play the fruit machine. We had great fun together. People were forever coming up to us and asking for photographs of Lauren with her daddy. I was so proud of my little girl I loved showing her off to people – her impish smile, the way she furrowed her brow and screwed up her eyes when she scrutinised people. Absolutely gorgeous.

Now, when I said 'we were out eating', that doesn't really include me. I had developed a sort of anorexia due to being depressed, and as Lynn ate her meals I looked out for Lauren.

Not eating, not really drinking, and having a small child to look after all day can take it out of you. In the evenings all I really wanted to do was chill over a glass of something and a Robert Ludlum thriller, especially as I felt that Lynn was giving me the cold shoulder.

On one particular evening – which was about to become one of the most significant in our relationship – I decided I had to make an effort to thaw the ice and suggested we all went out for an early dinner. Off we went, about 7 o'clock, and settled down in a lovely restaurant with a balcony overlooking the marina. It was the perfect place to have a lovely meal, a bottle of Chablis between us and watch the sun go down over the yachts in the marina, Lauren charming the staff around us. That's what I'd hoped. But no, again, Lynn wasn't interested in having a good time. She hardly spoke, she wouldn't have even one glass of wine, she played with her food and insisted on leaving before we'd had dessert.

I wasn't prepared to have the night ruined, however. It must have been around 8.30 p.m. when we got back to the villa. I sat out on the veranda, put on a tape, opened a bottle of bubbly, offered Lynn a glass, which she refused, of course, and settled down to read my book. It must have been about 9.40 p.m. when she came out again and announced she was going to bed and then asked why I was drinking. When I tried to explain I'd only had a couple of glasses, she started to call me every name under the sun, saying it was me who wasn't making any effort to save our relationship. She kept on nagging and it was driving me nuts. I'd had enough. I told her if she kept it up, I'd knock back all the tablets in the bathroom in one go. She didn't believe me and said something like, 'Always the drama queen, eh Alex. You won't kill yourself, you're too selfish.' And with that she slammed the bedroom door.

It was like a red rag to a bull. I grabbed the pills and swallowed the lot, washing them down with the remains of the champagne. 'I hope you're pleased with yourself now,' I said. 'Lynn, I don't care if I live or die,' and I walked out of the villa, found a bar, flumped on a bar stool and ordered a beer. I remember very little after that. I do recall sitting there not giving a damn what might come next. I felt beaten. Defeated. And annoyed at the same time. In my mind I'd tried to do the right thing on the holiday and yet here I was. Alone on a bar stool, perhaps waiting to die. My head was so fucked up I wasn't thinking straight – I was so beyond caring. I didn't even think of my beautiful little Lauren. And that's it. No matter how hard I try, those emotions are my only recollections of that moment. The next thing I knew I woke up in hospital with tubes sticking out of me. I don't know how I got there.

I was feeling giddy and confused. I didn't know where I was. There was a glass of water by my bedside and I had a sip. For some reason, that seemed to clear my head. I carefully removed the tubes – thank God, I didn't do myself any more damage, I didn't have a clue what I was pulling out – and looked in the closet for something to wear. I had no intention of staying where I was. My clothes were there and I quickly put them on and crept quietly out of the hospital, undetected. I found my passport and some money in my pockets and stopped at a shop a few hundred yards up the road for cigarettes. Looking back towards the hospital gates I saw a flurry of activity among the white-coated staff. It looked as though they might have spotted me, or at least realised I was gone. 'Time to make yourself scarce Alex,' I thought.

I shot off – as much as a man who has been out cold for two days can shoot off – in the opposite direction from where I'd been heading. I hid as an ambulance sped past me, and when the coast was clear I fooled everyone by heading back towards the hospital. The last place they'd look for me, I reasoned. I felt like the character Jason Bourne in the book I'd been reading. I hailed a taxi to take me to town and a bank where I had money wired to me immediately. From there, it was straight to the airport and on to the first available flight. To Lisbon.

Once I'd arrived I phoned Del Simmons to let him know I was OK and asked him to pass on the message to Lynn. Then, fuck it, I was going to enjoy myself. I booked into a nice hotel, went shopping and chilled out. I even got hold of a call-girl one night. We went out for a quiet drink and then I took her back to my room, but I couldn't go though with it. That's just not my scene. I enjoyed her company, but that was as far as it went. I wasn't interested in sex when it came to that point of the evening. I paid her some cash and wished her luck.

The rest of that time in Lisbon was spent trying to chill out. I knew I was lucky to be alive and I thanked God for my good fortune, but I couldn't get it out of my head that it had been Lynn who'd driven me to do something so stupid. Perhaps I should have been more self-aware, but as far as I could see, I'd done nothing wrong.

After a few days I returned to Manchester, found the key to the front door in the hiding place I always left it in – just in case – and climbed into bed. Later that day, the phone woke me up. 'Alex, what the hell are you trying to do us? Me and the kids are in a state over all this. You can't keep acting like this. I'm coming over to the house. Be there.' It was Lynn and she was spitting venom. I got washed and dressed and waited for her to arrive.

We had a very adult, calm conversation. The end result was that I agreed to go into a local mental hospital – what we'd call rehab now I suppose – to get an assessment and some treatment. It was a bit of a relief to be honest, and it meant Lynn was giving me another chance. That pleased me because, all said and done, I wanted our marriage to work. At least, I thought I did. And I wanted my babies around me again. I wanted to be part of a family. Most of all, I wanted to be normal again. I agreed to go into a nearby hospital, the Cheadle Royal, as a voluntary, private patient. If I admitted myself on that basis, I could sign myself out at any time, and after a few days I realised that the place wasn't for me. My room was nice enough, I read a lot and I had a very comfortable bed, which meant I got plenty of sleep. I even ate well, thanks to daily deliveries from a friend of mine in the area, Cosimo, who owned a fabulous trattoria. That resulted in me putting on about ten pounds, which I probably needed. No, it wasn't the set-up that drove me away. It was the fact that the place was full of crazy people. And that wasn't me. They had us sitting around in groups, playing silly games and talking about our problems. I stuck it for four days but couldn't stand it any longer.

I remember going into the group therapy room, looking at them all and just saying something like, 'I've had enough of this, I'm off.' As I went through the door I turned back and said, 'By the way, the answer is operation.' I was referring to the anagram they were trying to work out, which was one of the exercises they used to have us do. I never found out if I was right or not. I didn't even see the clue, but I couldn't resist winding them up for the last time.

I don't know what it was, but for some reason, after such a terrible year, I walked out of that hospital feeling positive. I was certainly refreshed, and somewhere deep inside me I knew that if I pulled myself together fully, there was a chance of some redemption. I wasn't about to let 1983 disappear without a fight. The second good thing to happen to me in the year was only three and a half weeks away – the Coral UK Championship.

I practised ten hours a day for that tournament. I was so focused that I even found myself becoming nervous and apprehensive at the practice sessions. I was so determined my game should improve that, as I stepped up to the table every day, I could feel the butterflies in my stomach. 'Would I be better than yesterday?' The answer invariably was yes. My game was becoming razor sharp. In my last session before the tournament, with Warren King, I chalked up five century breaks on the trot, followed by a 90, then another two 100s, with a maximum 147 thrown in for good measure.

My first-round opponent was a young Scottish lad called Murdo McLeod. I knew I was well prepared, perhaps better than ever, but when I arrived at the Guild Hall that night to start the match I was like a rabbit caught in the headlights. Stage fright. Call it what you will, I froze. Perhaps there was just too much adrenalin pumping through my body. Whatever the reason was, almost without me noticing, Murdo was 4–0 up. I got through to the break, settled down and went into cruise control, ending up a 9–6 winner.

Next came Paul Medati and by then I was fully into my stride. I beat him in a virtual whitewash. He managed to win just one frame. Tony Knowles was my quarter-final opponent and it is fair to say I wiped the floor with him. I flew round the table in true Hurricane fashion, and before I could draw breath I was 6–0 up. Tony fought back well, but he was no match for me in that mood and I marched into a semi-final encounter with Terry Griffiths with a 9–5 victory.

Terry had no chance of beating me. I had set my mind on that title and nothing was going to get in the way of my ambition. I wanted to prove to myself that when I practised and was focused, I was still the best. In addition, I had a feeling that Steve Davis was going to win his semi, and I wanted to exact some revenge for my annihilation at his hands months earlier in the World Championship. The £12,000 wouldn't be unwelcome, either. So in my mind, Terry was an obstacle that just had to be swept aside. I don't know if Terry felt intimidated by my play during the match, but he never really got into his stroke with any sort of rhythm and I polished him off 9–4.

The fans were cheering wildly at the end of the first session of the final. At least, the Davis fans were. He was 7–0 up, having played some sublime snooker. I know. I'd had to sit and watch it. They must have believed their boy had his hands on the trophy already. They might have thought that, but I didn't. Although it was obviously a horrible scoreline to face, and especially against someone as skilled as Davis, somehow I knew I wasn't quite done for yet. I'd been playing too well in practice and throughout the tournament up to that point. But for some reason, I hadn't brought that form to the office that day. Stage fright perhaps. All I needed was a chance to hit a few balls, get my eye in, put a break together, channel my adrenalin in a positive way and I'd be right back in it. So even though I had a mountain to climb, I was remarkably calm. I knew it couldn't be long before the hurricane was unleashed.

The following session started with a bang. I felt twenty-one again and stumped Davis by taking the next three frames. His face fell as I potted the balls just like he had done in the morning. His play had been disrupted, my eye was well and truly in and I knew I had him on the ropes. I won the session 7–1, leaving Davis with a narrow 8–7 lead. Steve, being no slouch himself, was shaken but not stirred. The next session was pretty much honours even as we duelled back and forth to establish supremacy. By frame 30, Davis was 15–14 ahead. We were both tired, but I detected that he was feeling it more than I was, and I felt I could take the pressure better than he could when the chips were down. I played the next two frames with the same gusto as the first two against Medati and it was too much for him. I potted the black to win the match and the competition 16–15. The noise, the cheers, everyone off their seats, Lynn, who had come along to support me, hugging me, people shaking my hand, clapping me on the back – all that will stay with me forever. I remember looking across at Steve during the presentation and thinking he looked like a little boy lost. He stood there, chalking his cue, bemused by the scenes of joy around him. I knew I had triumphed in one of the greatest comebacks in snooker history. I was back on top, and nothing was going to stand in my way. How wrong I was. This was just the beginning of the end.

That win was to be my last individual title in the UK, and within a couple of years or so, my marriage was over.

17

Travels around Ireland

•

During the mid eighties, for all that my life at times seemed to be spiralling out of control, and much of it in the public eye, I did have some fun adventures that the majority of the public never heard about. I say they were fun – but at the time I often didn't think so. One particular tale always puts a smile on my face – now.

The new year, 1984, couldn't come round quick enough for me, not that it was particularly awe-inspiring when it did eventually arrive. I didn't win the world title that year and if it hadn't been for the bad luck, I'd have had no luck at all. It all started one day when I got a call from my pal Tommy McCarthy.

'Alex, it's Tommy, are you well?'

'Hello, Tommy, what's up?'

'I've a booking for you. An exhibition over in Ireland in June. You'll be playing Pascal Burke and me. What do you think?'

'That seems OK, Tommy, what dates do you have?'

I was free and the fee was about £2,000, after you changed the Irish punts for sterling. I would be playing Pascal and Tommy in a series of frames to entertain a crowd of snooker fans including local dignitaries and members of the Irish government.

It was a disaster from start to finish. My plane was late taking off and, of course, I took the opportunity to have a few drinks. The bar was full of snooker fans and everyone wanted to buy the

Hurricane a pint. Needless to say, I obliged them. I don't think I fell off the plane, but I may well have staggered a bit. Tommy with his mate Noel O'Brien were waiting for me through customs and they drove me back to Tommy's house.

There, I showered and got changed before starting out for the exhibition. We'd travelled a good few miles when suddenly the car started to steam up, or rather smoke up. I don't know anything about cars, but I do know that smoke coming out the back and front isn't a good sign.

Noel pulled the car over and we all got out. The fact that a hangover was developing meant that I was not in the best of moods. In fact, I was pissed off and started having a go at Tommy. Then Noel said, 'If you don't fucking shut up, Higgins, I'll fucking knock you out.' Now this guy is a big bastard and I know my limitations so I backed down, but I was still moaning. It seemed to me that the whole thing was beginning to turn into a bit of a farce. So I grabbed my bags and cue, and stood in the middle of the road to thumb a lift, resplendent in my monkey suit.

Quickly enough, a car comes along with three old dears in it. It stopped for us, mainly because I was standing in the middle of the road waving my arms around.

'I'm Alex Higgins the snooker player. Can you give us a lift? I have a very important match to play.'

'You want to get out of the road, you'll get run over,' the driver said.

'Look, two thousand people are waiting for me to play,' I carried on, as I yanked open the back door and clambered into the back. Noel and Tommy were left with the car. So we're driving along, the four of us crammed into this mini, and me giving out to the driver. 'Will yer come on, babe. Put your foot down. I'm already late. I'll even pay you if that will help.'

iz Kendall

HURRICANE'S
THE TON-UP
CHAMP!

Alex is world king aga

ALEX HUR
as he won :

Higgins ov
to take the
yearned to r
And Higgins

Alex hits
a jackpot

BY JOHN HENNESSEY   Sheffield

o. 24,817
353 0246

ALEX TH!
GREAT

TH
e's champ-
ooker title
matic last-
last night.

pion Steve
5—15 in the

n that frantic
edible finals.

CHAMP
incredib
Higgins
Coral tr
his sup
over St
at Pres
night.

urricane blasts back to

...RRICANE BATTLES BEAT THE BOOZE

Snooker ace calls in wife for help

By JOHN KAY

SNOOKER'S wild boy Alex Hurricane Higgins is taking his wife to tournaments . . . in his bid to beat the booze.

Alex, 32, hopes the presence of his beautiful blonde wife Lynn will help him and a binge that has lasted 10 years.

Last week Alex spent three days in a private clinic at Rochdale, Lancs.

Torment

Lynn, 28, went with him at the weekend to Yorkshire where he was due to play two games — at Batley and York — against world champion Steve Davis.

She has watched him stage a desperate battle against the bottle in the last few months. And she said: "It must be a torment when so many fans want to shake his hand and share a drink with him.

"Lynn . . . I've been worried to death about Alex and his diet and his drinking."

DAILY MIRROR, Friday, August 21, 1987   PAGE 11

HIGGINS IN FIGHT WITH BOSS

Butting attack over drug test

By ALASDAIR ROSS

SNOOKER star Alex "Hurricane" Higgins head butted a tournament host in an ...

DAILY MIRROR, Tuesday, April 7, 1987   PAGE 3

BIRDS, BOOZE AND BRAWLS

HIGGINS HELD IN AIRPORT BATTLE WITH WIFE

Snooker star tries to...

SNOOKER wildboy Alex Higgins was arrested at an airport last night after a frantic bid to halt his children heading for a sunshine holiday.

He tried to gatecrash security barriers at Manchester airport's immigration control jetty...

THE SUN, Friday, April 17, 1987

HIGGINS DRUNK AS A SKUNK AT MATCH

Snooker ace was potted

SNOOKER wild man Hurricane Higgins was at the centre of a new storm yesterday after appearing "drunk as a skunk" at an exhibition match.

10   DAILY EXPRESS Monday July 27 1987   ★★★

HIGGINS BANNED FOR 6 MONTHS

£12,000 fine for snooker ace

RELIEVED: Alex yesterday

By EUGENE DUFFY

...AMED snooker ace ...x "Hurricane" Higgins ...s yesterday banned ...d fined £12,000.

...his punishment was the ...ost severe disciplinary ...tion ever taken by snooker

Higgins, whose offences included head-butting a tournament official, could have been expelled from the game or banned for years.

Instead his six-month suspen-

Night in cells for Hurricane

ALEX HIGGINS DRANK MY PERFUME!

My snooker room at Delveron House. A row over a nanny in this room ended with a TV being thrown through the window.

'A horse kicked me, honest ...'

'Business is fine, send more money.' Taking a call on my 'mobile' while facing the press after head-butting an official.

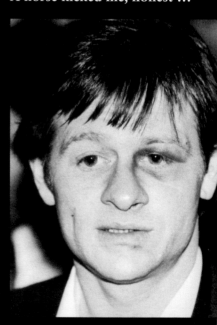

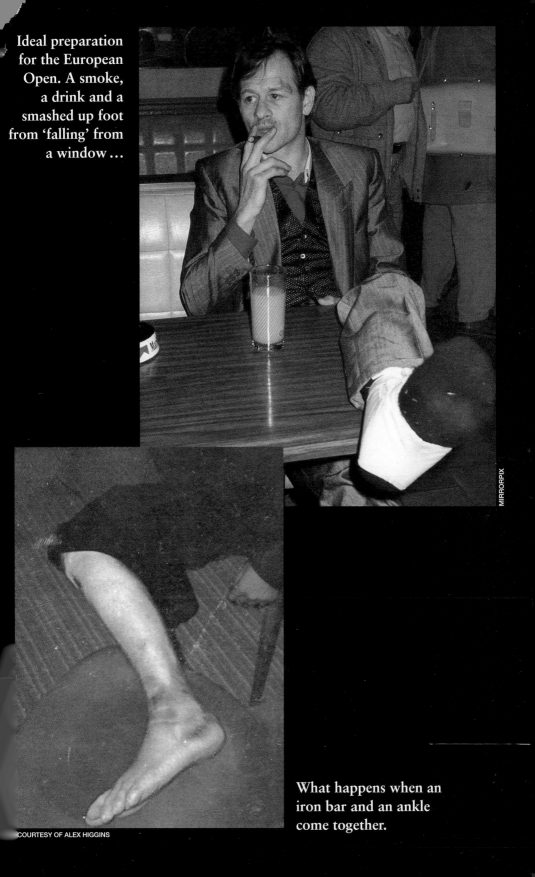

Ideal preparation for the European Open. A smoke, a drink and a smashed up foot from 'falling' from a window …

MIRRORPIX

What happens when an iron bar and an ankle come together.

COURTESY OF ALEX HIGGINS

Great pals. The Whirlwind and the Hurricane.

Wild Things.

The incomparable Ollie Reed. 'You can do it Hurricane the Pig. Just one more bar ...'

Making quite a sartorial splash at the Crucible... for the very last time. I didn't know that then, and I certainly didn't know the battles I would have to face a few years later.

Recovering from cancer with the support of my loving sisters, Anne and Jean.

She looked at me in the mirror. 'I'm not taking any more cheek from you, sonny boy. You can just get out and walk. I don't care about your two thousand people. We've two thousand people waiting for us at the bingo. So you can just feck off.' And she pulled over and threw me out. I was not a happy boy until, having walked a couple of miles up the road, I spotted a pub, in the middle of nowhere.

I'll never forget the place. It was a classic village pub and I don't think I've ever been happier to see one. I put the bags down at the bar and a fella came out from the back.

'Can I help you?' he said, and looking me up and down, he went on, 'Are you going to a wedding?'

'Fucking wedding, boss, I think I'm on my way to my funeral,' I said. I ordered a Guinness, and as the barman poured the drink he looked at me hard.

'Do I know you? Sure, your face looks awful familiar,' he asked in a real country accent. Normally, I would have been surprised back then if someone from that part of the world hadn't instantly recognised me, but this bloke was clearly as blind as a bat, with thick jam-jar-bottom glasses on. His daughter came in at that point and spotted me instantly.

'Da, that's Hurricane Higgins. Good to see you Alex.'

By that stage I'd resigned myself to being late, so I sat down with my pint and was introduced to the daughter. She was a lovely lass and we got talking about horses. Her father joined us, and the next thing I know I'm the proud owner of a race horse! I've bloody well bought it off him for the equivalent of £1,500. I never saw the thing and it certainly didn't win any races for me. But buy it I did. Not my best investment. But that holds true for much of my relationship with the sport of kings.

Word soon got round and within minutes half the village was in the pub and I was signing autographs and posing for photos.

No one was in much of a hurry, except me. That evening's do was a charity event and I didn't want to let them down. Eventually, I turned to the landlord, and explained my problem and asked, 'Can you help me, babe? I'm in a bit of a fix.'

'Ah sure, not a problem, the horse is a done deal boss, and sure you'll not regret that decision. And now it's time for me and the girls to get you on your way,' he replied in his wonderful accent. We went through the back and he pulled a truck out of a barn. The landlord's two daughters and I climbed into the back and sat on bales of straw in among tack and horse shit. I kid you not.

We eventually got to the venue one and half hours late and the place was in uproar. Tommy had made his own way there and was frantically pacing up and down outside waiting for me. People were already leaving as we pulled up, and the shout went up, 'He's here, lads, the fucking Hurricane is here.' I think they expected to see a limousine or something, but no, the Hurricane was arriving in his dinner suit in a truck full of manure. The people started going back inside and we followed them in. I was shown to the office of the owner of the place.

'You've cost me a fortune tonight, Higgins,' he snapped, but I wasn't in the mood for his cheek. I was trying to wipe horse crap from my shoes on his office carpet as I looked at him and replied, 'Do you want to get on with it or what?' Then I said I wanted the money in cash upfront, so he counted out 3,000 punts, put it in a bag, and threw it at me.

'Look after this, Tom,' I said, handing it over.

'Alex, I can't hold it,' he replied. 'I'm playing tonight as well don't forget.'

So I asked the owner to put it in his safe for me, then walked out to the arena where Pascal had already been for hours, entertaining this unruly crowd.

By this point, having sunk a few in the pub, my hangover was on the way out and I was getting merry again, and playing some great stuff. During one frame against Pascal I was on for a 147 break and the crowd was loving it. I missed the blue, but they didn't care. I was still their champion. I kept up a steady pace with the pints as the evening continued into the early hours. By then I was doing tricks and being silly, standing up on the table and showing off with all sorts of wild shots. Suddenly, the owner bloke comes over and tells me to pack it in. When I ignored him, he said that the Gardaí were outside and had told him to send everyone home.

I still carried on so he turned off the lights and the place erupted in boos and insults from the crowd. We had no choice but to call it a night, but when Tom came with me to pick up the cash from the owner, we were in for a surprise.

'You'll get no money here, Higgins. You were an hour and a half late and it cost me.' Then he turned on Tom, saying, 'And you, one-armed man, it's all your fault.'

'Look,' Tom replied, 'the delay was unavoidable, and Alex has already given cash to the charity, so what's your problem?'

Whether he thought Tom was about to have a go at him, I don't know, but he opened a drawer in his desk, pulled out the bag of cash and threw it at me.

'Go on, fuck off and don't come back here again,' he said. I know a thing or two about money, and the moment that bag hit me, I realised it was lighter that it should have been. I glanced at Tom, who, I think, had also sussed what was going on, and a look passed between us. We weren't about to be taken for a ride but at that very same moment we both suddenly became aware that all the doormen were standing in the doorway. We're not stupid. We knew we had no chance against so many fellas, so off we went, taking the bag with us. A local lad offered to give us a lift into the nearest town and we left with him. Tom told me to count the money and sure enough it was 1,500 punts short, so we asked the fella to drop us at the Garda station. By now it was about 3.30 a.m.

We knocked up the duty garda and he was a right rookie.

'I want to see the superintendent,' I said to him. 'I've been robbed of fifteen hundred punts.'

'Sure, the super isn't here, lads. He's gone to a snooker match to see Hurricane Higgins play,' he replied.

'I am Hurricane Higgins!' I shouted back at him. 'Look, just ring and tell him that I've been robbed.'

Off he went, leaving Tom and me in the waiting room. What we didn't know was that the superintendent and our 'host' at the venue were mates and did business together. Needless to say, our complaint wasn't destined to be successful.

Sure enough, our rookie friend came back and said, 'Look, lads, I've spoken to the super and he said to tell yous you've three minutes to get out of town or I'm to lock you up in the cells for the night.'

I was now really pissed off and shouted back at him, 'Listen to me, I've been robbed and I want to make an official complaint, so get your form out and take a fucking statement from us.'

'There'll be no complaints here tonight now, lads, so get on your way. Go on.'

I tried arguing with him, but he was having none of it. We had very little choice but to walk to a hotel up the street and book in.

'Tommy, get my book out of my bag will you and call Brian Madley at the *Sunday People* in London.' So Tom calls Brian and explains the situation to him. Brian's a journalist and is used to getting calls in the middle of the night. I was hoping that if we got Brian involved, the possibility of the story making the papers might get my money back. Brian made a few calls and we got some sleep. At about 10 a.m. the hotel was swarming with local media, eager to report the incident. It was probably the biggest event to happen in the area for years, but it all came to nothing. We never got our cash.

Round about noon our friendly landlord turned up to see how we were getting on. He'd heard what had happened and wanted to see if he could help.

'I'm not sure I can do much about your cash, lads, but I can entertain you. Come on now, I'll take yous to the horses. There's a meeting on today.'

So we left the shambles behind us and headed for the races – and another disastrous day. We lost 5,000 punts between us. After that, we were given a lift to the nearest large town track, and decided a few beers were needed to cheer us up. At 4 a.m. we were still out, but no happier. By then, I'd had enough. I was tired and wanted to get back home, so I took my cue out of the case and, holding it up like a lollipop man would, I stood in the middle of the road and stopped a truck. The driver rolled down his window.

'How're you doing, boss? I'm Alex and I'm in a bit of trouble here. Could you give us a lift to Dublin?' He looked at me and it clicked.

'Oh yeah, Alex Higgins. Sure, no problem. I'm going to the docks in Dublin, hop in.'

'Come on, Tom, we're going,' I said.

'You can go, Alex,' he said. 'I'm going back home,' and off he went to find a cab. God knows where from at that time of night. I climbed into the truck and straight into the driver's bed, where I fell instantly asleep and was out cold until I was woken at Dublin. I thanked the driver, jumped out of the truck and soon found another Good Samaritan to take me to the airport hotel, from where I called Brian Madley again.

'Brian, you've got to help me out, babe. Tommy has me

booked to play another exhibition match tomorrow night in Clonmel.'

'How can I help, Alex? Is there a story here?' he replied.

I went on to explain everything that had happened to me and said he could use it all but in return I needed to have someone with me with some clout, so I wouldn't get ripped off again. Brian flew over the next day. He agreed to cover all my expenses, and even gave me a few hundred punts spending money. It was getting late and we needed to get to Clonmel fast, but we wouldn't have time to get there by conventional transport. We only had a few hours and, in those days, the roads weren't that good. So Brian got clearance from his editor to hire a helicopter to fly us there – quite a step up from the truck full of horse manure. Brian was going to be my minder and he was loving every minute of it.

We were met at the heliport by Noel O'Brien and he drove us – in the same car, now fixed – to the exhibition centre, an old dance-hall in Clonmel. I was in bits. I was hungover and tired, although at least I was showered and clean-shaven. I vowed to stay off the booze. Milk was my poison that night. This time all went well. Noel paid me in cash as we got into the car and Brian looked after it. The Mayor of Clonmel turned up and after I had played for about five hours he made a great speech. It was so different from the Wexford catastrophe. Brian got his story and I was reminded that exhibition tours really could be fun and successful.

18

Heading towards debt

●

The next year, 1985, proved to be one of the worst years of my life. Break-ups, fights, booze, fines – sound familiar? I wasn't exactly learning from my mistakes.

In the Benson & Hedges Masters tournament at Wembley in February, I put out Steve Davis in an incredible match. The crowd were on my side and had been booing Davis, which I don't condone in any way. When I was asked about it in the post-match interview, I said that I don't like the crowd booing my opponent, and added, 'But personally, I hate Steve Davis.' Taken out of context, that sounds bad. What I was meaning – and, in fact, said at the time, although the press didn't report it the next day – was that I thought he was a very, very good professional snooker player but that we were miles apart and played a different style of game. I was also caught swearing on the BBC after the match with Steve. The whole place had been buzzing that evening and when it went to 4–4 with Steve at the table and well up, it looked like curtains for me. But no one should ever underestimate the Hurricane. Steve failed to close the frame, and match, and gave me an opening. I didn't need to be asked twice. The place went berserk when I potted the last ball and, carried away with it all, I blurted out something along the lines of 'I'm fucking back!' It wasn't meant to be broadcast but, of course, it was. More grist to the WPBSA's mill.

The next morning, although I was knackered, I went on breakfast TV to explain again what I'd said about Steve. Yes, I did say I hated Steve Davis, in the context of saying I admired his snooker skills, but we weren't friends off the table. All that did was play into the hands of the press. Inevitably, the whole thing was blown out of proportion – equally inevitably, a fine was on its way to me.

The WPBSA hearing on the Benson & Hedges tournament came up in March. This time I wasn't on my own. Jimmy White was up before the beak as well. Jimmy's 'crime' involved a dispute with the hotel management, which to me is a private matter. The board had no business getting involved. As it turned out, there wasn't enough evidence and the whole thing was basically dropped, with Jimmy just receiving a stern letter. As for me, I was up on a charge of swearing on the BBC plus the interview incident. I was fined £1,500 and got a dressing down. Water off a duck's back as far as I was concerned.

I had been banned from the Winfield Masters in Australia the year before, but I appealed the decision and won. I think it was more a case of putting up with me to get the crowds in, rather than keeping me out and seeing the arena half full. As it happened, I bombed out there anyway. I did play in a few exhibitions while I was there, in clubs owned by friends of mine, but before long I was ready to go home, although 'home' didn't hold all that much appeal.

Lynn and I were living apart and had been for about six months. She packed her bags for the second time in the autumn of 1984. She put it down to my bad temper and drinking, and always being out either playing snooker or golf. I don't think that is fair. My job was still keeping me away, and it wasn't possible to be drunk all the time, as some would have it. Lynn obviously felt that things had gone too far, though, and she was off with the kids, but I was determined to get us back together.

I wanted to buy a new house, partly as an investment, but also as a base from which I hoped Lynn and I could build our relationship back up. I was initially keen on a place near to where I played golf – Mere Golf and Country Club – but when I mentioned this to Lynn she didn't go for it. My thinking had been that I could play snooker at the club and keep fit on the course, but Lynn didn't really like the area. My doctor at the time used to meet me for lunch sometimes in Prestbury village, and it was on one of those occasions that I saw a lovely country house in an estate agent's window. 'Perfect,' I thought. 'If I'm not moving to Mere, this is the place for me. I am going to make this happen.'

A few weeks later Lynn and I were out having dinner with some friends and on the way back I persuaded her to pull into the drive of the house so I could look at it. It was beautiful and when I looked through the window and saw the panelled walls of a large room, I said to her that it was perfect for a snooker room. I begged her to give us another go. 'I'll be at home more practising if I can get this place. Please, Lynn, come with me to see it tomorrow.' She agreed and the house didn't let me down. We were both sold on it the moment we stepped through the front door. Was this the house that would mend our lives? We thought so, and within a short space of time we were the proud owners of Delveron House in Prestbury. Things were surely on the up for the Higgins family.

Fast forward to the night of 29 September 1985. I'd planned on having some dinner and watching the Barry McGuigan – Bernard Taylor world title fight with some friends, but Lynn said I was drunk and she didn't want to invite anyone round. I had been out at the pub earlier that day, watching horse racing, but I certainly wasn't drunk. When I've got a few bets on, it's the horses I'm interested in, not the Guinness. So I watched the fight and Lynn went to bed, much earlier than me, as usual. I wasn't tired so I decided to pop out to the local, the Bull's Head, for a couple.

Lynn later claimed I'd gone to chat up our Spanish nanny, which is absurd. I went for a couple of whiskies and to chat to whoever was there. That's something I did often. Lynn had a bee in her bonnet about that nanny. Previously she'd claimed that I'd been having an affair with her because she had come down one night when I'd been playing snooker with a friend and supposedly 'found the nanny joining in', looking as if she owned the place, apparently. What actually happened that night was that myself and a fellow pro, called Bob Harris, were playing for a few quid, and listening to some cassettes. Probably some Motown or blues, and possibly quite loudly. The nanny had woken up and come downstairs for a glass of water or something. Unbeknown to us, she peeked her head around the door of the snooker room to see what we were up to. She didn't cross the threshold, she just stood there quietly, watching us play. We hadn't even noticed her. She wasn't joining in in any way, and the first time I realised she was there was when I heard Lynn's voice demanding that the poor girl get back up to her bed. I was accused of all sorts, but Lynn wouldn't listen to reason. I categorically state here, however, that I wasn't having an affair with the nanny.

On that night in September I came back from the pub and found the nanny still up, and I asked her to make me a cup of coffee. I went to the snooker room to listen to some music and that's when all hell broke loose. Lynn appeared and started screaming and shouting. I had done nothing wrong and I just lost it. I guess it was years of pent-up emotion – on both sides – boiling over.

Heading towards debt

I did throw some things, because I was so frustrated and wound up and wanted her to shut up. At no point did I even slightly threaten Lynn but she locked herself in a room and called the police. And, yes, at one stage, I did throw the TV out of the window – twice actually. It would have been funny if it hadn't been so sad. Delveron House had lovely, heavy leaded windows. When I picked up the TV in a rage and threw it at the window in a grand gesture, I was expecting a huge shattering of glass. Instead, the TV got stuck, thanks to the leading, wedged tight. It took me a good few hard tugs to release it, and then it was on its way out, but my big moment was somewhat lost.

I hadn't realised Lynn had called the police, so when they suddenly appeared at my door, I didn't want to let them in. They later claimed in court that I was drunk. I maintain I wasn't. I believe the police manhandled me when they came in. I ended up with a fractured rib and bruising after being locked up for the night. I was charged with disturbing the peace, and later that year in court, I admitted to offensive behaviour and was bound over to keep the peace for twelve months. The Higgins wit didn't desert me, though. When reporters asked me whether I thought it would be difficult to stay out of trouble for a whole year, I replied that I was going to go for a drink with Ian Botham to ask him to sort me out. Ian was having his fair share of tabloid attention around that time. To my mind, the whole affair was blown out of proportion by the police and the press, but it was the end of Lynn and me. She'd moved out for good.

I always seem to entertain hopes of a bright new year but 1986 did not mark the dawning of a new age of happiness for me, I'm afraid to say. Quite the opposite. It is hard to believe, but things actually got worse, starting in January.

Even though I'd purchased the table on which I won the 1982 World Championship and had it installed at Delveron House, I still preferred to practise at the Masters, Paul Medati's club in Stockport. The night before the fifth round of the Mercantile Credit Classic in Warrington, I was in the club practising when Paul came over and we started talking. He asked me why I didn't play at home and I told him that Lynn and I were going through a rough patch. He started to goad me a bit about Lynn being too good for me and a huge row erupted.

Tommy McCarthy had been staying with me for a few days to keep me company and come to matches. We had been at Medati's club about a week beforehand and Tom had apparently got off with the barmaid, whom Medati was dating at the time. So, imagine the scene. There's Paul and I having a blazing row and it starts to get personal. I let my big mouth run away with me and blab about Tommy and the girl. No prizes for guessing what happened next. Medati whacked me one, giving me a black eye and we both started laying into each other.

It was well known that Medati wore a wig and during the fight I got him in a headlock and really started to punch him. All of a sudden his wig came off and for a minute I thought I'd scalped him. The whole thing suddenly took on a ludicrous aspect and we just looked at each other and stopped fighting. I'm sorry to this day that the incident happened.

A guy I was with was going to take me back to my house, but instead I asked him to take me to Lynn's place – the house I'd bought her when we split up after the police incident a couple of months previously. When I got there, I told Lynn that I'd been in a fight over her and asked whether I could stay the night. Not surprisingly, given the mess I must have looked, she said no. The next morning I turned up at the tournament as normal – apart from sporting a black eye – to play Dennis Taylor. The press were there in droves. News of my black eye had obviously leaked, as I knew it would.

God knows why, but I'd already come up with a frankly daft story to explain it. It went something like this – I'd been out horse riding that morning with a solicitor friend and my horse had reared up and thrown me off, I'd been kicked and the eye was the result. No one believed it, of course – especially Lynn. The *Sun*, in fact, called me a liar on their front page the next day. Hard to complain about that one.

The truth about the Medati incident all came out the next day and I had a call from Del Simmons, who wasn't very happy about it. He threatened to ditch me, again. Then, just to add to the drama of the moment, I got into a row with the tournament office at Warrington when I demanded my prize cheque. They didn't want to hand it over there and then and we got into a bit of a slanging match. I got a £2,000 fine for that one. It's true Del wasn't too enamoured with me over all this, but to be honest, I wasn't too taken with how he'd handled things. I should have been protected from the press, regardless of how I'd got my black eye, but instead I was put up before them and had to say something. OK, I admit the horse-riding story wasn't exactly watertight but I feel my manager, not me, should have fronted all the questions. My partnership with Del was on the way out and a few weeks later, at the Dulux British Open, I announced that we were splitting up and I was joining Howard Kruger's Framework management team.

I was pissed off with how things were going, and how the press seemed to be following me everywhere I went. I was constantly being photographed with women at exhibitions and tournaments, which is normal for all players. People just come over and ask for a photo, so we do it, except that when I did it the pictures ended up in the papers the next day, usually with a caption such as 'Higgins and a blonde out on the town'. That sort of attention could be regarded as flattering, I suppose, but it was getting way too much. So when the whole black-eye story blew up, I decided to try and use the press to my advantage for once. I let it slip that I was going to blow the lid on the corruption I felt was rife within the WPBSA. I offered the story for £300,000 but there were no takers. Perhaps I was asking too much, or maybe the WPBSA was too powerful and the editors feared a backlash.

Next up for me was a welcome reprieve abroad, at the BCE Belgian Classic. I played well and reached the semi-finals, where Kirk Stevens ended my run. When I got back home, it was like I'd never been away. Drugs, booze, fights, suicide attempts – you name it and the press said I was doing it. I wasn't. By this time I was with Siobhan – 'the Blonde' – and very much in love. I didn't have the strength to fight the press. You've got to be feeling robust to take them on. I couldn't manage it. I wondered if they were trying to get back at me for asking so much for my corruption story. Who knows? Perhaps it was nothing more complicated than the idea that a Hurricane Higgins story on the front cover sold newspapers.

The World Championship was upon us again. I won the first round and was drawn against Terry Griffiths in the second. Lynn and Lauren came along to watch me play, which pleased me, but unfortunately, my talisman didn't quite work her magic that year. Terry knocked me out of the competition in a close-fought match that ended 13–12.

I had a bit of light relief when Tommy McCarthy called me up one day, and asked me to come over and open his second snooker club in Waterford. It was good to hear a friendly voice for once and I agreed straightaway. To make the evening go with a swing he had managed to persuade a mutual friend of ours, Bal Moane, to do some cabaret as well. Bal was one of the funniest comedians I know. He died in Kilkenny in November 2006 and is very sadly missed. Tommy had also booked one of Ireland's greatest billiard and snooker referees, Paddy Comerford, a man I'd known and respected for a long time.

Tommy met me at the airport in Dublin and we went into town to meet up with Paddy and Bal at Heuston station to get the train down to Waterford. We managed to get a seat with a table and Tom went off with Paddy and Bal to get some beers. Around that time, to help me relax, I was smoking the odd spliff – only once in a while, when I felt it might help calm me down. I rolled one up for the journey and once we were settled I lit up. Paddy got a whiff.

'Janey mac, Alex, dat's a lovely aroma. What's it called?' he said, as only Paddy could. Before I had time to answer, Tom butted in and said it was a special blend. Now you have to remember that Paddy was a true, green-blooded Irishman and seventy-three years old at the time.

'Sure I'd love a smoke of dat, Alex, will yer ever roll me one please?' Now Bal and Tom were trying to suppress their laughter and encourage me to let Paddy have a toke. It was too good an opportunity to miss. Paddy sat there and smoked it like it was an expensive Havana cigar, and as he did so he got more and more stoned and started to giggle, like you do.

The next thing we know, Paddy is out of the seat and running the length of the train like a young greyhound. He was a train one minute and a plane the next, with all the noises. He had the entire train in fits, us included. He eventually fell asleep and when he woke up he was fine, after a few Guinnesses of course. We never let on what he'd been smoking and to his dying day he always believed that he had a special blend cigarette with Alex Higgins.

Back in the UK, I was ready for the beginning of the 1986/87 season, and things were about to kick off in a big way. If I'd thought the Medati situation, the argument over the prize money and the rash of tabloid headlines that had chased me throughout the year were as bad as it was going to get, I was woefully wrong.

There'd been some bad news earlier in the year when Kirk Stevens collapsed outside a club in London. It was all to do with his cocaine habit, which had come to light at the 1985 British Open. Kirk had lost in the final to Silvino Francisco. In a toilet break in-between frames, Silvino accused Kirk of taking stimulants and the press hounds were on to him. Within a few weeks, he admitted his drug habit. Then he collapsed. I liked Kirk and felt sorry for what had happened to him. I was delighted to hear that he had pulled though this horrible scare and has subsequently beaten the drugs. That takes a lot of courage. Kirk was also a member of the Framework management set-up and his problems affected me deeply. I'd heard rumours about where Kirk might have first been introduced to coke but I had no proof. That didn't stop me making a splash about it at the season's opener, the Langs Scottish Masters, though.

The holder of the title was Cliff Thorburn and I was determined to beat him. It is no secret that he and I do not get on, not since 1973 when we first had a fist fight. I have always considered him to be brash and full of himself. We met in the final and it was me in front, then him, me again and so on. In the thirteenth frame the referee called a foul, claiming I'd missed the blue. I was not a happy boy, and tried my best to have the call overturned, but to no avail. To this day, I still insist it was not a miss, but no matter. Thorburn went on to win the match 9–8 and retain his title for another year.

After the match we were having a drink upstairs and I was still complaining about the supposed missed blue ball. I got pissed off with Thorburn's attitude about the decision and I blurted out that I thought he was a lucky bastard even to be in the competition at all, let alone win it with the help of a dodgy decision. I said that after all the problems he'd caused with what I called 'the bags of white powder' he shouldn't have been playing. Thorburn did not take kindly to my comments, and the press were within earshot. I thought at one point he was going to smack me one, but he didn't. Anyway, apparently I wasn't as quiet as I should have been and the press boys got their story. It was all over everywhere the next day and Cliff faced a pretty tough time. I can't say I was too sorry. As an interesting aside, three years later Thorburn was fined by the snooker authorities for using coke.

If I was looking forward to the end of 1986, I shouldn't have been. The Tennent's UK Championship was held in Preston at the end of November. I started off well and was behaving, for once. It seemed that the press, the viewers and the paying spectators were all on my side again. There was some controversy about the size of the new pockets, and some of the other players, especially the newer, younger ones, were complaining. Tony Knowles and Stephen Hendry, who was just seventeen at the time, came under fire for daring to say anything about it, but it needed saying. So I held a press conference and reinforced their views, to the dislike of the WPBSA. All we were saying was that the Association hadn't really thought about the impact the new pockets might have on the game. I got a bit carried away and ended up slagging off the authorities. I think they deserved it.

From the press conference I went to the players' room and had a couple more drinks to celebrate my victory over Mike Hallett, possibly getting a bit merry while not being drunk. Anyway, there I was when Paul Hatherell, an official with the WPBSA, asked me to take a urine test. I told him that I had already been tested earlier, but he insisted that I take another one. I argued with him, but he wasn't having any of it. I saw this as a ploy by the Association to discredit me. I didn't want to take the test in case someone doctored the sample to make it look like I was on drugs. If that sounds a bit far-fetched, you have to remember that I was feeling paranoid at the time. It had been a terrible year. Lynn and I were over, Siobhan and I were on and off and the previous twelve months had been full of headline-grabbing incidents. In any case, I did have some justification for feeling picked on because it was unusual for players to be asked to take a test so near to a previous one, especially in the same tournament.

I got up and went to the cubicle where they conducted the tests. The doctor came in and tried to explain what to do, but by this stage I was too far gone. I'd wound myself up so tight I was about to explode, and the poor doctor felt the full force. I told him to fuck off or I would punch his lights out. Not surprisingly, he made a beeline for the door to complain to Hatherell that I had threatened him with a broken glass. That bit wasn't true. I don't know why he said that. I went back to the players' room to get another pint. Ann Yates, who used to help run the tournament, was there and she could see that I was upset about something. She came over and I told her that I felt I was being picked on deliberately and I wanted to see the administrator, Dave Harrison. Ann, very reasonably, tried to convince me that the tests were routine and that there would be no messing with the samples. I told her that I had already given a sample during the tournament, but she tried to explain that that really didn't matter.

I went to find Harrison and as I walked out I lost my footing and tripped, spilling my pint over someone. That just made me even angrier. Harrison took me into the main tournament office and tried to persuade me to give the sample. I was trying to explain to him why I was so upset but he wasn't interested. That got to me as well. I wanted to make some personal calls, but all he kept going on about was the test. At that point, Paul Hatherell came through the door.

As soon as I saw him, my last ounce of self-control disappeared. I was no longer reasoning properly. I grabbed him by his tie and head-butted him. A nasty gash opened up above Hatherell's left eye and I could see blood. The shock of what I'd done suddenly hit me. A security guard, who had been standing outside the room, and Dave Harrison, who was staring in disbelief, both reacted quickly but they couldn't have stopped the head-butt. It took no more than a second. I wish they had been able to. They both grabbed me, but I shrugged the two of them off and went back to the players' room.

Del Simmons asked me what the matter was but I was so pent up I couldn't explain. John Virgo tried to calm me as well, but I was a man possessed. I don't really remember everything that happened from then on. The red mist was blinding my eyes and my memory. I'm told, among other things, that I punched a door. I'm sure it's true. I went out into the corridor and saw a pile of plates so I started smashing them. Eventually, another security guard grabbed me around the waist and tried to calm me down.

The police were called and took me away. I offer no excuses for it all now. Whether I was having some kind of a breakdown or not, I don't know. All I do know is that there is no justification for taking out my frustrations on innocent parties. Of all the damage done that night, the most damage was done by me to myself. I don't question that I deserved to be dragged over the coals by the Association for what happened, but I do believe their retribution was far in excess of my actual crime. There was little or no effort made to take anything into consideration, no trying to find out why I had done it. This was only an opportunity to do some Higgins bashing. I was told I could continue in the competition and that I would be dealt with later on. I knew it would be severe.

After Ronnie O'Sullivan walked out of the UK Championship in December 2006 – and I am not saying that is the equivalent of the physical assault I was guilty of – he offered as a reason that he was under tremendous personal pressure and apologised for it. The WPBSA of today, under the chairmanship of Sir Rodney Walker, took a different view from the one the Association would have taken in my day. Sir Rodney said that before they would even consider any charges, he would be asking his colleagues to see if there was any help the Association could offer Ronnie in his hour of need. That is the right approach to this kind of behaviour in the initial stages, and not the kind of knee-jerk reaction the WPBSA used to jump to in the bad old days.

The police let me go and I went back to Delveron House, with Howard Kruger in tow. The next day the press were camped out on the doorstep. I knew the WPBSA would be giving their version of events, so I decided to give my own press conference. I put on my long sheepskin coat and a rather stylish fur hat, and strolled outside with Howard to give the Higgins side of the story. I pleaded with the public through the press to pressurise the WPBSA into not banning me. 'If they ban me from playing, the interest will leave with me,' I told them in a vain hope they would listen.

Halfway through the questions my mobile phone rang. I say 'mobile' phone but that would indicate that it was easily transported. This thing was one of those huge house-brick numbers. Weighed a ton. Anyway, I hit the button and holding the thing to my ear I just said, 'Business is fine, send more money,' then clicked off. The press boys loved it. It was pure Alex Higgins. As I turned to go back inside the house, a voice shouted out to me, 'Alex, could you live without snooker if they banned you for life?'

Quick as a flash I retorted, 'Could snooker live without me?' Now that may sound arrogant, but time did eventually tell us the answer to that one.

I was knocked out in the semi-finals by Davis. My slice of the prize money was £18,000. I was going to be thankful for that cash when I learned, five months later, what my punishment was going to be – an unprecedented £12,000 fine and banned from five tournaments. The police dealt with me a lot quicker than the WPBSA. I was charged with assault and criminal damage, and given a conditional discharge and fined £200 at a court hearing in January, with an additional £50 fine for the damaged door. I believe that has been preserved by the staff at the hall.

I was on TV-AM a week or so after the disciplinary committee hearing to promote my recently released video *I'm No Angel*. The presenter asked me, inevitably I suppose, about the ban and the incident itself.

'What are your feelings about the head-butt now, Alex?'

'Well, it was the most expensive head-butt in history. Cost me about £80,000.'

Never a truer word was spoken in jest . . .

19

Feeling the pinch

•

Even after the head-butting incident I was still invited to play in charity golf events. It seemed my celebrity hadn't been diminished by the events of 1986. I remember one such event, in Northern Ireland, when I was feeling particularly low. I shouldn't really have gone, because when I'm in that sort of mood I can get myself into trouble. I didn't want to let the organisers down, though, so I went along.

The round itself actually proved to be great fun – lots of spectators, lots of photos, lots of autographs, everyone with a smile on their face. Mine was a little painted on, I guess, but smile I did. When the round was over I headed to the clubhouse to pick up my taxi to take me to my sister Anne's. I was on the phone to her when this fella came over to me. God knows how he recognised me with that gigantic telephonic monstrosity hiding three-quarters of my face. I saw him, but presumed he'd walk past me once he realised I was talking. Instead, he just stood there and stared at me, trying to get my attention.

'What is your problem? Can't you see I am on the phone? It's a private conversation,' I said.

'I'm a big fan, Alex, can I have your autograph?'

He obviously hadn't listened to me at all.

'Fuck off,' I said and walked away.

I know I was rude, but sometimes the public don't recognise

the difference between private and public space, and when that happens, it is not surprising that people can react. I am not a product or a pet to be patted and fussed over all the time. To my mind, he was the one being rude, so I gave him some of it back.

Now, the thing about this particular incident is that it came back to haunt me years later. I was at Manchester airport one day and Eamonn Holmes, the former GMTV presenter, was there waiting for a flight to Belfast. I needed to get to Belfast quickly and there were no seats available. So I went up to him and asked him to sell me his ticket. I even offered him three times the price of the flight.

'Alex, I would gladly let you have the ticket and wait for the next flight, but I don't want your money. All I would want is an autograph for my dad,' he said.

'That's great,' I replied. 'Do you have a pen and paper?'

He turned on me. 'Too late,' he said angrily. 'Now you fuck off.'

It turned out that the guy at the golf course was his dad. Fair play to him. He got his revenge and kept his seat.

As I mentioned in the previous chapter, what with the Medati black-eye fiasco and the manner in which both Del Simmons and I handled it, it was clear that the time was right for us finally to go our separate ways. Around then, the beginning of 1986, Howard Kruger strengthened his fledgling snooker management organisation – Framework – by recruiting Jimmy White, although I don't think Jim ever actually signed a contract with them. Kruger seemed to want to establish a stable that could compete with Barry Hearn's 'Matchroom Boys', but it became clear quite quickly that Framework was never going to be a match for the 'Romford Mafia', as Jimmy and I used to call them. Most things seemed to go their way around that time, perhaps best epitomised by the relative chart success of two competing singles. The matchroom crowd put out 'Snooker

Loopy' which reached No. 6 while the Whirlwind and the Hurricane (with a little help from Kirk Stevens who was only there because I'd arranged for him to get a lift down to London with me) weighed in with 'The Wanderer'. Best not to ask where we featured in the Hit Parade. It was all a bit of fun as far as I was concerned and the fact that we didn't take the *Top of the Pops* studio by storm didn't put me off recording at all. In fact, a few years later Ollie Reed, myself and Reg Presley from the Troggs recorded 'Wild Thing'. Can't imagine why we thought that was an appropriate song for us . . .

It seems Kruger had got involved in snooker after meeting Tony Knowles in Majorca in 1985 when they both happened to be staying at the same hotel. Kruger's father, Jeff, was a big-time music promoter. When Kruger took over his dad's role in the company, he saw potential in sports management and had already been involved with various athletes.

Tony was getting some stick in the press about his supposed bedroom habits, so Kruger put his PR people on it. They went to work and cleverly managed to make light of it all. Tony was impressed enough to ask Kruger to manage him and so Framework was formed.

I have to say I was impressed with Kruger when I first met him. Alongside the music management – and it was an impressive line-up that he was involved with, including Wham!, The Jacksons, Glen Campbell and Joan Armatrading – he also had sports management experience with swimmer Sharron Davies and ice-skaters Torvill and Dean. Snooker may have been new to him, but I felt that if he could bring some of that showbiz pizzazz to the sport, then we were all in for a better time. It didn't turn out as I'd hoped.

In the spring of 1986, having spoken to Jimmy White about how things were going for him, I was impressed enough with the

Framework set-up to buy out the remaining year of my contract with Del and sell it on to Kruger. It was sporting handshakes all round and looking forward to a new beginning. Again.

I wasn't sorry to see the back of 1986 and, as usual, when the new year came around I was determined to make a better fist of it. Getting older wasn't on my mind. I had a young girlfriend in Siobhan (God, I loved that woman), and I thought of myself as being in my late twenties I suppose, although in 1987 I was going to be thirty-eight. Siobhan and I were happy flitting between Delveron House and her place. We both felt we had enough space whenever we needed it. The year 1987 was set up well.

At the Benson & Hedges Masters in February I got to the final and felt good. Kruger was there with me and, to give him his due, he made me feel like a true professional. We stayed in a good hotel close to the venue, Wembley, so there would be no hassle getting to the tournament. Whenever I walked out of the hotel doors to make my way to my matches I could feel a more positive reaction from the fans. They were seeing me in a different light, smart again, sharp again and finally acting like a true A-list celebrity. That is what we had all become, celebrities but, unlike some of today's celebrities, we had a talent that truly entertained the masses.

I played some magnificent snooker in that final and Dennis Taylor could see what he thought was his winner's cheque slipping away. However, it all went wrong at the end. I had a chance to play a snooker behind the brown or go for the jugular and pot the blue. I chose the jugular option to kill off the match but as the cue ball struck the blue it took a slight kick. There is no explanation for moments like that – I'd played the shot well, the white ending up exactly where I wanted it. But the blue was knocked off course by the kick and missed the pocket by quarter of an inch. And that was it. My luck deserted me entirely.

Feeling the pinch

Taylor took the fourteenth, fifteenth, sixteenth and seventeenth frames with hardly a break over 40 and walked away with the title. As the final ball dropped, the first person to come over to me was Jimmy White, who had been watching in the audience. 'I can't believe what I've just seen Alex. I feel gutted for you mate,' he said, giving me a huge hug. I couldn't believe it either. I was shattered that I'd lost. I shook Taylor's hand, congratulated him, went through the presentation ceremony graciously, and then Jimmy and I went for a few drinks to drown my sorrows. Good lad that Jimmy.

I didn't have much luck in the Irish Masters, either, and was fined for an outburst at tournament director Kevin Norton. Then I was reported for being drunk and abusive at an exhibition match in Newmarket. At least I did win something that year. Taylor, Eugene Hughes and I successfully defended the snooker World Cup for Ireland. It was our third straight win.

In my view, the incident in Newmarket shouldn't have had anything to do with the WPBSA. It was much ado about nothing, but the facts of what happened aren't important. It was just another row. My point here is that I could never fathom why the WPBSA were so interested in its members' behaviour at private functions after matches. They should have been protecting their members, not going after them. The WPBSA were getting totally out of control with more and more rules, and no opportunities for members to complain or discuss these issues. It was a case of do as we say, or you're out. Hearings were held behind closed doors and there was no right of appeal. I wasn't the only one getting restless over their behaviour, but it seems that I was the only one brave enough to try to do something about it.

None of the Matchroom Boys were interested in saying anything. Why would they? Nothing they did ever seemed to make the press, and when they did do something wrong I always felt they weren't as harshly treated as I was. They would say that was because my misdemeanours were of a more serious nature, and that may be a fair point, but I can't help feeling that the fact that their manager also sat on the board can't have been a disadvantage to them.

Lynn was putting pressure on me, which I didn't need. She wasn't happy with the maintenance money I was paying, and when the payments started to get further apart she threatened me with court action. Howard Kruger told me he'd look after things, which was a relief. I didn't need to be worrying about making the payments to Lynn. I wanted to be concentrating on my game. The taxman had other ideas. It seemed I was way behind with my tax, and interest and penalties were accumulating fast, so as I got out of debt with Lynn, I seemed to be stepping into more of the same with the Queen's representatives.

My ban kicked in after the 1987 World Championship and it was having a devastating effect on my ranking. I couldn't accumulate points because I couldn't play in the qualifying tournaments. It seemed that I was heading for an enforced retirement from the sport I loved so much.

I was playing some exhibition matches but the money wasn't coming in and Lynn wasn't getting her payments. She took me to court and they threatened to lock me up for contempt. I kept telling them that my managers were dealing with it.

Lynn and I got divorced in 1988 and it was during that summer that Lynn did her piece in the *Daily Star*, leading to yet another huge row between Siobhan and me. My private life was in bad shape and so was my snooker. I got thumped by Tony Drago in the first round of the World Championship – and that was the best I'd played for quite a number of months.

At a tournament in Glasgow I was asked again to provide a urine sample, and thinking this was more of what had happened in Preston the year before, I insisted that the press be present to witness it. I was reported to the WPBSA by Ian Doyle, who managed Stephen Hendry, for abusive behaviour, insulting Glasgow and just about everything else. The WPBSA were at it again as far as I was concerned. Doyle was a board member and it looked to me as though he was out to get me. I vowed that one day I would expose these people for what they were.

Siobhan persuaded me to get some help with my temper and anxiety problems. I looked into hypnosis but it wasn't going to work. I am too strong minded. I had some tests done and the results were encouraging. I didn't have anything mentally or physically wrong with me, I was just highly strung. I'm sure a few of my enemies would have liked to see me 'highly strung up'.

I did, however, learn a lot about stress relief and being in control of your body from a friend of mine. He taught me breathing exercises and about the beneficial effects of pressure points on the body and how flexing and re-flexing certain muscles can be calming. I know it eventually helped my temper, which is saying a lot given the pressure I was under, and I've used the technique to good effect ever since.

The festive period was not far away and I was thinking about what I could do on Christmas day to appease Lynn and see the kids when a summons arrived ordering me to the high court for failing to pay maintenance. That was a shock. I was £14,000 in arrears. I kept on telling the judge and Lynn that Kruger was supposed to be making the payments from my earnings, but it all fell on deaf ears. The judge said I was looking at six weeks in jail.

I didn't fancy tucking into turkey with trimmings and pulling a cracker with 'Mugsy the blagger' in Strangeways prison, so I went out and managed to get £1,000 to appease the court and Lynn, with a promise that I would sort out the rest in a matter of weeks. It was around that time that I got into that fight with

Siobhan when I threw the ashtray. How she ever let me back for Christmas I'll never know.

The only real consolation I had at the year's end was that the taxman agreed to me making payments in stages on my out-standing bill – which, by then, was £100,000. I wouldn't be made bankrupt as they had threatened. That would have been bad because they would have been able to snatch any money I earned before even Kruger got his hands on it. Kruger and I finally parted company when he decided to sell my contract to David Hay, the ex-footballer. Hay had a company that managed sports stars and it looked a good move. However, after my shenanigans leading up to Christmas got into the papers, he shied off and it looked as if I would be managing myself again. Every cloud has a silver lining, though, and that's when I found mine – Doug Perry. I got to love him like a brother. He was probably the most honest and sincere manager I ever had. I wish he was still alive and I miss him so much.

As far as I was concerned, Kruger owed me money, even though he no longer represented me. He assured me I would get as soon as it came in. I'm still waiting.

20

My days in court

•

Howard Kruger was director of a company called Framework Management which ended up owing me and other parties a total of £460,000.

In 1989 I brought an action in the high court in London against Framework Management, as did other creditors. The case was unopposed and the company was wound up, but they only admitted owing me £21,000 in earnings that they had received on my behalf. I was actually suing for £51,000 and change. To my reckoning, those that ran the company should have been brought to court as well.

As far as I was concerned, money that I had earned, and was rightfully mine, had been misused by the company. That isn't right by anyone's standards. It was my money and they received it on my behalf. Sure, they took their agreed percentage, but that is all they should have kept. The law is an ass, someone once said, and they were right, from my experiences anyway.

I believe that the WPBSA behaved badly regarding the whole sorry mess as well. It's no secret that I have had a long-running feud with the WPBSA and throughout this book I have highlighted some very serious matters that I feel need to be talked about, but do not for one minute think that I'm whingeing at the loss of the thousands and thousands of pounds I paid them in fines or the bans I received. It's not that at all. I might not have agreed with all those decisions, but my complaints go deeper, and were, in my opinion, and the opinion of many others in private, fully justified. You will be the judge and jury of all this, and by the time you finish this book, I am confident that you will agree with most, if not all, of my grievances.

At the time of the 1989 court case, Howard Kruger was sitting on the board of the WPBSA. At no time did they ask him to stand down, at no time did they think to have a meeting about what the court action was doing to the reputation of snooker, or of the WPBSA and its members. As far as I know, in English law it is not deemed right and just for anyone to sit on a board of directors, a committee or a court bench while a conflict of interest is present. If you are an athlete and you fail a drugs test, you will have to appear before a committee of some kind, be it British Athletics, the IOC or some other body. Have you ever heard of a sports person's manager sitting on a disciplinary committee, especially when their own client is up before that committee? The answer is no.

I asked the committee to dismiss Kruger for bringing the sport into disrepute. That was something I knew about. I'd been fined for it many times, often just for swearing at people. This matter was much more serious than that. From my perspective, I felt Kruger had allowed his company to let players down badly. There he was, sitting as a member of the board of the WPBSA, the organisation that was meant to look after snooker players, and he had done anything but. That's why we were in dispute. Surely the public would see that as not being right. How could a disrepute hearing be refused? What right had the board got to dismiss my request for an investigation into Kruger? The WPBSA was, after all, my association, not his.

They wouldn't hear of it initially. Kruger stayed on the board and, not only that, but his other company, The Travel Bureau

Ltd, was awarded the contract for making all the arrangements for world-ranking tournaments in the Far East. The board told me to my face that the matter of Kruger and the players was a private matter between us and him. So how come when I got involved in that row in Newmarket in 1987 at a private party, I was fined for bringing the game into disrepute?

I wasn't going to let the Kruger matter go, however. I felt strongly that his actions had brought the game into disrepute and I kept at the WPBSA to hold a meeting to address my grievances. Eventually, a meeting was scheduled to take place at the end of November 1989. But Kruger was no fool. A couple of days before the disciplinary hearing, he resigned from the WPBSA. That pretty much put paid to my plans and, although he was found guilty, as I always knew he would be, there wasn't really any action that could be taken against him as he was no longer on the board. He'd escaped me again. I came away with no scalp.

I was disappointed with the Kruger situation. That feeling of being let down was compounded when I heard that, the very night that Kruger was found guilty of bringing the game into disrepute, John Virgo had gone to the opening of Kruger's new club in Brighton. He was there to promote the opening, to do trick shots, that sort of thing. I don't think he should have gone. Where was the solidarity of fellow professionals? Perhaps it was more of a case of solidarity to WPBSA board members (even ex-ones) as I think Virgo was on the board at the same time as Kruger. If the roles had been reversed, I would have refused to go.

Howard Kruger came to the fore again in recent years when he started dating the estranged wife of George Best. I told Alex about my dealings with him and his company. Alex Best is a lovely, charming lady and I felt it was my duty to say something to her. After that, what she does with her life is obviously up to her. Kruger then became involved in an awful sex case. He was convicted, but the conviction was quashed on appeal. I wouldn't wish that nightmare on anyone. Despite my personal feelings about him, based on our business dealings, to be found guilty of something of which you are innocent has to be one of the worst things that can happen to you. I've recently heard that he and Alex are now engaged, and I wish them the best, although that may sound strange, but I care for Alex and want her to be happy.

I also had to sort out the matter of financial arrangements with Lynn. She instigated the proceedings, not out of malice but necessity. She had to look out for the kids and their future. I had some investments in a couple of industrial units, which we divided up. There was also a tax break investment I made years earlier, which involved a forest. I had hoped to be able to pick out a special branch on my own tree and make the ultimate cue from it, a one-off. I had already bought Lynn a house near her parents for her and the kids, so she had no mortgage to pay. On top of that I paid maintenance, which had been sorted out earlier in the proceedings, when she applied for custody of the kids. I got reasonable access, which at first was always in the presence of the nanny or someone else. I bet no judge has ever had to accept that when they got divorced, but I had to and it broke my heart. I had to endure the humiliation of a stranger seeing my children more often than I could, the same stranger who would tell me when my time was up. I have had a good relationship with Lauren and Jordan over the years. We've had our fallings out, but what family doesn't? They all supported me when I had cancer and I believe it brought us closer together. I still wish I had done it all differently, but I can't turn back the clock, I can't be someone I'm not.

My next spate of legal action came against the WPBSA. I discussed the merits of the case with my solicitor, Robin Falvey, and he agreed to take it on. This was in 1997. I must have had a fairly reasonable claim because I was granted legal aid at one point to pursue the case through the courts. The main contention against the WPBSA was a procedural issue regarding the manner in which they dealt with me at a disciplinary hearing in 1994, which centred on my supposed refusal to take a drugs test after my defeat by Ken Doherty at the World Championship that year. I was very unhappy about being picked on again, and more so about how the test was conducted. I was 'escorted' from one toilet to the next – because each one in turn was occupied – and I felt degraded by the whole episode. When I eventually gave the sample, the bottle was broken. I was accused of smashing it deliberately, which was rubbish. Anyway, that July I was up before the disciplinary committee, with Robin conducting my defence, and he was brilliant. The case was thrown out. We thought that was it, but oh, no. Out of the blue, the WPBSA came up with two more 'offences' that hadn't been mentioned. I'd shown a packet of cigarettes of a brand other than Embassy at a press conference at the championship and that was against the sponsorship deal. I was also charged with the destruction of the urine sample. The two new incidents were introduced with no warning. We couldn't defend ourselves because we had no time to prepare. Needless to say, I was found guilty. Totally unbelievable. Our 1997 case, then, concerned the manner in which those proceedings were dealt with by the WPBSA. There was also a side issue regarding the additional legal costs I had incurred at a hearing in 1992, which concerned my supposed foul and abusive language against Stephen Hendry in the UK Open in 1991. But, as I said, that matter was not my main bone of contention.

There was a lot of to-ing and fro-ing of letters, and it dragged on and on. Eventually, in 1999, Robin wrote to tell me that the

WPBSA had offered to settle the matter in amicable terms. The offers was as follows:

1. I was offered the sum of £30,000 in respect of the stress caused by the false charges and the hearings (it was conceded that the offer could be increased).
2. That my complaints against board members would be dealt with.
3. That my wasted costs in preparing, with my legal team, a defence and cross-examination, would be paid to me.
4. That the 1994 hearing would be overturned.
5. That I would be offered some financial assistance towards any medical treatment that I may wish.
6. That I would be provided with accommodation at the expense of the WPBSA, with an option to purchase the property after an agreed period of time.

The letter from Robin went on to say that there were also discussions to invite me to certain tournaments. I refused the terms at a meeting in Manchester. I realise that it would have saved me a lot of hassle, but I felt it was a petty offer and I wanted my day in court. I wanted a platform from which I could say everything that I thought about the WPBSA. I wanted to face them in court with the press there to report it all. I could say what I liked about the members and the organisation, and there was nothing they could have done to stop me. Not even a libel or defamation action was possible. In English law, anything said in a courtroom is privileged and no actions can arise from any statement, whether it's true or not. That covers the press, too. Any evidence, no matter how explosive, can be published in a paper so long as it is reported as proceedings in a court case.

It wasn't to be, though. Having made the offer, the WPBSA

legal team knew that we had to inform the legal aid board so that they could decide whether aid should continue if the offer was refused. I was in a dilemma. It was a lot to risk but I still felt it should have been a much higher figure on the table. I was advised to accept but refused. I wanted to hold my ground. The legal aid was withdrawn and other solicitors got involved but ultimately nothing came of it. The whole thing was then interrupted by my having cancer and I never got back to it over the years.

It is strange how the fates – or the gods, however you want to view it – can play with you. The year 1989 was terrible in so many respects – court cases, financial worries and worst of all, Siobhan and I splitting up – and yet, whatever powers there are out there deemed it appropriate to grant me what I regard as the greatest snooker victory of my entire career. I've mentioned it previously, the Benson & Hedges Irish Masters at Goffs, where I beat Stephen Hendry 9–8 in a pulsating final. The prize money was welcome, of course, and lifting the trophy was very satisfying. But the real reason I rate this triumph above all others, even the two World Championships, is because of the Blonde. Siobhan Kidd. I'd never seen her so happy. I think back now, to the moment that she came down and hugged me after I'd won, and tears fill my eyes. She was the driving force for that victory. I did it all for her and she knew that and was so proud of me. That made me feel a thousand feet tall. Like I could walk on water. Fly though the air. Just the look on her face.

Within months, we were finished forever. Too much damage had been done between us, impossible to repair. As was my heart.

21

Going out in a baize of glory

•

1989 refused to go quietly. After the court appearances and breaking up with Siobhan, the year ended with a splash. I went out to Dubai to compete in the inaugural Duty Free Classic and one evening I was in the bar of the hotel, talking to a few journalists. I was asked my opinion of young Danny Fowler. I said something like 'I don't know him very well, but he seems a nice lad. I'm just not sure he's got what it takes to make the top grade'. It was that innocuous, but his manager took exception to my comments.

He was quite a volatile character and he marched over to demand an apology. 'For what?' I asked. He then grabbed me and dragged me outside, demanding that I apologise. By this point I was wound up by his behaviour and told him there was nothing I had to apologise for. We had a bit of a scuffle and the next thing I knew I was in the pool and he had jumped in after me. He held me under the water for what felt like minutes (but was probably only a few seconds) until I wriggled free. There was a moment when I truly thought he was going to drown me but I realise he was just making his point – in his own unique way.

That wasn't the only incident on that trip. The very next day I got into a fight with a journalist. I don't think it applies now, but over the years, there was something I noticed with the press when they went on trips like this one to Dubai. It seemed to me that some of them didn't actually enjoy sitting watching snooker. They'd much rather have been in a nice bar somewhere, having a few drinks and probably trying to pull some birds. What they used to do was delegate one of their part to actually attend the days play (probably the person who pulled the short straw) and the rest would disappear happily to a watering hole. After the match the journalist who had actually watched it would distribute his piece amongst the rest of them and they'd tinker with it sufficiently to make it their own.

I don't think that applied in this particular journalist's case and that wasn't what I had a go at him for. What had annoyed me was his report of my match a couple of days previously. He'd got the score wrong and I thought that was sloppy. I pointed this out to him when we were in the hotel disco. Everyone had been having a few drinks that evening and for some reason what I said to him sparked him off. I might have been winding him up a bit, I accept that, but there was no reason for him to lose it like he did. A fight erupted . . . well, when I say 'fight' but that wuold indicate it was a two-way thing. I'm ten stone dripping wet, and this bloke was about 6'4'', so it really was all one-way traffic. We spilled out into the reception area and were eventually split up by one of the doormen, who knew me from my previous trips, and Jim Chalmers, another pro player. My journalist 'pal' disappeared off to bed at that point, as did Jim, who had hurt his foot in the fracas. I was buzzing. The adrenalin was flowing through me and I was hyper. Really uptight. In the space of two days I'd been nearly drowned and attacked. I went back to the disco, sat with some of the other players, knocked back a large vodka and orange, and tried to calm down.

I really wanted to call the police and get them involved. I was so angry. I even thought about using some of my connections in Dubai to see if I could get the bloke deported. Not that the incident warranted that in any way, but I was in overdrive. John Spencer talked me down and we agreed that the best thing was to sleep on it all and have a meeting the next morning in my room. To be fair to him, I received an apology the next day and the matter was settled. I'd been there often enough myself and held no grudges. We all agreed that that would be the end of it. And it was.

At the beginning of 1990 my finances were really starting to worry me. The Revenue were threatening to bankrupt me if I didn't pay off the £100,000 I owed in the six-month period I'd agreed, and Lynn, quite rightly, was chasing the maintenance money that I hadn't paid. I needed a cash injection and thankfully that came at the Pearl Assurance British Open where I lifted the runner-up cheque of £45,000, losing to the Canadian Bob Chaperon in the final. I think I'm right in saying that was the biggest prize I've ever won. But going back over all my bank statements is too depressing a thought, so I haven't checked. That would be enough to sober even me up. Along with the money, my second-place spot also did wonders for my ranking. That had slipped so badly that I'd had to go through qualifiers for the 1989 World Championship, and didn't make it. Qualifying for this year's tournament was still a possibility, but to know I was secure for the 1991 championship, because of my position in the Top 16 after the points I'd earned for the British Open, was a real boost. As things turned out, however, I was destined not to play in the competition. And the Open proved to be the high point of the year.

For the 1990 world cup the Northern Ireland team was captained by Dennis Taylor. We got through to the final again, where we lost to the Canadians. I wasn't playing particularly well but, in one frame, I did have a chance to win the prize for the highest break in the tournament. I always play to win, and in this case that meant the team winning. So I opted to ensure I won the frame and didn't worry about trying to put together the big break. Anyway, as far as I was concerned, if one of the Northern Irish team won the £6,000 prize, it would be divided up between us all.

I finished the session and was walking over to my team-mates when Taylor said something like, 'Great, I've still got the highest break.' It was the 'I' that made me see red. To me, that said he wasn't talking about the team in any way. I believed he wanted that £6,000 for himself. I walked up to him and said, 'You're a greedy bastard, Taylor.' That sparked things off between us. We argued and then we argued some more. The row eventually spilled over into the players' lounge, where John Spencer and a few others got involved. Of course, they were supporting their big pal Dennis. I was fighting a one-man battle.

I was getting more and more angry at what I saw as the injustice of what Taylor was proposing to do, and at one point I leaned over to him and snarled, 'Look, you, if I had a gun in my hands, I'd blow your brains out.' That's what I said. So much has been reported and speculated about that moment, but that's what I said. I'm not suggesting for a second it was a nice thing to say, and I do regret it, but at no point did I say that the next time Taylor was in Northern Ireland I would have someone else shoot him.

Taylor claimed things happened very differently, and that is up to him. People have different recollections of events, particularly when the tension is so high. But I have explained exactly how I remember it. It is true that at a press conference after the match I said that I didn't think Taylor was fit to represent his country, but as far as I am concerned I did not threaten him with any form of sectarian violence as was reported at the time. I am well known for being neutral in matters of sectarian differences in the North of Ireland, and I wouldn't have brought it up.

Going out in a baize of glory

Dennis Taylor is from a Catholic background and I, as you know, am from a Protestant background, but neither of us had until that moment ever said anything that mentioned the Troubles. It was a thing that famous people from the North never got involved in. My opinion of Taylor is based on my knowledge of him personally. I have never, and will never, judge anybody on the grounds of their birth, creed or colour. I am a non-political person.

On the advice of Doug Perry, I eventually apologised for any offence I had caused, but Taylor wasn't having any of it. He was out for the kill and made an official complaint to the governing body. Looking back on it now, it is hard to blame him. I don't believe I threatened him in a sectarian manner – but I did say I'd shoot him myself. And that is not acceptable, although it was only done in the heat of the moment, nothing more.

Things then went from bad to worse. In March, I went to see Jordan at the house in Heald Green where Lynn now lived with the kids. It was his birthday and although Lynn came to the door she refused to let me in to see my own son. I'm sorry to say, again, that I lost my temper and ended up rowing with her and the police were called.

I met Taylor again at the Benson & Hedges Irish Masters at Goffs. I was defending my title and was drawn against him in the quarter-finals; it was as if someone up there was having a laugh at our expense. I desperately wanted to beat him and prove to him that I was the better player. I already knew it, I just needed him to know it. He beat me 5–2 and it was a sickening blow. I wanted another crack at him – ideally in the final of the World Championship, which was coming up, for which I'd managed to qualify.

The day of the opening rounds arrived and I was not feeling good. The pressure of Siobhan leaving, my finances, the Taylor incident – it was all getting too much and I was in a form of meltdown. Doug Perry was so worried about me, but could do nothing to help. No one could.

I drew Steve James in the first round and played like an amateur to begin with. By frame 6 the score was 4–1, but the survival instinct kicked in and I pulled back to 5–4 in his favour. I evened the score in the tenth frame, but that was as good as it got. When he potted the final ball to win 10–5 I shook his hand, sat back down and knocked back my vodka. I couldn't seem to get up after that. I didn't want to get up. I just wanted to sit there in the greatest snooker arena in the world and soak up the history, the history that I had helped make. Some audience members stayed on to talk to me, but I wasn't in the mood. I took some drinks off them and waved them farewell. They just went to the back and sat there watching me.

What was I thinking? Just about my life and the paths and roads I had taken, some very good, many bad. Most of all I was thinking about the Blonde. I so desperately wanted to win her back and I'd persuaded myself that winning the World Championship was the way to do it. And now I'd failed. All I wanted was her and it was at that moment I knew I'd lost her for good. When James finished the game off, I realised that was it. I remember ripping off a bracelet that Siobhan had given me that I was wearing for luck. It might sound dramatic, but anyone watching that moment saw my heart finally ripped in two.

Once again, something had to give if I was to have any chance of moving forward. In the past it had been a change of manager, or Lynn, anyone but me. This time I couldn't shift the responsibility. I didn't want to. This time it was me who was going to have to give.

My mind was made up. I went back to the dressing room and tidied myself up. Then I made my way to the press room for the nightly conference. The room was virtually asleep when I got there but it woke excitedly when I arrived. Colin Randle of the WPBSA held open the door for me. Some say that the next thing that happened was that I punched him in the stomach. I thought it was more like a tap on the belly to move him at of the way, but you have thought he had been shot the way he doubled over as I walked through the door.

The press sat up and took notice. They could smell the blood of self-destruction and they were baying for a few drops of it. The speech I made reverberated around the world within the next twenty-four hours. I covered a lot of ground in what I said. I congratulated Steve James on his victory. I suggested I was going to sue certain newspapers for stories they had run about me. I even suggested that I might go abroad to develop the game overseas. But the most important thing I said, the thing that everyone remembers, was, 'I would like to announce my retirement from professional snooker. I am not playing snooker any more because this game is the most corrupt game in the world.'

That was it. I was done. No notes. No rehearsal. I spole for almost 30 minutes. All I could hear were questions being thrown at me as I headed towards the door. 'Is that your final word, Alex?' 'Will you not reconsider, Alex?' I reached the door and Randle stepped aside. This time he wasn't going to be my doorman. I went straight to my hotel room and locked the door, took the phone off the hook and hit the pillow. I went out like a light. My conscience was clear. I believed it then and I believe it now – at that time, when I made my statement, the game was corrupt. Mainly in the way it was run but that wasn't all. Players were deliberately losing on specific scores for betting purposes and I also think a few referees might have been in on some of what was going on – for the promise of free overseas holidays and inducements of that nature. I am not saying that it was corrupt throughout, and I am sure it is very different today, but in the 80s and early 90s I believe corruption existed.

Doug Perry didn't let rip at me. He understood my psyche, and he knew what drove me forward. He was one of the few people in my life at that time who did truly care for me. Doug called a press conference to explain my actions of the night before. He said that it was a culmination of years and years of frustration, mainly fuelled by the way the governing body had been running the game. He went on to explain that my outburst wasn't a whinge, but rather a bringing to the fore the way things were.

In July, I rolled up to the offices of the WPBSA. The hearing concerned various complaints levelled at me for bringing the game into disrepute, and threatening Taylor and 'punching' Colin Randle were top of the list. They considered banning me for life from ever playing in professional snooker tournaments, but they knew that the fans wouldn't stand for that. They couldn't just let me off, either. I had to be punished like the naughty boy I was or others might do the same. In the end, I was banned for the rest of the season from competing in any tournament matches. I was also docked 25 ranking points and had to pay £5,000 in costs.

I accepted the decision and didn't moan about it, although I wasn't pleased. I would have no income from tournaments for the rest of the season, but at least I could make a living doing exhibitions. Doug said that if I wasn't playing the tournament circuit, that would make the public hungry for me at exhibitions, so what I was losing on one hand I would make up on the other hand, hopefully.

While I was making my living playing all and sundry, in some of the best, but mostly some of the worst, snooker clubs in the UK, I was thrown a very exciting lifeline – for a short while anyway – by Barry Hearn of all people. Barry was one of the few people who still knew that I was the face of snooker and he invited me to compete in the £1 million Mita World Masters, which he was promoting for Sky TV and which was supposed to feature all the world champions. This event was not within the remit of the WPBSA and, accordingly, my ban had no effect. Hearn still wouldn't take me under his wing, but he knew my drawing potential. Some of the other players, led mainly by John Spencer I believe, and Stephen Hendry, objected to my taking part. Hendry's stand was basically that he didn't want sponsors dictating who should play in what tournaments. If I was banned from playing snooker, he argued, then I was banned. After all, he went on to say, 'it is our governing body and we must support it', or words to that effect. Hearn spoke to me about the situation and said he didn't think I was being fairly treated but that the decision was mine. I thought about it and decided that the tournament needed the current world champion – Hendry – more than it needed me. I had had enough of all the backbiting anyway, so I told Hearn I wouldn't be coming along. That seemed to sort out the problem and I carried on touring the country.

My ban meant that I had to qualify for tournaments in the 1991/92 season. Not qualifying would be a better description because I failed miserably, over a humiliating couple of months, to make any impression at all in the snooker world. Almost the only tournament I succeeded in making was the Dubai Duty Free in 1991, where I reached the last 16. I had some fun out there at least, when I was invited to lunch by the crew of a ship, which had been active during the Gulf War. The booze was running freely as I was entertained by the crew and we decided to fit in a bit of a show. They decked me out in full uniform and we were all having a ball, especially when I found the control panel for the missiles. I sat there and pushed all the buttons, like a kid at Christmas. The whole mechanism was switched off but the crew were in fits as I aimed the missiles in jest. 'There's one for the WPBSA,' I said as I pushed a button, and another for . . . well, the list was too long to go into here. I'm sure you can guess most of the names. The cheers rang out each time I did it. It was hilarious.

In November, I was drawn against Hendry in the UK Open, the only other tournament I qualified for. He was the young professional who had once admired me, had once been inspired by me. I so wanted to beat him, to make a point about the World Masters event, but more importantly, I needed the ranking points to avoid the horrors of qualification for the next season.

I lost 9–4 and was devastated, but being a good loser is as important as being a good winner, so I walked over and shook his hand and said in a low tone, 'Well done Stephen, but just wait. I'll fuck you the next time. I'll play like the devil.' I'd lost but I didn't want him to think I was defeated. I didn't mean anything by it at all but Stephen was a bit taken aback I think. Anyway, his manager complained to the WPBSA that I had said 'up your arse, you c**t', which I have always denied saying. Needless to say, the case against me was pursued by the authorities and eventually it got to a hearing in August 1992. This was the hearing that the WPBSA later accepted had been handled incorrectly. The charges relating to my supposed comments were all dropped, in my view, confirming my account of what I said.

And so a bad season withered away. I failed to qualify for the World Championship and lost in the final tournament of the year, the Irish Benson & Hedges, held at Goffs, to Ken Doherty. Something was required to raise my spirits.

22

Cancer

●

Goffs is a venue I love, partly because it is fairly easy to get from there to Dublin city centre. Whenever I was playing in Dublin I used to frequent a club called Lillies Bordello, which is the top celebrity club in Ireland. After my defeat by Ken Doherty in the 1992 Benson & Hedges I went into town and ended up at Lillies, which is just off the thoroughfare of Grafton Street. There are three parts to the club. The first part is the public area, which has a long bar and a dance floor, then to one side is the members' bar. Farther down the public bar is a doorway that leads up to another level. This is the piano bar, which is one of the most exclusive rooms in Ireland, frequented by the rich and famous.

It was in the public bar that I got into a conversation with a fella about clothes. He was wearing what can best be described as a hippy outfit – flowery, open necked shirt, bright coloured trousers. That sort of thing. As for me, I was wearing a rather sober, double-breasted suit and tie that I'd bought the previous day for around £80. Louis Copeland quality it certainly wasn't, but this fella took a shine to it. I said I'd do a swap with him if he'd strip down to his undies and run round the inside of the club. He was up for it and when he came back I congratulated him and stripped off myself. A deal is a deal. Everyone was watching us and it was great fun. One minute this bloke looked like something from the Woodstock generation and the next he looked like a very serious business man. As for me, I kind of liked my new peace and love persona – for a few days at least.

That was an interesting few days I had in Dublin. The day before my quick change at Lillies, I'd bumped into Marianne Faithful. Many people will remember Marianne for her well-publicised relationship with Rolling Stone Mick Jagger in the 60s. Well, I'd have a brief, but very energetic, romantic enganglement with Ms Faithful myself, a couple of years earlier. It was in Reading, where it is fair to say she won the 'bout' by a technical knockout in the fourteenth round, leaving the Hurricane flat out on his back after a fantastic night, but I hadn't bumped into her since. I was delighted to have the opportunity to catch up. Her sharp nails had left a long-lasting impression on me, literally. We went for a drink in a pub in Temple Bar, Peter's Pub, which is frequented by actors and showbiz types. She explained that she was in town appearing in the show *The Threepenny Opera* and invited me to come and see it the following evening. I did and loved it. Afterwards we headed out with a few members of the cast to Peter's Pub again for a few beers, before Marianne and I made out excuses and left. We wanted to relive old times, and we did . . . Marianne had to leave very early the next morning and although I haven't seen her romantically since, we remain good friends to this day. The song 'The First Cut is the Deepest' always reminds me of Marianne. I wonder why.

I went back to Manchester the next day as I had to get ready to meet the Queen, I kid you not. I was invited along with most of the living sportsmen who had achieved greatness during the reign of the Monarch – mostly footballers, cricketers and athletes with a few snooker players, including Steve Davis and his missus, Judy. When they saw me they must have had kittens, but I drank nothing all day except the tea on offer, and was the soul of discretion. I wasn't even tempted to give the press the story of the year. Can you imagine it if I had said something outrageous across the lawn to Prince Philip?

I hadn't played in the World Championship since that first-round exit to Steve James in 1990, and although I had to accept that some of the old magic had been lost from my cue, I wasn't ready to hang up my boots quite yet, no matter what I had said in public. I am a fighter and always will be. Thank God, given what was about to happen to me.

I was determined to make a return to the Crucible in 1994 and so I entered the qualifiers in Blackpool, where I needed to win three matches. I had a hard game against Colin Kelly in the first round but managed to beat him, just, 10–9. Next I was drawn against Andrew Cairns, whom I saw off 10–5. All I had to do was win the next match to qualify. I was drawn against Tony Knowles and I was feeling quite good. After the afternoon session I was down 6–3, so I decided I needed a breath of fresh air and a pint in the pub up the road. I was running across the car park, heading towards the pub, and decided to hurdle the wall to get on to the pavement. I say hurdle, but I actually tackled it more like a steeplechaser, aiming to plant my foot squarely on the top of the wall to get over. And I misjudged it. Badly. I came crashing down on my arse. Well, my whole left side to be precise. It was a nasty one and I'm sure I could have broken some bones but fortunately my cue case broke the fall. I knew I'd hurt my arm and my ribs were aching, but I thought I was okay, until I reached the pub that is. I ordered a whisky and water, which I knocked back in one, and as I began to calm down I became aware that my left arm felt very sticky. In the loo I took off my top coat and jacket and had to peel my shirt off to assess the damage. I was covered in blood and as I washed it away in the sink I looked at the cut and realised that it was my bone that I could see. That gave me quite a dizzy turn I can tell you. I knew there was no time to go to casualty to get it looked at so I headed back to the B&B I was staying in and administered my own first aid, bandaging myself up. I was friendly with the owners and they kindly washed my silk shirt, which I knew would dry quickly, giving me just enough time to get back for the evening session.

No one was any the wiser about my mishap when I entered the arena and I played out of my skin. By about the fourth last frame my wound was weeping blood and I noticed some flecks dripping on to the green baize. Strange the things you remember, it looked brown to me. I refused to let the blood distract me and I concentrated on winning, and win I did, 10–9 to qualify for Sheffield. I showed the press the cut afterwards. 'There you see, I do bleed, I am human,' I jokingly told them.

Bloodied I might have been, but I was going to be back at Sheffield. I was determined to do well and make a big impact. I think it is fair to say I achieved the latter.

I entered the arena sporting a rather fetching fedora, tipped my hat to the crowd – and lost to Ken Doherty. During the game I felt that the referee, John Williams it was, was standing too close to me. I was livid. As I've said before, that sort of behaviour annoys me so much when I am trying to play. I kept catching him out of the corner of my eye and couldn't concentrate. But he refused to budge. Williams' behaviour really put me off my game, it was very distracting. Ken was the worthy winner, there's no doubt, but I don't think he would have had a four frame margin if it hadn't been for Williams. Although I was out in the first round, I thought I'd acquitted myself pretty well, and as I told the press after the match I would be back better and stronger the following year. Only thing is, I wasn't. I never played in the final stages of World Championship again.

As for making a big impact, it wasn't merely the natty headgear that did that. You'll remember that this was the tournament where I was once again accused of abusing one of the WPBSA officials and smashing my urine sample after I once again was chosen for a drugs test.

And so the 1990s drifted along. There were some good times to be had and some good friends stood by me. A couple of years before Doug Perry's devastating death in late 1996, we were in a bookies, losing, when two big fellas came in and recognised me. We got chatting and it turned out they were minders for Lennox Lewis, the boxer.

'He only lives just up the road, man. Why don't you come along with us for a game of pool. The big man's just chilling today.'

Now I love boxing. And I loved the way Lewis approached the game so I jumped at the chance. 'You're on. Doug, let's get moving. We can win it all back tomorrow.'

The two of us had a great time. Lennox didn't recognise me at first but when I started shooting some pool, it clicked into place. I played a few games with the minders (and lost) and with Lennox. Then his mother came in and persuaded us all to have one of her Jamaican cocktails. It was pretty lethal stuff but it sure helped me play better pool after knocking it back.

I was so excited about meeting the great man. He was a gent, and signed an autograph for me and some extras to take to my boxing-mad friends. It was a genuine pleasure to spend time with the heavyweight champion of the world. A bad day at the bookies had turned into a day to remember, a day that Doug and I talked about many times afterwards. I just wish I'd kept the recipe for that cocktail.

In 1997 Ken Doherty and Louis Copeland showed what good people they are when they got together and organised a benefit night for me in Belfast. I played Ken and he beat me; it was just after he won the World Championship title. They raised £10,000 and Louis said he would see that I spent it right. I didn't, as it went mostly the way of nearly all my money – in effect, handed over to the bookies.

Then, in June 1998, my world changed. No, 'changed' isn't the right expression. Turned upside down? Blown apart? There is no expression that is adequate. I was diagnosed with cancer. I have smoked cigarettes most of my life and, like all other smokers, I never really thought about the health issues of it. Even when Roy Castle died and there was all that publicity about his getting cancer from breathing in secondary smoke, it never dawned on me that I would get the disease. Be honest with me now, if you are a smoker, have you ever really sat down and considered you may get cancer and die from it? I first got a sore throat that wouldn't go away early in the year. Typical of me and most smokers, I paid it no attention, until eventually I just had to do something about it. The tickly cough was driving me crazy.

I was living in Manchester at the time and had some tests at the hospital there. Somehow I just knew what the results were going to show, but I hoped against hope that I was wrong. As I waited for the hospital to call me to let me know that the tests were back, I just kept thinking 'This is it Alex. You are going to die.' I couldn't stop myself. I was frightened. It was the most agonising period of my life.

It was cancer. Cancer of the palate and throat that had spread to my neck nodes. When the doctor told me it felt like he'd slapped me in the face. More than that. Smacked me with a sledgehammer. Everyone in Manchester was fantastic but I knew I had to get back home, back to Belfast, for my treatment. I remember telling Anne and Jean about the results and that I was coming back for treatment. I remember Jean saying 'Come home

Sandy, love. Come home and we'll get through this together. Don't worry, we're here for you and we love you. We won't let anything bad happen to you.'

So in July I started a daily course of radiotherapy that was to last seven weeks. It was horrible. That is the only way to describe it. Truly horrible. I was going through so much pain, I couldn't eat, the weight – what there was of it – was falling off me. But I had to endure it. My life was in the balance. Anne visited everyday and Jean, who can't drive, came when she could. Isobel, in Australia, was on the phone all the time, checking up on how I was doing. Sending encouragement and love. It was those three girls who got me through it.

The treatment finished towards the end of August and I moved into a flat in Drumard Park, Lisburn, that Anne and Jean had arranged for me. I am a very private person and didn't want to be a burden on anyone, so living on my own suited me. I could just about manage it, with the support of my sisters. Lynn, Lauren and Jordan also visited and I was very grateful to them. We cried a lot, tears of happiness and sadness at the years gone by, and I promised my kids I'd get through whatever else the cancer might throw at me, and I'd get better. Having them all there meant so much to me.

But even though the radiotherapy was over, and I thanked God I didn't have to face going through that every day, I continued to feel dreadful. I still couldn't eat and the pain, the dreadful pain, was constant. Eventually it became too much for me and I was readmitted to hospital, for four days of pain relief. That helped but the way my throat felt, with the glands on the left side so swollen, meant I knew I was still in trouble.

I was referred to another doctor who examined me immediately and admitted me into the Royal Victoria Hospital. The nodes in my neck were so enlarged that they had to be removed.

If the diagnosis of cancer and the radiotherapy had terrified me, the thought of this operation was ten times worse. I had lost so much weight and I was terribly under nourished, that I didn't think my body would take it. Alex Higgins doesn't just give in and admit defeat, though, so I refused to say my goodbyes to everyone, but I remember lying in that operating theatre, waiting to go to sleep, thinking that I would never wake up. There was many people I would miss, family, friends, strangers even who come along and shake my hand. I didn't think I would see any of them again.

And I was right to worry. It was touch and go. My doctor refers to it as a 'stormy post-op period'. That has been the weather front of my life. And it was nearly the one of my death. Apparently I was actually administered the last rites at one stage. But to everyone's amazement, I pulled through. Obviously, or it would be tricky to be writing this now. I stayed in hospital for over a week after the operation and I received the best news possible while I was there – while removing the nodes they had done a thorough examination of my throat and the results of the pathology report showed that there was no residential tumour. The world was going to have to put up with me for a while longer.

I was still in a bad way but at least the danger was over. I know I should have quit smoking at this point but I just couldn't. The stress of the previous five months had been so dreadful that I found I needed cigarettes more than ever to help calm my nerves, and a pint of Guinness was just the right thing to soothe my throat and give me some relief from the burning pain of the operation. The powerful painkillers that I was prescribed also helped, although they could put me into a sort of a trance. I wouldn't know what was real and what wasn't. At times I'd wake up from a nice dream, feeling positive, only to see the bottle of pills on my bedside table and the reality would come crashing down around me again. So the pills, the smokes and the Guinness all played their part in my recovery, but what really got me better was Jean, Anne and Isobel. Their help, support and belief in me during those dark times was what made the difference. I can't thank them enough. I hope they know how I feel about all three of them.

Alongside my sisters, my friends also played a huge part in my recuperation. Cecil Mason would come round and help out Jean and Anne, and I received so many calls from people I had met over the years. For instance Ollie Reed and Josephine would ring every couple of days. Ollie was always his usual self and he would tell me all about his latest project or what he was doing to the house. At the time he was in negotiations to appear in the film *Gladiator* with Russell Crowe. He was so excited about it. He said it was being filmed in Malta and I should come out so we could show them Aussies how real men drink.

Ollie would have me hooting with laughter as he went on about my cancer, he had such a way about him. He could say the most terrible things to you, but he never made you feel that he was actually insulting you. It was a knack he had. Ollie would tell me that I couldn't die till at least the end of 1999, because he was far too busy to come to my funeral till then. Little did we know that in the not-too-distant future I would be going to his funeral. I miss Ollie very much, as does everyone who has ever had the privilege of meeting him.

I also got calls from Jimmy White, Ken Doherty and so many others. Those people don't have any idea how much those calls meant to me. When you are recovering from an illness as deadly as cancer, it is very easy to feel isolated and alone. You feel that no one can possibly understand what cancer really means, unless they have had it. Those calls from these famous, and let's face it, very busy people, often meant the difference between a good day and a shitty day.

Jimmy and Ken were on the blower virtually every day. Sometimes I couldn't talk to them as my throat was so sore, but they would still tell my sisters to give me the phone. Then Jimmy would proceed to tell me, in that typical London accent of his, some new joke he had heard, or he would talk about something he had been up to that week. I used to be in stitches and pain at the same time, but I wouldn't have changed it for the world. It is nice to be thought of so much that people will go out of their way to make sure they let you know it.

As I got better and stronger, I began to come to terms with the fact that I wouldn't ever be as strong and articulate as I had been in the past, that cancer really had changed my life. It is so demoralising to look in the mirror and see your former healthy frame reduced to a pathetic bag of skin and bones. I had aged a hundred years in just a few months and it was scary to say the least. What a mess I was in. I often used to say to myself, 'Alex, you've got into big trouble this time kiddo, big trouble.' I was glad that Mum and Dad weren't here to see it because it would have upset them so much to see me suffering like this, while being so helpless.

I was approached by someone who asked me if I would be interested in being part of a huge court action against the tobacco companies. It turned out that an action was being launched by a Dublin legal firm. They apparently saw my involvement as being a useful element in swaying public opinion against the big corporations.

I was introduced to a brilliant Dublin lawyer named Peter McDonnell. Peter had been hired by a few people originally and then more and more had joined the throng. By the time my name was added to the list in July 1999 there were about two hundred litigants suing the tobacco companies.

Our claim was based on the fact that they encouraged us to smoke through advertising tobacco as a product that was glamorous and appealing to the opposite sex, while all along they knew from their own research that it was killing us. I was due to get around £200,000 from the claim. Mind you, had it come off I would probably have spent it all in a year or two on cigarettes, drink and gambling. So, it was probably a blessing that in 2002 the courts ruled against us and the claim failed.

My recovery was slow, but I got there in the end. In March 2002 I was readmitted to hospital for further tests as my throat was painful and I was having difficulty swallowing. I am not sure how I would have reacted if I'd had to face it all again, but the biopsies indicated that all was clear.

There are so many people I want to thank for helping me beat the cancer. Family, friends, the doctors, nurses and surgeon. You know who you all are. Thank you from the Hurricane. I might not blow as hard and as ferociously as once I did, but I am here and it is thanks to all of you and also the fans who, to this day, wish me well and give me encouragement to fight on. That's the way I like it.

There were times when I was very ill, and really didn't think I was going to make it, that I looked back on my life. I realised I'd messed some things up. I'd hurt people I didn't want to, and to them I wanted to apologise. Still do. Some people had hurt me, and to them, well you can guess what I wanted to do. But even as I lay there, perhaps dying, I thought it had all been worth it. And I hoped the world agreed with me. I'm still around, and I'm still finding out if that's true or not. I think it is.

23

Oliver Reed

•

I couldn't write my autobiography and not include a chapter on my good friend Oliver Reed, the actor and king of the hellraisers.

I got to know Oliver through Dessie Cavanagh in the seventies. I met Dessie because of our mutual love of the horses – he was an ex-jump jockey – and I used to visit him in his place in Dorking, where he ran a local mini cab firm. Oliver was one of his best clients. On one occasion when I was staying with Dessie and his wife, Sue, Oliver got wind of the fact that the Hurricane was in town and called, demanding my presence, post haste. He was not an easy man to refuse.

Oliver lived at that time in the most extraordinary rambling mansion, Broome Hall, with the ballet dancer Jackie Daryl and their daughter, Sarah. The place had something like 45 rooms and stood in nearly 70 acres of countryside. I loved it. When Dessie and I arrived that first time I must admit to being quite apprehensive. Like everyone else, I'd read all sorts of stories about Oliver Reed in the papers, and all they told me was that I didn't know what to expect. We went in through the back door, straight into the massive kitchen that comfortably housed two giant aga cookers. Oliver was standing in the centre of the room, staring straight at me when I walked in. He looked very ominous and serious. I just stood there, trying to look cool and probably looking more like a little boy lost.

And then Oliver spoke. 'I am going to call you Hurricane the Pig. We are going to play snooker, you and I, but first we must drink.' Needless to say, I was somewhat taken aback by this. I later learned that when Oliver called anyone a 'pig' it was because he liked that person. It wasn't an insult in any way. Oliver then threw me over a half pint glass, which I nearly dropped in my nervousness, and approached me with a bottle of whisky. All I could think at this stage was, 'My God, this man is crazy.' But I held my ground.

Oliver then filled up my half tankard glass, almost to the top, with the whisky. 'Drink you Pig,' he instructed. I was too scared not to obey, and took what I thought was a healthy sip. 'Drink properly Hurricane you Pig,' he insisted. He wasn't satisfied until I'd downed virtually the whole glass. It nearly killed me. I like water with my whisky, so knocking back the hard stuff neat was not fun.

But I seemed to pass the test, if that's what it was, because Oliver then put his arm around me and lead me out of the kitchen door and on a tour of the grounds and house. I slowly began to relax but I kept on my guard the entire time. He was so unpredictable that you had no idea what Oliver might do next. He showed me every one of the bedrooms and I swore that I would have a house like it one day. Delveron House might not quite have equalled the splendour of Broome Hall, but I always thought I did OK on that promise to myself. For the next three hours it was talk mixed with drink, snooker, darts, draughts – almost any game you could think of. Oliver was very competitive and loved to take on his friends at just about everything. At one point we engaged in a somewhat one-side round of arm wrestling, for which Oliver was infamous. I did not come out on top in that one. Then came the craziest challenge of them all, disco dancing.

By this time Sue Cavanagh had joined us and so Des and Sue were our judges, and I managed to get them to vote me the winner, which Ollie hated. Then we were off to see his granny. Fair enough, I thought, but seems a bit late to disturb her. I needn't have worried. Ollie took me down to the cellar, which was full of junk and cobwebs, and there lying in a casket, was a skeleton. 'That is my granny,' said a very pissed Ollie. 'I dug her up so she could say hello.' I mouthed a quick greeting and went to make my exit from the room.

'Not so fast Hurricane the Pig.' Oliver then handed me the most disgusting, festering, mould-ridden glass I have ever seen. Louis Pasteur would have been fascinated by it. He filled it with gin and said, 'First you must have one more drink, and then you will be my friend.' I duly obliged, just hoping I'd survive to tell the tale. Well I did, and many more besides.

I spent a crazy and drunken two days there and it had a profound impact on me. I liked Ollie so much I started to copy his ways. And by that I'm not talking about his drinking. Although it would be fair to say some of that did rub off on me . . . What I mean here is that I used to watch how Oliver moved, how he carried himself, his stage persona, how he spoke and held himself. He had such presence and I learned a lot of professional tips from him in that capacity.

After he moved to Guernsey I used to go over for a week at a time. That was often a big mistake, as I'd find I couldn't play for a few days after I got back home. I needed the time to recover. I would have a rest from drinking for a few days, but Ollie never did. It was there that I escaped to after I got banned for head-butting Paul Hatherell. I knew Ollie would look after me. I spent a week there on that occasion before I was due to catch a plane back to London to appear on TV-AM. On the morning I was due to leave, Ollie dragged me out of bed at the crack of dawn and insisted that we have a farewell drink. He poured a half pint glass of whisky for me and ordered me to down it in one. Now when Ollie orders you to do that, you do it, no questions asked. 'Thank God it's only a half,' I thought, 'I'm the Hurrcane, not Hercules.'

The tricky bastard had put most of a bottle of his new wife's perfume in the glass and I, like a fool, downed most of it before I realised. Too late, I tried to bring it back up, but it just wouldn't come. Josephine, his wife, just shrugged her shoulders when I told her later. 'Don't worry, Alex,' she said, 'I'll get some more sent over from Paris.' I was sick hours later and for a few days afterwards, and the poor presenter of the show that morning had to interview me while I silently belched. I'm told he even remarked to the director through his lapel mike that I smelt like a goddess.

Oliver and I often got ourselves into daft and sometimes potentially serious situations, but we always escaped any actual injury, which was more by luck than judgement. I remember one visit to his place in Cork, Castle McCarthy, while he was on a short break from filming *The Return of the Three Musketeers*. We started drinking in a few pubs on the island and ended up back at his house, where we passed out in chairs in the huge lounge. The next thing I remember is Ollie jabbing me with a sword. Yes, a real sword. I think he'd been practising for the film with it.

'Get up, you fucking Hurricane the Pig,' he said. 'How dare you fall asleep in my company. For that insult, sir, I require satisfaction.' He stepped back and threw another sword at me. 'Now, sir, prepare to die,' he said with one of his wicked smiles. The next thing I remember, I am swishing this sword around for all I'm worth. 'Fight, you pig, fight like a gentleman,' he shouted at me. Of course, he was just playing, but I was genuinely scared for a moment that he had at last flipped and was going to kill me.

That wasn't the only time Oliver frightened the shit out of

me. During one of my 'restful' visits to Guernsey Oliver and I were following our usual routine of getting pissed in the pub before going back to the house. As often happened during these sessions, Josephine wasn't best pleased with the state he was in, and let him know it. I got on well with Josephine most of the time and she often told me she didn't blame me for Oliver's mad ways.

We'd had a great afternoon in the pub that day, drinking, arm wrestling the locals and generally having huge amounts of fun. We were in fine fettle and once Josephine had let off her steam we all settled down to one of her lovely dinners. The drinking, of course, continued afterwards, and I was just beginning to doze off in my seat when I became aware of Oliver getting to his feet. He looked at me strangely and I knew he was going to do something crazy.

'What . . . what?' I said in an effort to calm him down.

'Fall asleep in my company would you, Hurricane the Pig,' he said. Then he went into the utility room and came back with a huge hatchet. 'I know how to wake you up,' he said as he approached me with the axe.

There are many cures for hangovers and for sobering up, but this was one I hadn't come across before. My head cleared in 1.5 seconds and I ran upstairs to my bedroom and locked the door.

'Come out here, Hurricane the Pig, I fancy a pork sandwich,' he shouted. Then he started to thrust the blade into the door, which was solid oak, made to withstand an invasion. I was just praying it was also Oliver proof. After a few minutes he started to weaken the wood and the top of the axe started to appear through the door.

Josephine had made herself scarce, finding refuge in the sauna. She'd seen Oliver in these moods before, he was a man possessed. As for me, I was terrified. I honestly thought I might be about to breathe my last if he got through. Jack Nicholson in *The Shining* has a lot to answer for in firing up terrifying images.

The door held, thank God, and I silently thanked the carpenter for his fine craftsmanship, as it all went quiet out in the corridor. After half an hour or so I worked up the courage to unlock the door and poked my head outside. There was no sign of Oliver – he had evidently given up and disappeared downstairs for a drink. I decided that discretion was most certainly the better part of valour, and that I'd leave him to it. I'd had enough excitement for one night. I was wrong.

There were some wonderful views from Oliver's house and I was sitting in my room, nursing a whisky nightcap from the bottle that Oliver had very kindly supplied in my room, looking out on the night sky, contemplating the complexities of Mr Reed, when out of nowhere the fucking hatchet sliced through the air inches from my head, and wedged itself firmly in the window sill. It scared the shit out of me.

'Night night Hurricane the Pig,' declared a very soft-footed Oliver. 'You didn't think you would escape me, did you? I play to win. Always remember that.'

And with that he theatrically waved me farewell, and went off to bed. I just sat there, staring at the still quivering hatchet, embedded in the wood where seconds before I'd been resting my hand.

The next morning I came downstairs and there he was, the mad bastard, laughing at me.

'You're a mad fuck! I thought you were going to kill me,' I told him. He just laughed it off and insisted we go down the pub again. And of course went. Ollie had that effect on people.

When I got my cancer, Ollie used to call almost every day and chat for ages. He was an inspiration at times when I was low and a godsend when I was feeling good. He sent gifts of booze,

chocolates and fancy foods to fatten me up, and insisted that I
keep up the drinking habit. He had me in stitches at times with
his stories of his latest antics. I miss him very much.

On the evening of 2 May 1999, I got a call from a friend,
which went more or less like this:

'Have you seen the news, Alex? About Oliver Reed?'

'No, what's he been up to now?'

'Jesus Alex, he's died in a bar in Malta.'

After a long silence, 'Are you sure? Is it definite?'

'Yes, Alex, I'm afraid it is. I don't know the details, but he is
dead.'

'Is Josephine with him?'

'I'm not sure, Alex, put the news on and see.'

I put the television on and sure enough he was all over the
news. I couldn't believe it. Only days previously we'd been
talking about me possibly dying from the cancer. Now, out of the
blue, he was dead. Instead of him coming to mine, I'd be going
to his funeral. I was devastated for Josephine, his children and
myself at the same time. He loved everyone he met, even those he
didn't like. His children were his life, as was Josephine, and now
he was gone, my friend and soul mate.

Oliver Reed died on his way to hospital in Valletta. He had
been on a break from filming *Gladiator* with Russell Crowe. He
was in a bar called The Pub, 136 Archbishop Street, Valletta, arm
wrestling with some Royal Navy sailors by all accounts. He'd
have been having fun. I am glad about that. That pub is now a
shrine to him, as it should be. So if you're ever there in Malta, go
and pay tribute to a great actor, man and drinking buddy. The
pub sign now says 'Ollie's last pub'.

I went to his funeral service on Saturday, 15 May, which was
held at St James' church in the town of Mallow, Cork, and it was
one of the saddest days of my life. They played the song

From the Eye of the Hurricane

'Consider Yourself' from one of his greatest films, *Oliver*, in which he played Bill Sykes. When that came on, I cried. I felt privileged he'd considered me a friend. He is buried in the thirteenth-century graveyard of Churchtown, a town he loved so much and a town that loved him back. I was heartbroken at losing such a good friend. I don't have many close friends, so those I do have are very dear to me. The wake was held in a marquee in the grounds of Castle McCarthy. It went on until the wee small hours, family, friends, fellow actors all mingling and telling tales. That would have been Oliver's wish I'm sure. 'The party goes on, even in my demise,' he'd have said. God bless him.

24

Belfast boy

•

The new millennium arrived full of hope for the future, but I was feeling more alone than ever, having buried some very good friends over the years since retirement from professional snooker. My absence from the circuit was not keeping me away from the table, though. I continued to love playing in exhibitions and charity events, the only difference being I was now playing to much smaller crowds and for expenses only or a lot less appearance money for the exhibitions than I used to.

I missed being a professional – more accurately, I missed the adrenalin rush of the big tournaments, I missed the fans and, of course, I missed the money. But if I am honest, the loneliness of being a professional player was something that I had never really come to terms with. I am not the only one who has felt the isolation of the game, being constantly on the road, often staying in awful hotels and not eating properly. All these things go a long way to explain why sometimes snooker players have problems holding down relationships.

I didn't do too many exhibitions or charity dos in the first couple of years of the new century, mainly because I couldn't, due to the toll that the cancer had taken on me. It felt a real strain at times to play Matthew Stevens, Joe Delaney or Ken Doherty over seven frames, and then sit and sign autographs and have your picture taken with dozens of people. I have to admit, though, that it gave my ego a big boost that people of all ages still admired my playing, even though I didn't really have the panache and quickness I used to have.

The problems associated with my cancer continued to plague me as I underwent my recovery, sometimes quite dramatically. In April 2000 I was invited to go out to the Dubai World Cup horse race and was asked to stay for a few days, as some people out there were interested in talking to me about doing some coaching. I started to feel ill one night as we were having dinner. I'd been having problems with swallowing, but sitting there in that restaurant, my throat suddenly seemed to close entirely and it frightened me. Fortunately, there was a doctor at a nearby table and he took me to my room and gave me some medicine. I stayed a day more and then decided I had to get back home. I asked to be taken to the airport, but when I got there I began to feel as though I was dying. No matter how hard I tried, I was gasping for air. I couldn't seem to get my breath. I really thought I was a goner.

I collapsed in the departure lounge and was rushed to hospital. It was touch and go for a while, or at least it felt like it. After eight days in hospital, where I was treated like a king, and looked after fabulously by my good friends Khalid Bin Suliem and his brother Mohammed, I left to come home. I was flown back by air ambulance and I don't think I've ever been happier to see Belfast. Anne and Jean came to the rescue once again and after a week's stay in the Ulster Independent Clinic, it was them who nursed me back to health. The reason for my collapse was that I'd run out of my medication and that, combined with the heat and dehydration, was too much for my body. I think it was at this point that I finally grasped the truth about the cancer, and the toll the treatment had taken on me. Even with all the care and attention I'd received, I was three and a half stone under weight. It was a scary thought.

In 2002 I went to see a play in Belfast – *Hurricane*, written and performed by a Lisburn actor/writer by the name of Richard Dormer. I went on stage to congratulate him afterwards. I made my point about how I felt about his performance and impersonation of me by grabbing him by the balls. It was all in jest, of course, and I knew it would make the papers. The publicity did him no harm at all and in 2004 the play moved to London, to the Arts theatre in Soho. I was delighted for him. The London play also got great publicity because it is good, but also because I was caught smoking a joint in the place. It seemed the powers that be were more concerned about the fact that I was breaking the 'No Smoking' safety policy. Oh well, that's London for you.

I am constantly being asked to enter tournaments still, as a wild-card entry, simply to boost up the number of spectators. In 2006, I played against Joe Delaney at the Spawell centre in Templeogue, Dublin. The place is run by Richie Dunne and his lovely assistant Tracie Tolbert. They now stage the Irish Open there. I was beaten by Joe in the first round and was back in the bookies for the last race. I played Ken Doherty at the Spa Hotel in Lucan as well last year. He went on to win the tournament at the Spawell a few weeks later. He is such a nice fella, Ken. I have even been and had tea with his mam in Ranelagh, Dublin. Ken will be a force to be reckoned with in snooker for some years to come. I wish him all the best.

I don't know what the future holds. No one does, of course. For me it held less of a fascination because I expected to be dead by now but for some strange reason I'm not. I'm still here. I expect the cancer to return one day, and if so, I might not be in the mood or have the strength to fight it again. I don't know. That isn't me feeling sorry for myself. I am just being honest with you. I don't know if I have the energy left any more. I often sit in my little flat on the Donegall Road, and reflect on the times I have had travelling round the world, playing a game I love and being paid well for doing it. I have been truly blessed with a great life. However, I have to admit that I haven't always been good to those who have helped me get there or tried to look after me when I got into trouble. That takes its toll eventually.

I try to look after myself although I'm not sure I make a very good job of it. I know I shouldn't smoke but I've found that impossible to pack in. I don't drink that much these days, but it is still probably too much, given my health. But again, it is so hard to stop. I'm on a lot of medication and food supplements to try to help me put on weight. You see, I find it very difficult to eat, because of one of the side effects of the radiotherapy. I am very sensitive about this aspect in my life.

The treatment made my teeth weak and they gradually fell out one by one. I was devastated. I was gaunt in appearance anyway, skeletal even, but that I could cope with. But the loss of my teeth, to me that was the last semblance of looking human. People who have seen pictures of me, at Oliver Reed's funeral, or subsequently, have commented that because of the way I look, I must be on drugs. That is just not true, but some people believe it because they've read it somewhere. That hurts, as do the snide remarks that are made about my appearance generally. But I have to take it on the chin and carry on.

I now wear false teeth, but I find them awkward and embarrassing and it means I can't eat many types of food. I would kill for the opportunity to be able to take a nice lady out for a steak or a chinese meal, but that is impossible at the moment. I'm determined to do something about it. Tired I might be, but I'm not giving up. Not yet. I have decided to have new teeth fitted. I would love to have a full set of real teeth again and that is what I am planning for the future. Unfortunately, I have to have some tests first. A side effect of those massive radiotherapy doses is that my jaw bone may be weakened. So before I have any teeth fitted, I have to go into a pressure chamber and sit there for hours to see if my jaw can take the pressure of the drilling I need. If that is a positive result, I can go and get a full set of artificial teeth screwed into my jaw.

I'll be a lot happier if I can have the dental work done. At the moment I am very conscious of the fact that my false teeth don't fit properly and my cheeks are so sunken that I cannot smile with any confidence. That has had a big effect on me. Almost everyone who remembers me from the old days tells me I always had a wicked smile. Just getting that small part of me back would have a huge impact on how I feel about myself. I am ashamed of having no teeth, and that shame is hard to live with. It is not the Alex Higgins I want people to see. But as I've said, I refuse to give up. I might not have the dazzling smile any more but I still care very much about my appearance. Although most of my clothes no longer fit me, I make a point of always being smartly dressed nonetheless. That's always been important to me. But the fact that it is all so hard these days depresses the hell out of me. But I'll fight it.

I mostly spend my time these days in pubs and betting shops. I like to think of them as my offices for my hobby, betting. I am very well clued up on most sports. All my life I have been a victim of gambling, but it has been a great pastime as well as a millstone around my neck. When I am in Belfast, I usually walk across the Donegall Road from the flat to the Royal pub. In there, I have my own little corner by the television screen. Like most pubs these days it has Sky TV and the channel that is usually on is At The Races, but as I have the remote control, I flick between that channel and Racing UK. The rest of the locals know me well enough not to try to take the remote from me. I like this pub. It is like a throwback to the seventies, but a nicer bunch of people you won't meet anywhere.

Despite what some people may think, Northern Ireland hasn't only produced infamous people on both sides of the political battlefield. The country I was born in and love has produced many very talented people, who were also great ambassadors. The most obvious is George Best – and of course myself – but let's not forget the pentathlete Mary Peters who won Olympic gold in 1972, author C.S. Lewis, actor Kenneth Brannagh, world-famous flute player James Galway, musician/songwriter Gary Moore, actor Stephen Rea, and my dear, and very sadly missed friend Derek Bell who was, although small in stature, a giant in my eyes, a multi-talented musician and composer and member of the Chieftans (I used to call Derek 'Genius' and he used to call me 'Maestro'; I know I was correct at least) to name but a few. I am so proud of the fact that when people from all over the world start talking about Northern Ireland and its famous sons and daughters, my name is lumped in with the greats, such as those I have just mentioned.

Belfast doesn't forget us, either. It is a city that has always recognised those that have represented the place worldwide. I had the privilege a few years ago of having a tree planted in my honour right opposite the Europa Hotel; there is a plaque on the pavement to celebrate the occasion. It is very humbling to think that when that tree is fully grown and blooming in hundreds of years from now, people will still be able to see that it was planted for me.

There are lots of other places around the city where I am quite well known, so let me take you on a little trip to a couple of my favourites, where you might find me on any given day – and one where you probably won't.

Belfast boy

In the city centre is the Europa Hotel on Great Victoria Street. Opposite the hotel are two great city-centre bars. The first is The Beaten Docket. The name means a losing betting slip, of which I have had many. Perhaps that's why I feel such an affinity with the place. In there, I have my own snug and TV set. I view the pub as one of my city-centre branch offices, where some days for a few hours I conduct the business of being a punter at the local bookies. The other pub is called the Crown Bar, just yards away from The Beaten Docket. When you go inside you will see it is unchanged in design since the 1930s, probably even longer. The bar staff are always friendly and it has real tradition that pub – to the point that it still closes on a Sunday.

The Crown was the setting for a classic 1947 James Mason film, called *Odd Man Out*. The film is about a bank robbery that goes wrong and the main character, Johnny McQueen, is chased all over town by the police. At one point he is holed up in the pub and the snug he is concealed in is still there. I love sitting there knowing that the late, great star also sat there. Maybe one day they will also talk about me in that same vein. Maybe.

If you do visit Belfast any time, you should go to the Ulster Museum. It is a great place generally, and one thing to look out for is whether my portrait is hanging. The last I heard they had taken it down and stored it away. Maybe they will bring it out again when I am gone. It was painted by fellow Irishman Rodney Dickson, who made a name for himself in America before coming home. He was watching me on the telly one night, managed to get hold of Doug Perry's number and called to arrange a meeting. He said he wanted to paint me, but I would have to sit for him for sketches.

Now Rodney Dickson wasn't a sports fan. He is an artist pure and simple. That was his sole focus. He had no interest in anything else. He saw me as the epitome of the dark spirit that lurks in us all. The picture is of me emerging from the darkness into the limelight, in a menacing sort of way. That's how he envisaged me, coming to a snooker table to take my turn. He gave me a haunting look, a man in pain, caught up in both passion and distress. I like the painting but its ownership has been a bone of contention from the very start and that is why it doesn't hang in the museum.

The last time I met Rodney was in 2001 in Belfast. I was sitting in a cab and saw him walking along the street. I asked the driver to pull over and ask Rodney for directions to a street, any street. As the cabbie spoke to him I just emerged and said, 'Hello, Rodney.' He was dumbfounded and looked at me for a second before it hit him who I was. 'Hello, Alex,' he muttered. I walked away and we have never met since. It is a shame as I'd love to sort out the problem surrounding the painting. Maybe one day. I'd love to see it again in all its glory before I am dead.

So let me just end on this note, a note of recognition for my native Belfast, my home. It has had its fair share of troubles, we have lived through a lot of turbulent times and for decades it wasn't the nicest place to live or to visit. That's behind us now and we are all looking to the future, without looking back. I love this city, which is why I choose to live here. I count my blessings that I am living in the kind of Belfast that my parents would be proud to call home. I hope that you will come and visit us some day and see what I mean. If I am still around, come and look me up, shake my hand and have a drink with me. I'd like that.

Career record

•

World Championship

1972
First qualifying round: beat Ron Gross 15–6; Second qualifying round: beat Maurice Parkin 11–3; First round: beat Jack Rea 19–11; Quarter-finals: beat John Pulman 31–23; Semi-finals: beat Rex Williams 31-30; Final: beat John Spencer 37–31

1973
Second round: beat Pat Houlihan 16–3; Quarter-finals: beat Fred Davis 16–14; Semi-finals: lost 23–9 to Eddie Charlton

1974
Second round: beat Bernard Bennett 15–4; Quarter-finals: lost 15–14 to Fred Davis

1975
Second round: beat David Taylor 15–2; Quarter-finals: beat Rex Williams 19–12; Semi-finals: lost 19–14 to Ray Reardon

1976
First round: beat Cliff Thorburn 15–14; Quarter-finals: beat John Spencer 15–14; Semi-finals: beat Eddie Charlton 20–18; Final: lost 27–16 to Ray Reardon

1977
First round: lost 13–12 to Doug Mountjoy

1978
First round: lost 13–12 to Patsy Fagan

1979
First round: beat David Taylor 13–5; Quarter-finals: lost 13–12 to Terry Griffiths

1980
First round: beat Tony Meo 10–9; Second round: beat Perrie Mans 13–6; Quarter-finals: beat Steve Davis 13–9; Semi-finals: beat Kirk Stevens 16–13; Final: lost 18–16 to Cliff Thorburn

1981
Second round: lost 13–8 to Steve Davis

1982
First round: beat Jim Meadowcroft 10-5; Second round: beat Doug Mountjoy 13–12; Quarter-finals: beat Willie Thorne 13–10; Semi-finals: beat Jimmy White 16-15; Final: beat Ray Reardon 18–15

1983
First round: beat Dean Reynolds 10–4; Second round: beat Willie Thorne 13–8; Quarter-finals: beat Bill Werbeniuk 13–11; Semi-finals: lost 16–5 to Steve Davis

1984
First round: lost 10–9 to Neal Foulds

1985
First round: beat Dean Reynolds 10–4; Second round: lost 13–7 to Terry Griffiths

1986
First round: beat John Spencer 10–7; Second round: lost 13–12 to Terry Griffiths

1987
First round: beat Jon Wright 10–6; Second round: lost 13–10 to Terry Griffiths

1988
First round: lost 10–2 to Tony Drago

1989
Fifth qualifying round: lost 10–8 to Darren Morgan

1990
Fifth qualifying round: beat James Wattana 10–6; First round: lost 10–5 to Steve James

1991
Banned for season

1992
Fifth qualifying round: beat Wayne Martin 10–3; Sixth qualifying round: beat Paul Gibson 10–6; Seventh qualifying round: lost 10–7 to Alan McManus

1993
Seventh qualifying round: beat Steve Judd 5–1; Eighth qualifying round: beat Murdo Macleod 10–9; Ninth qualifying round: beat

Kirk Stevens 10–5; Tenth qualifying round: lost 10–1 to Brian Morgan

1994
Seventh qualifying round: beat Colin Kelly 10–9; Eighth qualifying round: beat Andrew Cairns 10–5; Ninth qualifying round: beat Tony Knowles 10–9; First round: lost 10–6 to Ken Doherty

1995
Sixth qualifying round: lost 10–5 to Tai Pichit

1996
Eighth qualifying round: lost 10–7 to Surinder Gill

1997
Fifth qualifying round: lost 10–9 to Darren Limburg

1998
Eighth qualifying round: v Justin Buckingham withdrew

2003
Fifth qualifying round: v Chris West withdrew

Professional titles

By year

1972	Irish Professional Championship
	Park Drive World Championship
1974	Watneys Open
1975	Canadian Open
1976	Canadian Club Masters

1977   Canadian Open
1978   Irish Professional Championship
        Benson & Hedges Masters
1979   Irish Professional Championship
        Tolly Cobbold Classic
1980   Padmore/Super Crystalate International
        Tolly Cobbold Classic
        British Gold Cup
        Pontin's Professional (Camber Sands)
1981   Benson & Hedges Masters
1982   Embassy World Championship
1983   Irish Professional Championship
        Coral UK Championship
1984   World Doubles Championship (with Jimmy White)
1985   World Team Cup (Ireland, with Dennis Taylor and
        Eugene Hughes)
1986   World Team Cup (Ireland, with Dennis Taylor and
        Eugene Hughes)
1987   World Team Cup (Ireland, with Dennis Taylor and
        Eugene Hughes)
1989   Irish Professional Championship
        Benson & Hedges Irish Masters

By title
Benson & Hedges Irish Masters   1989
Benson & Hedges Masters   1978, 1981
British Gold Cup   1980
Canadian Club Masters   1976
Canadian Open   1975, 1977
Coral UK Championship   1983
Embassy World Championship   1982
Irish Professional Championship 1972, 1978, 1979, 1983, 1989

Padmore/Super Crystalate
International   1980
Park Drive World Championship   1972
Pontin's Professional
  (Camber Sands)   1980
Tolly Cobbold Classic   1979, 1980
Watneys Open   1974
World Doubles Championship
  (with Jimmy White)   1984
World Team Cup
  (Ireland, with Dennis Taylor
  and Eugene Hughes)   1985, 1986, 1987

Professional finals

1972   Park Drive World Championship beat John Spencer 37–31

1972   Irish Professional Championship beat Jackie Rea 28–12

1972   Park Drive 2000 (1) lost 4–3 to John Spencer

1972   Park Drive 2000 (2) lost 5–3 to John Spencer

1974   Watneys Open beat Fred Davis 17–11

1975   Canadian Open beat John Pulman 15–7

1976   Embassy World Championship lost 27–16 to Ray Reardon

1976   Canadian Club Masters beat Reardon 6–4

1976   Canadian Open lost 17–9 to John Spencer

1977   Dry Blackthorn Cup lost 4–2 to Patsy Fagan

1977   Canadian Open beat John Spencer 17–14

1978   Benson & Hedges Masters beat Cliff Thorburn 7–5

1978   Irish Professional Championship beat Dennis Taylor 21–7

1978   Champion of Champions lost 11–9 to Ray Reardon

1979   Benson & Hedges Masters lost 8–4 to Perrie Mans

1979   Tolly Cobbold Classic beat Ray Reardon 5–4

1979   Irish Professional Championship beat Patsy Fagan 21–13

1980   Padmore/Super Crystalate International beat Perrie Mans 4–2

1980   Wilson's Classic lost 4–3 to John Spencer

1980   Benson & Hedges Masters lost 9–5 to Terry Griffiths

1980   Tolly Cobbold Classic beat Dennis Taylor 5–4

1980   British Gold Cup beat Ray Reardon 5–1

1980   Embassy World Championship lost 18–16 to Cliff Thorburn

1980   Irish Professional Championship lost 21–15 to Dennis Taylor

1980   Pontin's Professional (Camber Sands) beat Dennis Taylor 9–7

1980   Coral UK Championship lost 16–6 to Steve Davis

1981   Benson & Hedges Masters beat Terry Griffiths 9–6

1982   Irish Professional Championship lost 16–13 to Dennis Taylor

1982   Embassy World Championship beat Ray Reardon 18–15

1982   Langs Scottish Masters lost 9–4 to Steve Davis

1982   Coral UK Championship lost 16–15 to Terry Griffiths

1983   Smithwicks Irish Professional Championship beat Dennis Taylor 16–11

1983   Coral UK Championship beat Steve Davis 16–15

1984   Coral UK Open lost 16–8 to Steve Davis

1984   Hofmeister World Doubles Championship (with Jimmy White) beat Cliff Thorburn and Willie Thorne 10–2

1985   Guinness World Team Cup (All Ireland, with Dennis Taylor and Eugene Hughes) beat England A (Steve Davis, Tony Knowles and Tony Meo) 9–7

1985   Benson & Hedges Irish Masters lost 9–5 to Jimmy White

1985	Irish Professional Championship lost 10–5 to Dennis Taylor
1985	Carlsberg Challenge lost 8–3 to Jimmy White
1985	Fosters Professional lost 8–3 to Jimmy White
1986	Car Care World Team Cup (Ireland A, with Dennis Taylor and Eugene Hughes) beat Canada (Cliff Thorburn, Kirk Stevens and Bill Werbeniuk) 9–7
1986	Irish Professional Championship lost 10–7 to Dennis Taylor
1986	Langs Scottish Masters lost 9–8 to Cliff Thorburn
1987	Benson & Hedges Masters lost 9–8 to Dennis Taylor
1987	Tuborg World Team Cup (Ireland A, with Dennis Taylor and Eugene Hughes) beat Canada (Cliff Thorburn, Kirk Stevens and Bill Werbeniuk) 9–2
1988	WPBSA non-ranking event (1) lost 5–4 to Gary Wilkinson
1988	Rothmans Grand Prix lost 10–6 to Steve Davis
1989	Irish Professional Championship beat Jack McLaughlin 9–7
1989	Pearl Assurance British Open lost 10–8 to Bob Chaperon
1990	British Car Rentals World Team Cup (Northern Ireland, with Dennis Taylor and Tommy Murphy) lost 9–5 to Canada (Alain Robidoux, Cliff Thorburn and Bob Chaperon)

World ranking tournaments

Titles (1)

1982	Embassy World Championship

Runner-up (5)
1976   Embassy World Championship
1980   Embassy World Championship
1984   Coral UK Open
1988   Rothmans Grand Prix
1990   Pearl Assurance British Open

Losing semi-finalist (5)
1975   Embassy World Championship
1983   Embassy World Championship
1985   Dulux British Open
1986   Dulux British Open
1986   Coral UK Open

Losing quarter-finalist (5)
1974   Park Drive World Championship
1979   Embassy World Championship
1984   Jameson International
1986   Mercantile Credit Classic
1989   Dubai Duty Free Classic

World ranking season by season

1976–77: 2
1977–78: 5
1978–79: 7
1979–80: 11
1980–81: 4
1981–82: 11
1982–83: 2
1983–84: 5
1984–85: 9
1985–86: 9

1986–87: 6
1987–88: 9
1988–89: 17
1989–90: 24
1990–91: 97
1991–92: 120
1992–93: 72
1993–94: 61
1994–95: 48
1995–96: 51
1996–97: 99
1997–98: 156

Note: Higgins is still on the ranking list as a WPBSA member despite not having played in a ranking tournament since 1997. Players with zero points are listed alphabetically.

Career statistics compiled by David Hendon

Index

•

The abbreviation AGH is used in the index for Alex Gordon Higgins, as in (AGH sister).

Index

Index

strategy in snooker 43–4
television impact 6
Snooker Loopy 236–7
Snooker Promotions 84, 94
Spawell centre 283
Spencer, John 51–6, 83–4, 105,
  112, 115, 117–18, 129, 158, 166,
  253, 254, 259
  early exhibition matches with
    42, 44–5
spoof game 86
Sportsworld 164, 166–7
Sproule, Alan 7
Stepney, Alex 61, 141
Stevens, Kirk 118, 133, 226,
  227–8
Stevens, Matthew 281
sticks game 7
Suliem, Khalid bin 282
Suliem, Mohammed 282
Sunday People 216–17
'Susan' 18–19
Sutherland, Donald 119

Taylor, David 123
Taylor, Dennis 43, 100, 105,
  113–14, 120, 123–4, 129–31,
  166, 193–4, 238–9, 239, 253–5,
  255
Taylor, Joe 87–8
Thames Television 56
The Who 63
This is Your Life 158–60
Thorburn, Cliff 71, 105, 115,
  117, 123, 133–4, 163, 198,
  228–9
Thorne, Willie 71, 101, 107–8,
  168, 174, 198

Thorpe, Jim 100, 120–1, 129
Threepenny Opera, The 262
Times of India 91
Timms, Bill 109–10
Tin Hut, The 23
Tolbert, Tracie 283
Tolly Cobbold Classic
  1980: 129–30
  1983: 193–4
Top of the Pops 237
Toronto 117–19
Torvill, Jayne 237
Travel Bureau Ltd 244–5
'Trevor' 4–5
Trinidad 149–51
Troggs, The 237

Ulster Independent Clinic 282
Ulster Museum 287
Ulster Queen 15–16
United Kingdom Championships
  1977: 119–20
  1978: 123–4
  1980: 136
  1981: 164
  1983: 207–10
  1986: 229–33
  1991: 260

Virgo, John 101, 153, 158, 231,
  245

W D & H O Wills 101
Wake, Peter 'The Mathematician'
  62–3
Walker, Sir Rodney 231–2
Walsh, Mr 3
Walthamstow dog track 29

Index